The KID ACROSS the HALL

The
KID
ACROSS
the
HALL

The Fight for Opportunity
in Our Schools

REID SAARIS

REDWOOD PRESS
Stanford, California

Redwood Press
Stanford, California

Printed in the United States of America on acid-free, archival-quality paper

Library of Congress Cataloging-in-Publication Data
Names: Saaris, Reid, author.
Title: The kid across the hall : the fight for opportunity in our schools / Reid Saaris.
Description: Stanford, California : Redwood Press, 2023. | Includes bibliographical
   references.
Identifiers: LCCN 2023003035 (print) | LCCN 2023003036 (ebook) |
   ISBN 9781503615274 (cloth) | ISBN 9781503636118 (ebook)
Subjects: LCSH: Saaris, Reid. | Equal Opportunity Schools (Organization) |
   High school teachers—United States—Biography. | Educators—United States—
   Biography. | Educational equalization—United States. | Education, Secondary—
   United States. | Discrimination in education—United States. | LCGFT:
   Autobiographies.
Classification: LCC LA2317.S23 A3 2023 (print) | LCC LA2317.S23 (ebook) |
   DDC 370.92 [B]—dc23/eng/20230208
LC record available at https://lccn.loc.gov/2023003035
LC ebook record available at https://lccn.loc.gov/2023003036

Cover design: David Drummond
Cover photograph: iStock
Typeset by Motto Publishing Services in 10.25/14 Freight Text Pro

NOTE ON SOURCES

This book is not fiction. And it is not strictly nonfiction either. I set out to write the truth as I experienced it, and found out along the way that doing so in the context of this story is complicated.

Students have an expectation of privacy when they attend school, and so in this book, character names and features have been changed to protect their privacy. Schools, districts, and states with whom I have partnered over the years also have an expectation of privacy, so their details have been changed as well.

As in most schools, teachers where I taught often served hundreds of students a year. Simultaneously, they interacted with a significant portion of the other seventy teachers in the school, as well as with administrators and parents. I found it difficult to keep this many people straight in my mind, even while spending most of my waking hours with them. To share a breadth of stories and keep things manageable for readers, I've created character, class, dialogue, event, and school composites.

During the writing process, we engaged dozens of readers and asked them to assess the accuracy of the text, and to help ensure that it conveys what the experiences they were part of were actually like. Their edits have improved the book tremendously, and brought it closer to nonfiction.

Beyond reading and editing the manuscript, a group of six of my former students collaborated on the actual writing of the student dialogue. Instead of eliminating dialect, they endeavored to convey different ways of speaking more genuinely, in the hope that doing so honors the diverse language and heritage of students.

Any profits this book may generate will go to my sister, my students, and not-for-profits.

Contemporaneously with the events described, my family and I kept journals, and those have been consulted to help reconstruct events and experiences.

The statistics, analysis, and research studies directly included in and informing this book have been carefully developed and reviewed for accuracy, including original analysis of public and private data pertaining to millions of educators and students across a wide variety of variables, and comprehensive research reviews and meta-analyses conducted by the author, by the United States Department of Education, by the team at Equal Opportunity Schools, and by hundreds of academic scholars.

Though I didn't use to think I'd ever fess up to such a thing, there will probably still be mistakes in the text, as there were in many of my actions recounted in it. And that's on me.

PART ONE

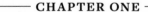

When she first graced the doorstep of our house in the woods, six-year-old Erin Marie was joining her tenth family. I was a lonely only child, nine years old, who'd never had to move, and I loved my new sister.

We ran child-wide smiles and imagination all over our garden, which overflowed with plants native to Washington State, like story-tall rhododendrons of a dozen colors beneath hundred-foot-tall firs.

I showed her the treehouse and the sandbox, all the best places to play. I showed her the bunk beds, Big Bear, and my carpeted loft with a window that looked down onto a streetlamp by a cluster of vine- and flower-covered mailboxes.

From my Auntie Suzy, I had my most prized possession: an old coin dispenser used by train conductors. You'd put the pennies, dimes, nickels, and quarters in the top, and press a little lever below to release them one at a time. Once I'd shown Erin how it worked, I extended it to her with both hands to say, *Here—this is ours now. It's all ours.*

With a steady diet, her own room, good sleep, and a regular schedule, Erin rebounded from malnutrition, growing several inches in her first months with us. She was in the spring of her life.

We took a trip to play in the tulip fields. We went to the rocky ocean beaches and I showed her how to find the best little crabs, to hold them on her palms and feel the tickle of their soft scuttle. How to keep her hands over water in case they fell. And how to clean off with kelp gel.

Her energy and her curiosity were enchanting. She wanted me to read her every book, show her every game. We traced all the known paths in the woods behind the house and made new ones, restrung an old swing between two giant evergreens with two long ropes and one thick plank to connect them. Then I sat on the plank and she sat on my lap and we pumped our legs way up into the budding maple leaves in front of us, and back over the huckleberries, Oregon grapes, and stands of sword ferns.

Finally—after so many years living next to an empty bedroom while my parents had looked far and wide to find my sister—things were as they should be. We seemed to have all we needed: family, food, and the space to grow, love, and learn.

———

I wish I would have always followed my instinctual love for Erin, as I did in those early days as her brother, when it seemed that, together, we could make the world wonderful for the both of us.

"How were your days, you two?" my mom, a school counselor, asked us over dinner at a round teak table, which seemed to grow out of our moss-green carpet, next to our forest-filled windows.

"We went over to Ardmore and played on the slides and stuff."

"How was it, Erin?"

"Fun," she said, smiling back politely.

"What was your favorite part?"

"Playing with my brother." She looked over at me, and then when I looked back with a smile, she looked down and scooped up a bite of microwaved scrambled eggs.

"What'd you learn?" my dad, an engineer, asked us, wiping his beard with a paper napkin.

"That I like playing with my sister," I said. "When're we gonna do the adoption, anyways?"

My parents looked at each other while Erin and I studied them.

"Well, like we said," my mom responded, "we need to think about that and figure out what's best, Reid."

"What do you mean, 'what's best'? Is there something better than this?"

"..."

"Well, aren't we ready?" I pushed.

"I can talk with you more about it later, Reid," she said softly. "How was your day, Gary?"

He told us about a wind tunnel and some of his friends' latest ideas about how to give tons of metal enough lift to fly, while Erin and I ate our peas, carrots, and corn—just warm enough to melt the pat of butter we'd each been given as a topper.

When I talked later with my mom, she said that we'd be doing foster care for a while with Erin, and then hopefully adoption. But I didn't understand it. They'd searched the world for years to find a daughter to adopt—Romania, Peru, Colombia, Guatemala, Texas—and finally found Erin right here. *So what's the problem?*

She said some things about professional case workers and recommendations and the idea that what was best would be to try things out and build from there. When I told her it didn't make sense, she said there were things about Erin's history that were, "well . . . complicated and potentially challenging. And it's important to be thoughtful. We'll see how things go, sweetie, and hopefully it'll all work out."

Since I had no idea what the complicated things might be, or how such things worked, I shrugged *OK*.

<hr />

I gave Erin my first bicycle, which had rainbows painted on it. My parents upgraded me to a black mountain bike with more gears and thicker treads to ride the jumps.

My best friend, Jamie, became her friend. We all rode bikes together by the school one day, Erin following us off-road, even though her bike wasn't made for it. When she fell off and crumpled up, crying in the dirt next to the dry grass, I raced back to get my parents while Jamie waited with her.

Feeling guilty that my little sister'd had the wind knocked out of her, I nearly knocked myself out crushing the pedals homeward and swerving up into our driveway to find help as quickly as I could. *So stupid of me.*

I leaped off, slamming my new bike down on the pavement. "Mom, Dad, come quick and get Erin." After telling them, "She fell," I started heaving out tears. As my mom put a hand on my face to comfort me, I pulled away and said, "No! We have to get Erin!"

Not knowing how hard it would get, I felt that being a good big brother meant I should try my best to take care of my little sister.

<hr />

Physically, Erin was fine. Though I was unusually tall, that first year she grew more quickly than I did. And because now we both had a 6'2" mom and a 6'5" dad, I figured we'd both get to be tall. But my parents told me that even with her growth spurt, Erin couldn't get there. Her biological parents were short, and she'd lost important growing time in the first six years. The doctors forecast that I would always be in the ninety-ninth percentile, and that Erin would never be close to tall enough to get into the Tip Toppers Tall Club, where my parents had first met.

I had just qualified for a program for "gifted and talented" students, which my mom got me into by having me retested after I hadn't qualified the first time. Meanwhile, I heard that the testers had concluded that Erin was "mentally retarded."

So they wanted to pull us both out of "regular" classes and put us in "special" classes. My type of special was talked about as being full of high capabilities and endless possibility, while hers was discussed in terms of disability (which sounded like the opposite of ability).

I didn't see Erin and her classmates when I was at school. They had separate classrooms, and I'm not sure how much her teachers even took them to recess. I don't remember seeing them out there.

I went to recess with the "regular" kids, but as soon as the bell rang, my group got to enter the first classrooms on the leading edge of the school, with the most external walls and tall windows. My teacher seemed to have the most training and experience, and took us on the most incredible trips (like to Washington, DC, Monticello, and her very own log cabin). And while she talked a lot about social justice, she never mentioned how it was determined who got to be in what were considered to be the good-special classes with us. So the fact that kids who looked and dressed like me were the ones categorized as "talented" seemed at the time as natural as the leaves outside our tall windows being green.

————

My mom believed that the testers had been too hasty in their judgment, calling Erin "retarded" when maybe she'd been reluctant to engage with adults because she was traumatized. After my mom had the school retest Erin, they decided she wasn't "retarded" after all.

Together, Erin and I had now gotten every result on these supposedly rigorous tests of intellectual capability. She'd been "retarded" and "normal," and I'd been "normal" and "gifted," our designations changing when we were retested at the request of my mom, who worked in—and knew how to work—the system.

My friend Jamie went the other way, showing up at the summer school for "gifted" kids, where we met, and then getting put in "regular" classes when he started middle school.

I'd been told time and again that I was talented, that anything was possible. And I just assumed that applied to others the same way—that Erin and Jamie could also accomplish anything they wanted.

———

In the intensive family therapy that Erin's caseworker assigned us to, I was told otherwise.

Two therapists, a man and a woman, led us.

"Erin, I understand that this week you were disobedient to Carolyn and Gary on several different occasions. Why do you think that is?"

"I what?" she asked, some of her freckles folding into flinch-wrinkles around her eyes as she scanned the room to try to see what this panel of four adults (and me) might have in store for her.

"For this to work out, you would need to do a better job of listening to Carolyn and Gary. They're responsible for you and they know what is needed. And it's your job to listen to them and respond appropriately . . . to do what they say. OK?"

"OK?" she asked, perhaps recalling all the adults who'd told her to do things that were not appropriate.

"You want to do a good job in the family, don't you?" the other therapist asked.

Erin didn't immediately respond.

"Erin, I said you want to do a good job in this family, don't you?"

"Yes . . . uh . . . I'm not doing good?"

Feeling immense tension, I offered, "I think she's been doing a pretty good job!"

"That's good, Reid. That's very nice of you. Maybe we can come back to that. For now, let's focus on the two incidents that you raised, Carolyn. Do you want to describe what happened?"

"And Erin, we need you to listen carefully, because I'm going to ask you why you chose to behave the way you did."

I slid farther back on the couch, next to my parents.

We all watched Erin, hunched in a little chair, nod slightly at the floor, her neatly folded hands in her lap, where her knee-length skirt met her navy blue cotton tights.

"So, my concern . . ." my mom started in. Then, noticing Erin, she restarted: "I think there's been a lot of progress. Things had been going better for a while, Erin. I appreciate how you've been picking up after yourself in your room. And how you'd been listening better. But I don't understand what happened these last couple days in particular. Like yesterday, when you had a meltdown and threw that big tantrum about your hair."

I couldn't sense Erin moving at all; in her stillness she seemed alert, absorbing everything.

"I've told you that if you want to keep your hair long, then you need to take care of brushing it. Otherwise, it gets tangled in knots and it's unmanageable. Does that make sense?"

". . ."

"Erin, Carolyn is asking you a question," offered one of the therapists.

Erin looked up timidly at the therapist, who pointed a thumb at my mom. Erin scanned over to her and then back to the floor.

My mom repeated her question: "Does it make sense that if you want to keep your hair long, you need to be taking care of it?"

". . . Yes?"

"And when I told you that you haven't been successfully taking care of it and that we were going to have to cut it, then you started yelling and screaming and were throwing pillows around your room, and you wouldn't calm down. What was going on for you?"

Erin said something.

"Pardon?"

"I don't want short hair," she said to the painted cement exposed at the edge of the area rug.

"I understand that," my mom responded, "but you need to show that with your actions, and you haven't been doing it. And we've given you lots of chances, so, like I said yesterday, we're going to have to cut . . ."

Things happened quickly from there.

Crying from Erin.

Commands from the therapists.

To stop screaming.

To please get up off the floor and get back in the chair.

That if she didn't improve her behavior and stop the noise, the rest of us would leave the room until she calmed down.

Then we were all watching Erin from outside the room through what I had mistaken for a mirror on the wall of the therapy room.

Eyes wide and teeth clenched, I stood back while the therapists explained what they believed was happening. "I think we may have some oppositional defiant disorder elements here, triggered by severe attachment disorder. She just doesn't want to listen anymore, and she won't respond and do what's being asked of her."

I thought of my biggest tantrum. My parents had told me over and over that I needed to wear a helmet if I was going to be allowed to use my bike. And when they caught me riding without one for the third time in a row, they locked up my bike. Jamie and I had been planning to ride down to the lake. I was screaming at my mom through the window, saying I wanted my bike back so I could go, and when she refused, I'd told her it was too bad that I was a son of a bitch, and then I ran off.

That was way worse than my little sister not brushing her hair and crying about having to get it cut short.

"Can't we just go in there and give her a hug or something?" I asked. "She's really upset."

"Reid, lisssten," said one of the therapists to me before breathing in, then smiling. "The pattern of Erin's behavior is quite concerning. You're probably not aware of all that's happened to her, but she is very much in need of treatment. Attachment therapy and more. If we're to prevent. . . . Well, I'll let your parents discuss that with you."

Erin sobbed on the other side of the glass. She lay on her side, holding her hair in her hands.

———

To prevent Erin from becoming a predator like her father, they said that my mother should hold Erin tightly in her lap and bottle-feed her. It seemed really weird to me, them on the couch like that, while I ate a bowl of Kix at the kitchen counter.

I witnessed a forced "rebirth" therapy session, in which Erin seemed to be getting smothered in blankets by the male therapist. They said she was supposed to fight her way out, to go back to the beginning, after which she would in theory be ready to bond, like a new baby, with my parents. I walked out partway through the session, while Erin was struggling to emerge from the pile that the therapists were manipulating around her.

I wanted these "treatments" to end, but what did I know?

One therapist was grilling Erin about why she'd tied up our cat in a chair, while the other whispered to us on the other side of the glass that "this type of behavior could presage sociopathy." I didn't understand her, but she seemed to know what she was talking about. And they'd tell Erin that she needed to behave better if she wanted to stay in the family. But I didn't muster a word in her defense, thinking about how I once stuffed Noche into a pillowcase long before Erin had done anything to him—hoping no one would find out, so that I wouldn't get kicked out of the family.

When I saw how mad my mom got after Erin chewed up a bunch of her chicken and peas and spit it back out onto her plate, I imagined that anger turning toward me, and her raised hand pointing "Out!" I didn't dare say I'd told Erin it'd be funny if she did it in front of our parents.

I didn't possess the loyalty and love that Erin did. Though I refused to put "foster" before "sister" and said I was committed to her, I wasn't doing the types of things she'd done for her baby brother. She'd risked beatings and getting lost trying to find him food after their mom had gone out looking for drugs and left them alone for days.

It was said that Erin couldn't really love, while I was the one standing by, not helping my sibling when she got in trouble.

———

Worse than just standing by, I began to flee when my little sister got in trouble, locked in her room.

One night, when Jamie and I were sitting in the hot tub soaking, he asked me, "Is that your sister watching us?"

"I don't know—is she?" I hadn't seen her since lunch.

"I think I saw the shade move up there."

I looked up from the tub to the silhouette of my sister pacing her room. "Oh yeah. I think I see it. That's probably her. Maybe she's still in timeout?"

"Creepy."

"Yeah," I said. "Let's get out of here. Maybe go to your place for the night?"

We biked away.

———

The reason to fear Erin's roaming freely never seemed quite in hand. There were fleeting insinuations of what might happen, that we had to be careful— in terms that came from the professionals' case files in a language of expertise inscrutable to children.

Over time, I picked up on some of the terms, but what was happening still didn't make sense. "Sexual molestation" was something that had happened to her, not anything she'd done.

But she might, they suggested. You have to watch for these things. We have to be sure that doesn't happen.

So we watched, locked the locks, left her alone to cry, told her she needed to get it together. Built the little things she did wrong (though I'd done worse) into a phantasm that was too scary to let out. Too scary to get close to. Too scary to keep in the house.

Really, she was just a loving little girl wishing behind a window for a family to choose her, to see all the good in her and thereby let it out.

———

Eleven seasons passed instead of the two Erin would typically get with a family. A few Christmases, with socks and sweaters and coats wrapped and piled up under the tree. Tangerines in the toes of our stockings, one of which had Erin's name sewn into the white velvet top. Chocolates and ChapSticks. Tops and pterodactyl puzzles. Under our fifteen-foot Christmas tree that climbed anew each year to the vaulted ceiling, Erin and I found just about everything we needed—and sometimes more. A cozy pillow that unfolded into a blanket with lions on it, with a pocket to keep your toes warm. A snowboard to go out and get cold. We delivered Thanksgiving dinners and Christmas presents to families seeking holiday help. Though she hadn't always been able to provide for her crying baby brother when she was just a few years old, now she lit up with the ease and joy of taking Tupperwares of potatoes and tins of pumpkin pie out of the trunk of our minivan and carrying them up a few steps to set them on the table of another family with a baby of their own.

———

Then we met for our final family therapy session.

"We have decided that Erin will need to go and live in a group home, where she can get the full-time support that she needs. She's just not able to be successful in a family at this point."

Wailing "Noooo," Erin and I slipped together from the furniture down to the place where the rug met the cement, where I'd seen her crying alone. All those times when I'd wanted to go to her—when maybe I could've made it better—and I'd been told to stay back.

My parents, suddenly no longer hers, cried quietly on the couch, looking at us, then up at the therapist.

I didn't know what "group home" meant or understand any of the explanations for why my sister would be sent to one the next week.

I knew from Jamie and his siblings what the bond of brotherhood was supposed to entail. Taking care of one another. Stepping into the toughest places to pull the other out. The responsibility of love was to fix things for the younger ones.

Though I had tried to change the adults' minds and find a better way, I unwrapped my arms from Erin when I was told to let her go, and headed home.

———

On the way to the bathroom we used to share, I felt the bottom of my rib cage collapsing in. I stood just outside the door frame of her dark bedroom but didn't go in.

I didn't understand.

My parents had helped me come to terms with other awful things, like my grandmother's death or a broken arm, by explaining how it worked, the stages of grief, how long an injury would take to heal. What we might be able to do next time to prevent so much pain.

This time, though, it just didn't make sense. This had been our house. Our mirror in the bathroom where we'd brushed our teeth together, making faces, laughter and toothpaste frothing over. And now she was somehow someplace I'd never see.

She came back to my one and only childhood house a handful of times, on special occasions when, I guess, it's too sad to be in an institution without a family: Thanksgiving, Christmas, her birthday.

And eventually, during the increasingly long stretches between visits, I crossed into her room and onto the brown-orange-and-green carpet. I approached the windows that looked out on the hot tub and the woods where I'd gotten to grow up. The view through the trees of the lake, the foothills, and, on a clear day, the snow-capped mountains.

Even on windless days, when the evergreens presided stilly outside her windows and no one else was around, the quiet room felt chaotic, full of lingering tumult.

Someone amazing had once been here. Had been playing Chinese checkers and, giggling, jumped up and down on the bed with me. Had been torn away from here.

Now I had two bedrooms to myself.

I no longer had to share anything, but I didn't get to share my life.

I thought about how, one day, when my parents would die and I would be wrecked—as my mom had been when Grandma died—no one would understand. No one would share the pain with me; no one but me would survive this family.

Why me? And why her? Like *this*?

We had been a we. And now she was she; and I, incomplete.

CHAPTER TWO

Since Erin's old room had my old bunk bed in it, Jamie and I eventually started going in for sleepovers, filling the darkest hours of the night with whispered wonderings about the reaches of the universe. We tore through the somberness of the space with farts and laughter.

What was I to do but gradually stop thinking about her?

I'd been given answers that I didn't know how to question, by professionals and parents who treated me really well. I was becoming a teenager, busy trying to figure out my own life.

After summer overnights at my place, Jamie and I would hop on our bikes and speed around the corner, where I stashed my helmet in a bush and rode the trail down to his place.

On previous trips alone to Jamie's house, on the last hill before his cul-de-sac, I'd turned around after hearing his mom from a block off, yelling things like: "Jamie, you little shit, get your ass in here and do these dishes NOW! I'm not playing!"

Jamie's house seemed full of a volatile, raucous love that I'd never experienced. I never knew what was going to happen, which was exciting, coming from a relatively quiet and mild-mannered home and always able to bike back there.

On this trip down, he sat up straight as we rounded the corner and said, "I better stop to check in before we go down to the lake. Just wait here." He threw his brother's bike down onto the grass and sprang over the gap in the deck to disappear through the red front door.

I sat crisscross next to the bikes and picked up a worm. *So far, so good*. I didn't hear "Get your ass in here!" or "You little shit!" or "You're grounded!"

And eventually Jamie slipped quietly back out of the house, jumped down the steps, and told me to bike fast across the neighbor's lawn so they wouldn't see us.

Emerging onto a dirt road, we sped by an old, burned-out house. But I saw only good things: the tread of our tires integrating perfectly into the two dirt tracks we rode, fast, side by side, pedal for pedal, separated only by a ribbon of grass with daisies and dandelions. Cascades of blackberry bushes with handful-size clusters of fresh, free fruit. Though we were sometimes pricked picking them, the blood just ran into the color of the juice and disappeared.

We were as expansive as the abundant foliage. It was full summer. Every drop of rain from fall and winter had been channeled into something incredible, quenching a tiny root's thirst perfectly, lifting higher a plant's green shoot. We were amongst millions of shoots as we rolled down the hill alongside an undulating creek.

At the edge of the creek were soggy crabgrass shoots, then blue-button forget-me-nots, ferns, azalea bushes, and eventually trees. The cherry trees had enough water to push up over the roadway, flower, and then turn those flowers into extra-juicy cherries. The apple trees bore hundreds of big, green apples filled with water. Nesting colonies of green caterpillars with green feet and green eyes.

We rolled past tree trunks far too big to reach around, over gravel, and on down the open field that merged into the sand of our lake shore. Pitching towel-capes and bikes aside, we pulled off our shoes and shirts, running for the dock. People looked up as the dock ramp rebounded loudly beneath us. We gained speed on the pontoon and dove in simultaneously. All sounds and colors immediately disappeared. There was nothing here underwater but the internal feeling and focus of pulling handfuls of frigid water from above our heads down to our waists again, again, again, returning toward the sun, kicking up into the sky.

Jamie had made it farther underwater than I had. So I heard the whistle and bellow of the lifeguard before he was back up. "No diving! Didn't we tell you yesterday?!"

Jamie popped up at the wooden pillar at the edge of the swim zone. "Let's see if we can make it all the way to the bottom," he said. The pillar climbed ten feet out of the water, and probably at least as far below our toes.

"I don't know, man. We've tried this before. It's really . . . far." I didn't want to seem scared, but I also didn't want to do it. There were messes of seaweed fields down there in the unknown dark.

"But I haven't tried it headfirst before," said Jamie, lifting his dense brown brows and showing white all around his irises.

"Why is that better?"

"Well, I was thinking about it," he said. "If we keep our eyes open, it's less scary because we can see what's coming. And we can get more speed going headfirst. OK, I'll go first."

". . ."

"But then you'll go, right?" he asked.

"Yeah, if you'll swim out with me to the far buoy later, when the life-guards leave?"

"I'll do it if you'll do it. As always!" he shouted out, making room for an immense inhalation, then doubling over at the waist, kicking his feet up into the air, and then hard against the water, until his pale soles disappeared into the cloudy black.

Big bubbles crested suddenly, followed by Jamie in his faded plaid boxers holding up a fistful of lake grass. "I did it!! Ha-ha! Your turn."

I glanced at the snowy Cascade Mountains past the lush hills, avoiding Jamie's intense eye contact for a moment.

"Remember, I'll-do-it-if-you'll-do-it."

"Yeah, yes. I know . . ." I looked at Jamie, took my biggest breath, and—not knowing what I'd find down there—dove.

———

After our swim, while Jamie was talking to a girl, I lay on my towel on the sand. Salt-N-Pepa, Sir Mix-a-Lot, and Sublime played on different boom-boxes around the park, singing "yeah" and "uh-huh."

Seeing only my closed, illuminated pink lids, I smiled big and rode down sweet exhalations into my towel.

"That girl reminded me a little bit of Erin. How's she doing?" Jamie asked.

"Mmmh? Hey," I said, just cresting the sleep-wake line. "Go good over there?"

"No diggity. What's the latest with Erin, anyways?"

"Erin? Umm . . . I think she's still in, like, that group home?"

"Oh, that's a bummer. That's like an orphanage, right?"

I hadn't ever thought of it like that. But I couldn't think of any difference between what had been described to me and an orphanage. I also couldn't believe that my parents would ever send a little girl away to an orphanage, so I didn't answer.

"Does she still come by for Christmases and birthdays and stuff?"

I had to think. I opened an eye and saw Jamie, also on his stomach on his towel on the sand, looking back at me. "I guess she didn't last Christmas, no. And her birthday just passed . . ."

"Did you get her anything?" he asked after a moment.

"Naw." I'd barely thought of her when May rolled around this year.

"Isn't she, like, your sister?" he asked. He had two older sisters and two older brothers.

"I mean," I started, propping myself up on my elbows, "she was my *foster* sister."

"Oh, so you don't consider her your sister anymore?"

I wanted to. But I didn't want to be a jerk for not remembering my sister's birthday, and for not having kept up with her. "I don't know, man."

I rolled away onto my side to look at the water. After a few minutes, when I was back under the sleep-wake line, Jamie asked the question: "Why did they send her to the orphanage?"

It was an iteration of the fundamental question that used to come to me in the hall outside her old bedroom: Why was I here, and she wasn't?

"I mean, they could've taken care of her, right? They're doin' OK moneywise, and your mom's a school counselor and everything."

Yeah: wasn't it really my parents' responsibility? And weren't they more than capable? My dad could solve the toughest science problems to make hundreds of tons of metal and plastic hurtle peacefully through the sky at six hundred miles an hour. My mom had solved hundreds of kids' toughest problems in her job. If they had given up on Erin, did that mean they were bad? It seemed like they were great parents to me . . .

"Dude?"

He wasn't going to let me back to sleep now, so I rolled away from the lapping, sun-glistened water and toward the question.

"Look, man," I said sternly, "she had a severe disorder—more than one, actually. The therapists told us she wasn't capable of being successful in a family." I tried to remember some of the big words they'd used.

"Hmm," he said. "What does that mean? Like, we all have our issues. I feel bad for that time we made fun of her at Ardmore."

I felt bad about it too, but said, "What're you talking about?"

"You know, when we all went over to the playground and were riding the slide and, like, making fun of her short hair. And kept daring her to ride the big slide even though she was scared, and we made up that other stuff to scare her."

"That's just stuff kids do," I said. "Don't your siblings do that kind of crap to you all the time?"

"Yeah, for sure. But we're there for each other if shit gets serious. And it seems like Erin really needed help with stuff. And we were kind of jerks that time. And she's your sister, you know. Like, maybe you guys could've made a difference . . ."

"*Foster* sister," I said, wondering the same thing, but not wanting to fess up to doubting the family I had left. "You don't know all the history. My mom said before they made the decision, they were told by the therapists that they should give her some sort of deprivation therapy. Like"—I swallowed—"taking everything out of her room. Except maybe a cot. And then she would just get plain oatmeal and water passed in to her. And to do that for a long time until she learned that her needs would be met, and then she could earn anything beyond that with good behavior or something. I don't know. But, like, crazy stuff, man. She needed some serious professional help."

I think I wanted to scare Jamie off the topic, the way all the professional talk about diagnoses and treatments had intimidated me. He chewed on the tip of his pointer finger for a while.

Eventually, I calmed a bit and lay back onto my towel but couldn't sleep.

————

At the very end of elementary school, Jamie and I had both gotten glimpses of what school could be—a class that started to verge on some of the big questions we were trying to figure out on our own, like the injustices of Erin's situation, or the psychology of Jamie's mom, or how the ecosystems around us worked, or what made things beautiful. We got to put on Shakespeare plays and conduct real science experiments in creeks.

Then we were sent to different middle schools. My school gave me some standard classes, and also algebra, geometry, and "gifted" classes—enough to sometimes keep me engaged and other times earning Ds and walking the halls with my friends. The most interesting things Jamie brought back from his school to our time walking our paper routes together were sex jokes about the name of the school, the mascot, and the principal, and his budding idea that drugs might be the best way to expand your mind.

————

Our high school put us all in the same classes again, in individual plastic chairs bolted to laminate desktops. We finished our color-the-map assignment early and began to joust with pencils. The teacher shushed us and said,

Do your work! We told her we were done, but she didn't have anything more for us. So, after a while doing nothing, we started to joust again.

I honestly couldn't tell you a thing about the history of the world that class supposedly taught us. The only thing I've retained is a permanent mark on my inner arm from a piece of pencil lead that broke off there during a jousting match, and was stuck in me until sixth period gym, when I noticed it, pulled it out, and threw it away.

Why didn't we learn about the country one of our classmates had been adopted from? Or the several different languages spoken by students in the room? Or what history could tell us about the rapid changes that might be coming to our neighborhood of horse pastures, 1970s split-levels, and multi-family apartment complexes as Microsoft began to take off? I wish we had learned about the history of racial covenants in the area that had strictly segregated neighborhoods, or why, as the lowest-income school in the district, we had so many of these low-level classes that led me and my friends to joust the day away.

When kids say they're bored in school, it's not because they need teachers to turn every poem into a pop song or all the science into robots. But we do need far more than dittos and color-in maps. Like any learner, we thirst for genuine interaction with the teacher and other students about real and meaningful ideas.

To try to make students to do boring things, you can go full jailhouse—as some schools do. But like Play-Doh in your palm, the more tightly you grip, the more cause students will find to escape from between your fingers.

There's always competition for kids' attention: a hallway to walk, kids across the street to talk to; actual learning beyond the classroom, from discussing big ideas, undertaking explorations of uncertain destination, traversing the frontiers of the human mind, and following our innate drive to imagine beyond all past imagining.

In school, my friends and I wore T-shirts that said things like "Take Me Drunk I'm Home"—even though I didn't drink—to see if we could make something interesting happen. We rushed off campus for lunch at Uwajimaya or Taco Time.

Lots of people didn't come back to watch the clock after lunch. Instead, they hung out smoking by the bus stop or went to the house of an older kid who had snakes and drugs.

Jamie and I were super bored. We were into skating and making money on our paper routes. We'd walk the routes together a couple times a week, getting an hour to talk about interesting things like the secret of getting

Kool-Aid to work as permanent hair dye, new guitar chords, gun control versus gun rights, the kid at school who'd accidentally shot his brother to death, the girls down the street, and the next jobs we wanted to get: at the moving company, selling newspaper subscriptions, and maybe even one day as journalists who put muckraking writing into the papers we delivered.

———

I couldn't sit there for fifty-five minutes, with only five free minutes before the next fifty-five-minute stretch began. So I started chipping away at the time any way I could. A little at first, then more. By tenth grade, I knew exactly how much I could take from each teacher.

In history, I'd lean over to my girlfriend, who was slouched back in her chair really low, then half-cup her ear with my hand, whispering behind its wall. Half a minute later, without a word to the teacher, I got up, walked to the front of the room, past the bombs on the television screen, and out the blue metal door.

Looking back through the large pane of glass in the door, seeing the teacher glance at me through the crack between his lowered reading glasses and his crinkled forehead, I walked off into the forest.

I waited behind a cedar tree for only a minute, leaning on the fragrant trunk and tilting my head toward a sky blocked by a hundred limbs.

Then my girlfriend skipped into view, her shoulder-length auburn hair skipping behind her. Steam rose lightly from the cedar's prickly interwoven needles, adding haze to haze, and we kissed.

After twenty minutes, we slipped out from between a patch of ferns, back onto the old-gum-covered walkway. I swung the big door wide open and took one more breath of morning mist before we crossed back into the classroom.

I strode down an aisle to the back row, and sat in my seat. The same theme was playing. It was a Civil War song on a fiddle that we'd been hearing for weeks now in this class. The music had a faded urgency, as though the fiddler had grown bored and the war we watched was already hopelessly lost.

———

Having spent her whole career as a teacher and school counselor, my mom knew how to navigate the system on my behalf. Though I didn't initially want to, she eventually got me to enroll in an advanced program that started halfway through high school.

Early one morning of my junior year, my teacher Del Dolliver stood ready in front of the whiteboard.

Listening to a student talk, he grabbed a marker like a five-year-old at an open-field Easter egg hunt. The color didn't matter, as long as he secured the closest one as quickly as possible.

"Yes," he said. "Yes!"

FUNDAMENIAL AIIRIBUIION ERROR, he scribbled. Then he went back and crossed several of the I's into T's—some that needed crossing, and some that didn't.

A student said, "You missed the first T in 'ATTRIBUTION,' and at the end, you crossed the I instead of the T."

Another student asked, "It means, like, attributing something to a situation or to a person, right?"

Dolliver tried fixing the crosses and dots. "Yes," he said. "Good." Then he wrote SIIUAIIION and PERSON, and went back and put a bunch of dots and crosses over both clusters of I's.

As Dolliver turned his head to try to make sense of the last cluster, a student offered, "You've got too many there."

"Oh, for Pete's sake," said Dolliver. He tried adding another two dots, then wiped out the whole word with his palm. Accidentally erasing the P in 'PERSON,' he just kept going and cleared both words, then started again over pink marker smears, dotting and crossing more carefully as he went. "S, I with a dot . . . T with a cross, U, A, T with a cross, I with a dot . . ."

The class was fixated.

"OK. So what about situations and people?" he asked.

He slumped behind a student desk into its affixed plastic chair. As he wiped sweat from his big forehead ringed by messy white hair, he accidentally smudged blue marker around his upper face.

"Yes, Reid," he said, pointing at me.

I said, "Well, because of the . . . what's it? The self-serving bias? Like, we talked about how the mind's always looking for a reason why—to try to explain what's happening. But people kind of screw up the explanation for why with their self-serving bias. So, if someone's explaining why they did something bad, they'll blame it on the situation. And if they're explaining something good they did, they'll say it's because of how great they are as a person."

Del Dolliver had his eyes closed. His hands rested, markered palms upwards, on the small writing surface before him. He appeared to be asleep.

"Hm-mmmmmmm . . ."

The class watched him, his eyes still closed, while he scratched his white mustache.

"So . . . you're saying we explain things differently for ourselves than we do for others." His eyes flashed open. "How many of you have ever cut someone off in traffic?"

A raft of hands went up around me.

"Why'd you do it, Melissa?"

"I overslept and was trying not to be late for this early class."

"So you didn't set out to cut someone off. You had the best of intentions. It's not that you don't care. In fact, you were trying to do the right thing and get to school to advance your education."

"That's right!" she said.

"But what if someone cuts *you* off?"

"Honestly, I usually curse 'em out," Melissa said, then coiffed the ends of her medium-length brown hair, which were curled in toward her face.

"Me too," added Khan. "And I tail 'em and honk and everything. Those . . ." he started, then looked up at Dolliver.

"So, if you do it, Melissa, then you find it easy to understand why and to justify. You can't miss class! You're working hard to learn! But if someone does it to you, they're a bleepety-bleep-bleep."

"That's what I'm talkin' about!" said Khan, smiling, clapping his palms together.

"This double standard is so pervasive, and so significant, that we've labeled it the *fundamental*"—Dolliver slashed and starred the word with emphasis from a fresh purple marker—"attribution error. And if you do something good, like show up on time or earn a good grade, then who's responsible for that?"

"Well, I like to think *I* am," said another student.

I know I am, I thought to myself, taking credit for my good grades since things had gotten interesting in school, and ignoring that my mom helped me with Spanish and with writing and editing papers, and my dad helped me with all things math and science.

"Right. And if someone earns a better grade than you or makes a better decision, then they just got lucky, right?"

We shrugged and nodded a bit at one another.

"So, let me get this straight," said Dolliver, trying to finesse his way back in between the student desk and chair. "You're not responsible for your bad actions. You get all the credit for your good actions! And if someone else does something good, it was just circumstance. But if they do something bad, then, well, they're a total jerk."

"That about sums it up," smiled Khan, crossing his arms and nodding.

"So how does this fit into the broader set of cognitive errors that we make as people?"

"Look, Dolly Lama," I said. "You've been teaching us about all sorts of errors and mistakes that *some* people make. These people in these experiments about obedience, and about playing into their roles, and saying the obviously wrong line size to conform, and stuff."

"Yes," he nodded.

"How old are these experiments?"

"How old?"

"Yeah."

Dolliver rattled off the years of some of the experiments, and I interrupted.

"So we're talking, like, fifty years ago! It seems to me that you're doing some sort of attribution error applying these things to us. I mean, come on: who's really gonna say the wrong line, when, like you said, in the experiment it's made to be so obvious which is the right one? Just because someone else said it? We're not sheep."

He smiled as though he had something in store for us. "OK. How many of you relate to the people in the studies we've been discussing this year? How many think, *Hey, that could be me?*"

No one raised a hand.

Dolliver's wispy white eyebrows asked, *Really?*

"Yeah, I mean, those people are straight up duuuuuumb, Dolliver," Melissa said.

"Yeah, man. Where do they get these dummies? Are they, like, so desperate for $5 that they'll say whatever the experimenter wants or sumpin?" asked Khan.

"*Dumb?*" he asked us. "Whoa."

"I mean, no one would really keep hitting the shock buttons when someone's yelling to stop in that Milgram experiment," a classmate added.

"Or the guards-and-prisoners experiment. Those buncha college kids must've been clownin' around, man. And you go and take it all serious and stuff," said Khan, scratching his left temple.

"Whoa now. Whoa," said Dolliver. His palms up and open at us, he wiggled some of his fingers. "How many of you feel this way?"

I looked around and noticed everyone's hand up. Our advanced class was smaller than most. No Black students. As far as I knew, none of the folks in this class lived in apartments, like most of my middle school friends had. And none of them talked about big families trying to make ends meet, like Jamie's.

"Now, I'll have to think about this some more," Dolliver said. "But it seems to me that we're not seeing ourselves reflected in this research. This is an immense body of work. Take Asch, for example. This study has been replicated across many decades and all around the world, in a wide variety of cultures. I wonder if it's a failure of imagination here, of empathy. As smart as you may be, you simply have to understand that you, too, are missing things when viewing the world from your perspective. You are making cognitive errors. I need to find a way to show you . . ." He trailed off.

"It's no big deal, Dolliver. It's interesting to read about and all. But I'm just saying, it's not how *I* would act," I said.

"But that's the very point. This is about our common humanity. The evidence about how we as people do make mistakes." He held up the textbook, and the packet with today's experiment. "These *are* about you. You can't simply project the bad aspects of humanity onto others and keep the good things for yourselves. That's the epitome of the fundamental attribution error."

"A-pit-o-what?"

"I don't make most of these errors we're talkin' about, is all," I said.

"You don't attribute good choices and behavior to yourself, and blame bad stuff on others?"

"Not me!" I announced gleefully.

CHAPTER THREE

The next day, we found Dolliver meditating—or sleeping—in a student desk again. Once we were seated around him, he recited, eyes closed, the intellectual trajectory of the previous day, paying special attention and respect to our original ideas, and their connection to the ongoing scholarly dialogue as he saw it.

"One of my students last year conducted an experiment to test whether one of these cognitive errors could be overcome through direct education about the error. And he found that to be the case. What I heard from you yesterday..." He smiled and nodded to himself. "I heard the hypothesis that deeper education in the nature of these cognitive errors could possibly make people altogether immune to such errors."

He seemed to be eating the idea. His jowls flexed and unflexed. He groaned in satiety. Seemed to swallow. "Mmm..."

"You OK over there, Dolliver?"

"Mmm, yes," he said. "It's a fascinating idea. And I would love for one or more of you to design some ways to further test this powerful and important hypothesis."

There was a sense of pride in the room.

He opened his eyes, walked slowly to the board, and drew a rectangle in black, then asked, "What is this?"

"Uh ... a rectangle," we said.

"Actually," he said, "from my perspective, it's a circle."

"What the ... ?"

"Dolliver, you're wacky as ever, man."

I snickered and said to Khan, "You gotta love this guy."

"OK, I'll bite," said Melissa. "How's a circle sposta be a rectangle?"

"Because that's what it is. From my perspective," Dolliver said, picking up a can of Diet Coke from his desk and taking a sip.

It took almost ten minutes—during which his gestures and subtle pointing at the Coke can escalated—for us to notice that what he held in his hand was the same shape and size as the rectangle on the board, when viewed from its side (our perspective). And from the top, where he looked down on it, it was in fact a circle.

I sighed in epiphany as the two perspectives, together, became something greater.

"It's important for us to understand that people with different vantage points can have radically different answers," Dolliver noted. "And even when they seem incompatible, they can be component parts of something closer to the truth than any individual can muster on their own.

"And to get perspective on yourself—to 'know thyself'—from any angle other than your own, can be the most difficult truth of all to pursue. I mean, the front of your brain—your eyes—is literally pointed outwards, and cannot face backwards. It takes a multiplicity of perspectives, and a humbleness, to begin to develop your perspective on yourself as a scholar, a citizen, a member of a community."

He told us that our ideas were interesting and our hypotheses worth testing, that we could approach truth through dialogue about differences of opinion. Then he went mostly silent, encouraging us with an occasional "mmm."

As the discussion went on through sunrise, I learned not just about self-serving biases and the limitations and possibilities of perspective-taking. I learned that as a student, my ideas and experiences mattered and could even be tasty. And this was a direct contradiction to what I'd experienced in earlier years of schooling.

Del Dolliver showed us that our mark on the world needn't be constrained to tiny ticks in a few lettered bubbles on an answer sheet. We could fill in big open spaces thinking, trying out ideas, and developing them with others.

————

Jamie's mom had dropped out after eighth grade, and during some of Jamie's formative years she raised him and his four siblings on her own. Though she cared for him as much as my mom did for me, she didn't have a lot of time to help Jamie figure out how to navigate a high school system she'd never been part of.

So I tried to help him navigate it. One day, we were riding back from a moving job, sitting in the cab of the truck next to the driver, Benny, a self-declared ex-con who had just walked us through his plan to make more money by taking some of our hours off the books.

"Jamie, man," I said, "you should sign up for some of these IB classes. They're amazing."

"Huh?" He lifted his heavy brows and turned his head toward me.

"Like, these classes are legit. This is the kind of stuff we've been lookin' for for a while. It's so friggin' interesting!"

"..."

"Are you listenin'?"

"I'm listenin'. You're talkin' about IB. Like 'I Be a little high,' right?"

"No," I said, frowning.

"I'm glad they're workin' for you, brother. But this school stuff isn't for me. I'm having a good time with Melanie. And pole-vaulting is pickin' up."

"I got sports and my girlfriend too. This isn't about any of that. You would rock this big time. You're smart and passionate and . . ." He shook his head, but I said, "I need you to just hear me for a minute about this, OK?"

"Sure." He watched the cars across the median.

"I'm saying that this is about, like, good books—like, the best ideas that people have ever had. It's about . . . uh . . ." I struggled to explain. "It's not something I can really explain, cuz it's, like, the knowledge of the whole *world*, and our chance to be a part of it and make our contribution. They call us scholars, and it's kinda true. I wrote a paper the other day about how Fidel Castro had this communist idea and fought in the woods, guerrilla style, like we used to play in the woods, but he actually beat the president of Cuba and took over the whole country! And he was sharing the money and the land, but then it got corrupted in some ways and turned into totalitarianism."

"Total-eh-what?"

"He tried to control everyone's minds: art, music, holidays, these speeches that went on for hours and hours."

"How long a paper we talkin'?"

"Five pages."

"By hand."

"No, typed."

"No way, dude. You think I wanna write a five-page, typed paper?! I've had too much of this school shit as it is. I'm not about to sign up for *more* of it."

"But it's not *more*. It's . . . it's totally *different*."

"I bet you had to do a bunch more work on top of that to even be able to write that essay. Like research and stuff?"

I wasn't sure whether to be proud of my answer or whether I was about to wreck my chances with Jamie: "I read two books on Cuba and Castro and compared the authors' perspectives."

"Heh," he exhaled, looking at me. He seemed to be feeling a couple of things. I caught a glimpse of interest, then he forced a hard, heavy laugh. "Heh-heh-hahaha!" He fully extended his arm and pointed at me. "You crazy, meng! I'm out. Ha-ha!"

"You said you would listen to me, jerk!"

"I've *been* listening, asshole," he said, serious.

"OK, you listened. But will you think about it? Please."

"Yeah, sure, man. You got it. Benny, we still stoppin' for food, and—you know?"

———

At this point, other than his one good class in elementary school, Jamie had had about a decade of time-wasting low-level classes—being told to be quieter, be stiller, listen better. To get in a single, straight line, instead of weaving complexity.

If I hadn't gotten into IB when I did, I would've gone from missing half of class wandering the halls to missing the whole thing, like Jamie was now doing some days.

He'd intermittently show up to classes just across the hall from mine, and I started to feel desperate to reconnect with him, to bring him over.

But then we didn't see each other for a long stretch. Someone said he might be moving. I'd hear that he was skipping to smoke out behind the school, but I didn't have time to go check before the start of my next class.

I went home after running practice and sat next to my mom on a glider bench on our back porch. Some days, I'd feel in awe that she could identify every single error in my essay with her erasable pen. And then something awful would come up—like a fist fight in a friend's family—and I felt haughty teenage disgust for my mom. After all, she was my tour guide for the world. She'd arranged my life trip and set me out in search of great, big things. And some days it was as if I were looking for whales but saw only a lone seagull that flew by and shat on me.

"Mom, uhhhh, no! I'm not saying Jamie might be a friend for a season or whatever. I'm saying I'm pissed off but I'm not going to give up. This is important!"

"OK, I hear you," she said patiently. "So he's not returning your calls and you want him to take IB with you. Why do you think that's so important to you?"

"I really like my classes these days. I know I don't say these kinds of things much, but I do appreciate your getting me to go into IB."

"Oh! I'm glad."

"And I guess I've been trying to do the same for Jamie, you know? And he's kind of being a stubborn jerk about it."

"I bet he would like IB. And it sounds like he's got a lot going on in his life too."

"Can you keep a secret?"

"Unless someone's in danger, yes," she said, ever the good, clear counselor. That made me think. "Well, technically . . ." I started. "Hmm."

"Is someone in danger?"

"I don't think so. But you might think so, so never mind," I decided. The last thing I needed was Jamie and his family getting pissed off at me for telling my mom a rumor I'd heard about what'd happened. "But yes, he does have a lot going on in his life."

"I hope you would let me know if someone is in danger."

"Yes, Mom. I would," I said. I'd told her when a girlfriend was cutting herself, and my mom had really helped with that.

"So, sometimes when people are struggling, we're able to help them directly. And sometimes the best thing that we can do is to give them space."

"Uh-huh."

"If you put yourself in Jamie's shoes right now, what do you think he might want from his friend?"

"That's a good question." I tipped my head back, trying to loosen my neck. "I don't know."

I tried to imagine Jamie's perspective, even though what he was doing hurt. All that came to me was the hurt.

"I'm going through this stuff with Jess, and he won't even call me back! What kind of a friend is that?"

She started to rub my shoulders. "You said he might be moving? You've never *had* to move. How do you think you might feel if we moved to another city right now?"

"Oh, that'd be horrible. I mean, my friends are all here. It's the middle of high school! His parents shouldn't move. Jamie should be able to stay here, right?"

"Sometimes, when people have to leave, they do this thing called spoiling the nest. That's when you try to make it easier to leave something by wrecking it. Then you think maybe you won't have to be so sad about leaving. Maybe Jamie is going through some of that. He might be comforted to know that you think he's a forever friend, and that even if he's struggling and acting out of character now, you're still going to be there for him."

"Yeah, I will."

". . ."

"But what about this IB stuff? He needs to get in now if he's going to do it, to be ready for college and everything."

"It sounds like you've done your best to try to help him with that," she said, looking at me kindly. "And he might not be ready to do it at this point. Some of these things are out of our control. All we can do is try our best."

I didn't agree. After all, my mom loved me, and she didn't just *try* to help me. She actually got it done.

———

I admired Jamie. He took me from a kid who got made fun of to someone who listened to good music, had cool clothes and hair, and eventually a couple girlfriends. The anthems of my childhood were from albums he shared with me. My first crush was his sister. Jamie took me out of my lonely house and into a social world where he thought I could belong. He poked and prodded and forced my physical and intellectual boundaries wider. He taught me how to share even when I didn't want to, to care deeply about what's fair even when it's hard.

We called arguments "discussions," and redefined maturity too: "Some people think it's immature to laugh at farts. But they're immature by letting the idea that something's immature get in the way of laughing and having fun with life and farts and friends!"

Because he had done so much for me as my best friend, I felt a responsibility to get through to him about IB. I rehearsed all the things my mom and dad had said to me when they were about to sign me up. All the things about IB that the teachers had told us to keep us motivated: the stuff about colleges liking it, about being among a community of scholars.

Then, one day, we saw each other in the hall by the locker bay, under a fogged-up plastic skylight, and I had my last chance before class registration closed.

I wanted to talk about how language was communication, community. How science was how everything worked, and math was about how much of everything there is . . . and about perfect balance, the ideal shape of things. And once you understood how things were and how they could be, history was the stories of how people brought imagined could-bes into reality—how maybe we could too.

But I couldn't get any of that out. So I just said, "Hey, man! I want us to do this IB thing together. It means a lot to me. And I just know it will mean a lot to you too. You have to trust me on this. I'm serious here."

"This again?"

"Yeah, man."

"Naw."

We'd been over all this before and gotten nowhere with it. Passing time was almost over. So I decided to wager our biggest call-out—one neither of us had dared turn down in six years. If one of us said it, the other came along: "I'll do it if you'll do it."

"Man, this can't be one of those things. Don't say that, because I just—"

"I *am* saying it, man. It means that much to me."

He tried to warn me. "But this is different. I'm totally pissed at my psychology teacher right now, who won't even let me talk. She tells me to shut up and to just label parts of the brain all period. I can't stand it. And here you're sayin' do *more* of this crap! More bullshit school when I already can't stand what I have of it. Maybe it's not bullshit to you. Maybe you like that stuff, and more power to you. But I'm about to—"

"That's exactly the point. This is different. This is what school's *supposed* to be about. All these dozen years so far, this is what it was for. It's real. It's actual conversation where they *want* you to talk. It's all about our ideas and real, actual learning. So I'm sayin' it: I'll do it if you'll do it."

Jamie walked away. "Naw, man. Screw it. You're not hearing me. This school stuff is not *for* me."

———

While Jamie sought his something more in the damp woods behind campus, Mr. Dolliver introduced the project that was to culminate my high school experience: the Extended Essay. He was trying to be helpful by asking us what topics we were thinking about, what subject area we each wanted to focus on, and whether we had found advisers yet to help us with our projects. But inevitably, our collective anxiety took us off a cliff of self-doubt about whether we could really do anything substantial, interesting, or meaningful.

"Is there any way we can finish up this program without doing the Extended Essay? Anything? I mean, throw us a bone here, Dolliver!"

"Yeah, this is so messed up, man!"

"How many pages is four thousand words, again?"

"It's around fifteen pages."

"*Fifteen?!* No friggin' way, dude."

"This essay is a unique opportunity that each of you has," he told us, "to join the broader international scholarly conversation. Your essays will receive feedback from around the globe, from experts who want to know what you have to say." Dolliver's huge, tan, freckled forehead wrinkled as his eyes widened with the possibilities of what we might write.

"So, we've talked about prejudice and discrimination and in-group biases, and the nature of enhanced liking through proximity and mere exposure effects—"

"Dolliver, whatchoo talkin' about, man?"

"Well, last year I advised a psychology essay trying to apply some of our knowledge about those tendencies in order to reduce prejudice." He twisted his mustache, and his smiling mouth opened, ready to taste the idea, then pass it around for each of us to try as well. "They created integrated groups in which new bonds could be developed by performing team tasks. And the results?"

"They quit the IB program so they wouldn't have to write the Extended Essay?"

"NOT!" Dolliver said, pointing dramatically at the student.

"Did the subjects in the integrated groups reduce their prejudice?"

"YES! And not only reduced, but she virtually eliminated the in-group biases demonstrated by Tajfel, and replicated by her own control group! And she posed a fascinating question in her discussion section. By both learning about cognitive biases like prejudice and practicing the power of contact theory, how much could we reduce the impact of prejudice and discrimination in our lives?"

"Wow, that is fascinating," someone said, rolling their eyes and swirling their finger around their ear in the sign for "cuckoo."

"That's just one example. The world is your oyster! You can write about anything from all of your studies to date—anything that tickles your fancy. And you get to make an original contribution to the thinking in that field."

"I saw Roger's girlfriend tickling his fancy in the hall before class. Can he write about that?"

"NOT!"

"Dolliver, I like you and all, but this project is just completely whack. No kids like us are gonna write fifteen pages, least of all me."

"Hear, hear! Same for me."

"Mmm-hmm."

"Me too."

"So, what options do we have here, Dolly Lama?"

"Yeah—what can we do if this Extended Essay thingy is just too long for us?"

"Just focus on this next step of picking a subject area," he said. "A journey of a thousand miles starts with just one step."

"Yeah, and my journey of four thousand words may never end."

"The essays will come to an end. But the insights you gain can last you forever, trust me. Have a nice day."

———

At the same time as I was struggling to come up with an Extended Essay topic, Jamie was stuck on the other side of the hallway, still doing dittos. He wore hand-me-downs from his older siblings, who'd been through our high school before him, and also hadn't been given the good stuff. Teachers handed down to Jamie the same low-level, boring schoolwork they'd tried to get his brothers and sisters to do, apparently not realizing that he and his siblings could do so much more if really given the chance. Never understanding that his misbehavior, his D average, was the *result* of the crummy schoolwork they gave him and not a justification for it.

He paid little mind to classes that offered his mind so little, and instead sought something more, elsewhere—he focused on girls, sports, drugs that were causing him intermittent full-body paralysis. More and more often, he was waking up unable to move. Trapped inside his mind, unable to take it anywhere.

But as much as I tried, I hadn't been able to do anything about that.

So, as the only kid around my house, and with my parents off at work, there was lots of time for quiet study, looking for answers. I'd set myself up just right, make a smoothie, string up a hammock between two evergreens, under a bank of honeysuckle. A pillow under my head, me under a book. I'd read and take notes, nestling the cordless phone between myself and the multicolored weave, hoping for a call so Jamie and I could ride off to the lake again. I would drop all the books if I could just have that. But the phone didn't ring. Jamie had moved.

CHAPTER FOUR

My Extended Essay was the project that would get me into Harvard College. Working on it, lonely at home, and lonely at school, where I seldom saw Jamie anymore, I began to fill the void with myself and my ideas—building myself up as a very special individual, sometimes at the expense of others.

I took as much credit as I could for things that went well. I may have begun to believe that I'd gotten to stay in our home when Erin hadn't because I deserved it and perhaps she didn't. Because I had important work to do. That Jamie not being in IB wasn't my fault—maybe it had resulted from him lacking a special spark that I had.

Never mind that my project had come from a newspaper clipping that my mom had left on my place mat at the kitchen counter. She kept up with the news every day and found that there had been a wildcat walkout strike at a slaughterhouse in eastern Washington State. And she knew I'd become interested in meatpacking because of a book I'd read that my dad kept on the shelf in his basement office.

I wanted to believe the book, but my teachers in the IB program were telling me I needed to question sources, understand motivations—to go back to primary evidence if I wanted to be an individual thinker who really understood what was going on in the world.

But was I really an individual thinker by doing what my teachers told me to do? I took interviews that an older friend of mine had conducted with the striking workers as my primary source. My parents paid for clerical assistance to transcribe them.

I only took transcriptions and quotes and a whole bunch of other people's work and pasted it all into a big Word document. And added some words around it, like "Gail Eisnitz said." Or I did simple math to say, "Workers at different points on the line reported that 15 to 50 percent of cows . . ." The project was a conglomeration of other people's words, ideas, suffering, money, and support. My mom edited the essay with me, and had long ago taught me to turn in early drafts for feedback from the teacher before the final draft was actually graded.

I received the praise when I'd gathered together enough of other people's stuff to turn the project into a short book, which a local nonprofit paid to publish.

The evidence revealed that the stories from *The Jungle* were still happening a hundred years later, just down the highway. That most of the people who worked in these factories got injured—often losing fingers, arms, or legs. That they were told to go to the bathroom in their pants so that the disassembly line wouldn't have to stop. That, due to the pace at which management drove the line, a third of the cows didn't get knocked out at the beginning, and were partially dismembered and gutted alive, kicking and screaming, and injuring the workers with their machetes. This work scarred them physically and emotionally, leading to depression, domestic abuse, and even suicide. That the meat produced was filthy, nasty. That this wasn't an aberration—this was the largest meatpacking company in the world, and they set the industry standards for meat in America.

A college admissions coach my parents hired taught me how to aggrandize myself in the story of what had happened. To tell admissions officers about how NBC sent in undercover reporters and how the governor formed a task force to investigate things shortly after *I* wrote about it (even if none of them had read what I wrote). To make a lot out of the fact that senior special agent Frank Weeks of the Office of the Inspector General at the United States Department of Agriculture had interviewed me.

To claim that I had boldly gone after the truth, uncovering hidden facts, and piecing the puzzle together!

And after they let me in, the admissions officers told me, over a fancy dinner, how my work on the meatpacking industry had been what impressed them.

I desperately wanted—as I think we all do—to feel special. And so I laughed, and smiled deep inside when they told me how they liked my work. And I started to think I was pretty great.

Lonely, across the country, knowing no one, I started to become best friends with myself. I enjoyed praise from folks who liked my assemblages of other people's work, edited by my mom, enhanced by the extra time I had to work on it because my parents paid for everything.

Folks who sang my praises didn't seem to understand—and I, myself, soon began to forget—that Jamie or Erin or lots of other folks would've done work at least as good as mine if they'd been enrolled in decent classes and been given the resources to work on things they cared about.

————

In college, I became so focused on myself that it would take me decades to figure out what'd really been happening to those I'd left behind to research and write my college thesis from the top floor of FDR's old dorm.

So as not to disturb my roommate, who was working on a big paper, I stepped out onto the fire escape with the cordless phone to take my parents' call about Erin. I had no idea that what I'd just been inside writing about for my senior thesis was her. Or that the teaching degree I was earning was motivated in part by a nascent desire to ensure that kids from backgrounds like Jamie's got to take on big ideas in school too.

If I'd known what was really happening to Erin while I perched atop my bell-towered dorm chatting casually with my parents, I'd probably have hurled myself off the fire escape in despair.

But it was so far away now.

My parents asked what I was working on.

"Well, I've been running lots of mathematical models to try to explain the life courses of the people in the National Education Longitudinal Studies of the high school classes of 1972, 1980, 1988, and 2002."

"Wow, that sounds impressive! What does that mean?" asked my mom.

"Actually," I said, trying to sound impressive, "it's these multivariate, multistage regressions designed to explain where political influence in our democracy comes from and what inhibits and what unlocks political voice."

Political voice was my adviser's idea. He'd written a big book about it, exploring the origins of political inequality. I was trying to apply some of it to new data sets.

"And I've been doing multiple-imputation fractals," I added.

"It's above my head!" my mom said.

"I'd love to check it out," said my dad.

"Yes, and I'll definitely need your help with editing, too, Mom," I said.

"OK, just let me know when," she replied. "Do you want to hear the latest with Erin?" She sighed.

"I guess so . . ."

"Well, we just heard from Sagebrook that this was her last week in the system."

"And why's that?"

"She turned eighteen this week and signed herself out."

Oh yeah. I could always remember when her birthday was if I thought about it. But I just hadn't been thinking about her anymore.

I looked through the window at the stacks of books and papers on my desk, charts and tables full of information tracing out the life courses of tens of thousands of people, across several decades.

What educational degrees do you have?

Do you vote? Volunteer?

What is your income?

Did your parents read a newspaper most days when you were a child?

What was their level of education?

What were their jobs?

What's yours?

Though all the people who were tracked through various levels of schooling and beyond into young and middle adulthood were asked hundreds of different things about their lives, they were never asked the direct question I most wanted to know: Why? Why did some people get to go one way, and others another?

"So, what's she doing," I said flatly.

"That's the thing," my mom said. "She hasn't told us a thing. We don't know, actually. Apparently, she's just gone off on her own—"

"The people in the group home should be keeping in touch with her," I said hotly.

"Now that she's eighteen, I suppose that's up to her, whether she keeps in touch with them, or with us. You haven't heard from her, have you?"

I didn't want to talk about it. I'd been going around campus to tiny offices where postdoctoral fellows swam in data for a living to ask them how to make sense of these files of information, how to write the best data queries, what formulas they had that I might use. To ask them what I could do to make it all make sense.

And the numbers were starting to make sense.

What didn't make sense was why I was here—writing essays and looking past these bell towers to the Charles River—while Erin was on the street, without even a high school diploma, told to make her own way.

"We'd hoped that she would show some responsibility and maturity by this point, to keep in touch. The Sagebrook staff said they didn't know if she'd planned anything or really prepared for this."

"Shouldn't they have been preparing her for this?" *Shouldn't you guys have been there with her to prepare her throughout her childhood?*

"I'm sure they tried," my mom said, "but people have to take responsibility for their own lives at some point, and she hasn't shown that responsibility yet, in my opinion."

I didn't think it was because Erin was irresponsible. I knew her from six. It was so much more about how irresponsible others had been to her. But although I felt pangs of deep emptiness in my bottommost stomach when my mom talked about Erin this way, I didn't say I disagreed. I'd had some of those conversations over the years, and always got swift pushback about how hard my mom had tried and how Erin needed to take the responsibility to turn things around.

As I'd learned from my mom, and from Erin's therapists, it was much easier to implicate Erin than to feel implicated yourself.

And anyway, I didn't feel like I had the time to be implicated or to try to implicate my parents. I had an important essay to write.

"Reid?"

"Mmm?" I grunted, watching a seagull squawk by overhead.

"Will you let us know if she calls you?"

"Did you give her my number?" I asked.

"Did you want us to give her your number?" my mom asked back.

I hated to think about it all. How they'd sigh in resignation about the bad choices they said Erin was making. How they hadn't talked to her in months.

I hadn't talked to her in years. "Of course I do," I said. "Look, I gotta go."

I stepped through the window and pulled down the large pane behind me, sat down on the sofa next to our fireplace, and resumed leafing through tens of thousands of people's life stories, as told in numbers, a pencil behind my ear so I could mark the things that seemed to matter.

———

In college, I hung out a lot at the Institute of Politics, where a lot of powerful people were. Maybe they could do something to solve the problems I'd seen in the world. Maybe one day I would.

I got to see all of that cycle's candidates for US president, working as an usher to keep the aisles clear while listening in, careful not to trip over the TV camera cords.

I met the person who had been the US secretary of agriculture at the time I'd written *Meatpacking Mayhem* in high school. He'd been responsible for making sure that things were safe, for regulating the meatpacking companies. I'd heard of and written about corruption and complicity with the USDA, so I was confused when I came face to face with a kind and soft-spoken man in a pink tie who welcomed me to sit down, and told me how frustrated he'd been by the system that allowed the things I'd written about to happen. Wasn't he the person who should have changed that system? He talked about how his hands had been tied by a lack of funding and authority, as well as negotiated agreements with field staff he'd inherited that made it about impossible for him to push them to push the companies to do better.

"Yeah," I said, "even the governor's task force that went for a surprise inspection apparently got told to wait outside, while the company cleaned things up, and then eventually allowed the inspectors in."

I started to feel empathy for this person, who I'd been planning to skewer in an article I was writing for the *Harvard Political Review*. But he was saying he couldn't just solve the issues I'd raised, because it was hard and complicated. And what he was saying seemed persuasive.

But then I got to meet with a retired US senator from South Carolina. After a couple of years hanging around the Institute of Politics, I wasn't too nervous about meeting a senator. I felt as if I belonged in his office. Like my being there was disconnected from Jamie and his effort to make it off academic probation and up to college standing. Jamie's job on hot tar roofs was thousands of miles away, while I sat in the senator's air-conditioned office. It was all about me and where I belonged.

After we'd introduced ourselves, he asked, "What do you plan on doin' after you graduate, son?"

"Well, I plan to ride my bike across the country first. Then, I'm trying to find a place where people sit on their front porches and talk to each other. For most of the year here when it's so cold, people just seem to rush by each other on the street, and I'd like more sense of community. And probably I'll teach high school."

He studied me as I talked, then he smiled.

"Have you heard of Conrack?"

"Conrack, sir?"

"Well, really, it's Conroy." He paused elegantly. "Pat Conroy. When they made the film," he offered gently, "I believe they called it 'Conrack.' Like some of his students used to call him. When he taught in South Carolina, that is."

"No, I don't believe I have," I said, relaxing into the calming pace of the conversation.

He reclined a bit, took a deep breath in, and began to tell me the story of Pat Conroy teaching in Beaufort County after college. How "he'd simply made a tremendous difference to Black children out in the islands of the low country that were very underdeveloped."

I wasn't sure whether he meant the islands were underdeveloped or the kids were underdeveloped. And I knew enough from my classes at the graduate school of education—where I'd been earning my teaching certification on the side—to be skeptical of the idea of Pat Conroy saving the Black children of South Carolina.

But I listened intently as he told me about how many of the families had been afraid to leave the islands for fear that sea monsters would eat them. And how many of the students hadn't understood, before Conroy arrived, that they were in the United States of America, or that they were on a planet called Earth. How corporal punishment prevailed. And how—according to the senator—Conroy had finally given these children a chance to really learn.

I read the book that the senator recommended, and really enjoyed it.

Though I said I was no hero, and that the idea of a white dude coming down to teach everyone a thing or two was silly, and that I had far more to learn from the students than they could ever learn from me, the characters in the book connected with something deep inside me—a way of seeing the world I'd been taught for decades.

After all, when I was growing up, the richest man in the world was also growing his fortune in my hometown, building the biggest company in the world, and then the biggest charity in the world. He'd started building right after he left Harvard.

And when I was in college at Harvard, so was Mark Zuckerberg, who was starting to build his trillion-dollar company, and would later pledge to give away 99 percent of his money to help make the world a better place. When I saw those folks, I saw folks who looked like me. When I saw candidates for president, or strolled in to meet with the senator from South Carolina, or the Honorable Secretary, I again saw folks who seemed like me. I felt right at home in their offices asking them for reading recommendations, and where I could find the best front porches, and laughing, no longer thinking much about Jamie or Erin, or the question that had so bothered me when Erin was sent away from our home and Jamie's counselor hadn't signed him up for upper-level classes: Why am I here and they're not?

I had pretended to understand the USDA secretary's talk of systemic barriers to change, and regulatory regimes that needed to be enhanced, and complex consumer, corporate, and government incentives. I even referenced his comments about "systemic" issues in my thesis.

But the worst parts of how I'd gotten to be at Harvard were with me, shaping me, shaping what I worked on and how I would go about my life.

I'd come from the bedroom with the loft looking out over the woods and the flowers. But I'd also come from the next bedroom over—Erin's bedroom, which was emptied for me. And my heritage was not only three generations of educators on my mother's side, and immigrants, miners, an orphan turned dry cleaner, a carpenter, and then an engineer in my dad. Our heritage was also the harm that we'd perpetuated in Erin's life.

I'd come from two bedrooms—my own space, as well as the extra room just across the hall that I had but didn't need—while Erin had only a fraction of a room at an orphanage I'd never see.

No matter my efforts to play humble, I felt then that I should and would do something great with all I'd been given. And because it was easier, and flattering, and made me feel like I was better than others, I started to believe on some level that I'd rightly been given so much because of my talents and my efforts. That something inside of me just got things done—like my meatpacking book, and my award-winning thesis, my meetings with political leaders. Though I'd never have admitted it, I began to assume that where I was and what I had were due simply to the content of my character.

PART TWO

CHAPTER FIVE

An enormous field had been hollowed out of the surrounding marsh forests for Battery Creek's campus. Across a drainage ditch and an immense asphalt lot sits the unadorned face of the high school's two-story building. The main entrance has no arches, naming, or ornamentation of any sort because the school—designed in the shape of a T—is backwards. The builders had realized at the last minute that the wetlands at the front of the property wouldn't support the heavier side of the school—the top of the T. So they turned their diagrams upside down and built the thing backwards.

I walked up to the concrete brick building, squinting in the intense sun at what might've been a small group of teenagers through undulating waves of heat. One of the four blue metal doors slammed definitively behind me. The cavernous hallway was dim and dingy, its fluorescent panels incomparably darker than the Carolina sun.

I heard music down the hall. A trumpet muted by one of the many doors I passed. I felt a drumbeat, and adjusted my stride to match it.

In the front office on the other side of the school sat a woman who appeared to be a secretary. She sat quite straight, clicking her mouse rigorously at something I couldn't see.

I said, "Excuse me—could I please speak with the principal?"

She paused for a moment to look over at me, said, "Just a minute," then pushed her glasses up and continued working her computer.

After he finished talking animatedly to someone on the other side of the office, a man dressed in slacks and a collared school shirt with a dolphin leaping over the letters B and C approached the secretary's desk. He reached for a sticky note and jotted down some information.

"Burney," she said to him, "this man wants to see you."

He strode toward me.

"Hi," I squeaked as he squeezed my hand from across the counter. "I recently finished my degree and student teaching at Harvard, and I'm interested in a teaching position. Do you have a few minutes to talk?"

On the other side of town, my opening question had gotten me less than a minute of the departing principal's time—and a commitment that he'd make sure I'd get hired to teach at his school if I put in my application.

Principal Burney Johnston of Battery Creek High School went further.

I followed him on a full campus tour, during which he discussed the school's founding, the student population, and his appraisal of the Dolphins' strengths and weaknesses. We ended in his office, which housed a long, cluttered conference table, a side desk for a computer, and other desks and file cabinets around the edges. Papers covered every surface. There were two broad floor-to-ceiling windows, and through blinds I saw a collage of bark and palm fronds slitting sunlight.

Johnston sat in a high-backed chair and reclined a bit, hands clasped over his middle, below a full head and full upper lip of hair, which was beginning to salt.

Over the other papers, he handed me Beaufort's phone book and asked what I thought.

"OK . . . ?" I looked at the cover, then opened it, not understanding.

"Creek kids took that photo of the Lowcountry marsh." I saw a couple of Crest-white cranes hiding behind clumps of sharp grasses growing in acres of pale, flat mud. "We've won the cover the past three years now. We're laying the foundation for the best technical training program in the state," he said. "We partner with the ACE School, where kids can learn a mechanical and technical field of their choosing. We've even got some beauticians who want to open their own salon!" he glowed.

"Thing about this school," he continued, "is I believe these students have great potential. Unfortunately, some succumb to poor choices." He tapped his hand on a pile of pink slips, where I could see the word "SUSPENSION" scrawled next to someone's name. "One day they'll be an angel sitting in your class, and then the next thing you know, they're arrested for murder."

My breath stalled partway in. Johnston told me about buses that ran out of Beaufort to Hilton Head Island.

"They target our students," he gnashed. "And every time one of our kids decides that they don't want to go to school, all they have to do is walk across the street and get on one of those damn buses."

He'd lost me. *What buses?*

"They run people to Hilton Head—been doin' it for decades now. Took the kids' grandparents there, and now their parents and tomorrow the kids'll hop on the bus as soon as they get bored or upset with us. And they get caught out there for good."

I was engrossed and a little confused. I thought maybe I'd get a chance to be interviewed, that we'd talk about classes, about teaching.

"These kids know they got an eight-dollar-an-hour job waitin' for 'em in these fancy hotels. Problem is, eight dollars sounds great now, but there ain't no raises. And no benefits. Course, it's impossible to take care of a family on eight bucks, so that's why the guys don't stick around, cuz they smell failure, and they never tried it before. Hard to blame 'em when they learned it from their father, who wasn't there to show you can trip and then get back up."

My skin itched beneath my striped suit pants.

"Then they're stuck for life in these dead-end jobs, a lot of 'em. They offer just enough money to get 'em to drop out of school, and then there's no turning back. They're stuck and they'll be earning eight dollars when they're in their sixties. Got grandmothers doin' it now, and they're all stoop-backed from making beds for rich people for half a century. It's a family tradition. I've gotten in a little bit of trouble for calling them slave buses . . ."

What is this guy talking about?

"But that's exactly what they are: slave buses. They keep kids away from education and a meaningful future to labor for rich folks for practically nothing for the rest of their lives."

OK. He was talking about big forces and an educator's worthy battle—to win the hearts and the loyalty of the students who, each day, have a choice. How we needed to beat the immediate draw of that bus, which would drive them away forever if we didn't perform.

When I started studying teaching in college, Dolliver had talked to me about education like this. He'd conveyed to me some of his desperation to be a great teacher. To add new dimensions to the minds of the rising generation. Because learning really matters. The work of teaching is a sacred trust. And standing at the front of a classroom is a privilege that comes with an immense responsibility to create conversations, experiences, and insights that matter to students.

This idea contradicted most of the professors, who'd told us not to worry about teaching so much, because "it wasn't like we were doctors or anything," "it isn't life or death," and "the kids'll probably be fine regardless of what you do."

Johnston was on to something else: "This really happens. His mom's boyfriend had decided he didn't want the boy 'round no more. Turns out he's been sleepin' in a burnt-out car. Now, you tell me how a kid like that's spose to come into school and learn in the morning when he's sleepin' in a burnt-out car the night before!"

I hadn't a clue.

"Well, he sure can't, if you ask me. (But they don't ask me). Sometimes they expect . . ." His sentence wandered off with his eyes. "But these are good kids. Almost all of 'em are."

He looked back at me, squinting slightly for several beats, then said, "US history, advanced history, advanced psychology, and double economics. That'll be your load."

Oh, will it? I thought.

"Mr. Johnston, this is very exciting, really. I'd really like to come work with you . . . but I'm concerned about designing four different courses during my first year as a full-time teacher, while I'm just getting started. That's really quite a lot."

"Just let the assistant principal know by Monday"—he turned to his computer—"of your decision."

He was through.

———

He had hundreds of other issues to address on the hundreds of documents strewn around his office. From me, he needed someone who could sign a contract to teach five classes.

I fumed on my walk out, planning to contact Johnston again to argue that he should lighten my load, because prepping daily to teach four different subjects was just too much for a new teacher.

Maybe he'd seen in my eyes what I didn't yet know myself: that I was there because I craved redemption for all I'd been given. That I was desperate to do something worthwhile, so that all I'd taken wouldn't be wasted. And that there would be no chance of success unless I started to learn how little I knew, and how much I'd need to depend on the students, who I could but hazily see through the heat waves as I walked out of the school.

Having not yet signed a contract, I'd been sleeping in the ditch out back of the Super 8 Motel to save the $45 a night.

Friday morning, I woke up and wandered across the street to the Piggly Wiggly grocery store, which had a single carton of soy milk. I bought it, my favorite Reese's Puffs cereal, orange juice, and a bunch of too-green bananas and ate on the concrete in front of the store. I placed what was left of the food under the hood of my rear-engine 1963 Chevy Corvair, which I'd purchased with my thesis prize money. The car had long ago been dubbed "unsafe at any speed," but Dolliver helped me balance it out by pouring some cement into the front compartment.

Without a room, I didn't have a shower. So I walked over to the motel's oak-leaf-ridden pool, stood on its edge, then jumped gleefully through the debris.

Drying off, then buttoning on a fresh shirt, I took the Corvair out toward the main drag, smelled the bananas already starting to cook in the heat, and decided to head in to the job at Battery Creek High School.

During prep week before the students started, I found the teachers lounge: a narrow, windowless room with a fridge where I could put my milk and orange juice.

"What's your name?" asked a man short and burly as hell. His wide outer chest pushed against his upper arms, and the muscles on his arms pushed back. Far out from his pockets, his hands dangled freely.

"Reid," I said, reaching over the card table.

He reached for my hand and shook it hard. "Chuck Cutter."

"Good to meet you."

"First year?"

"Oh, yeah, first year. I did student teaching before."

"'Round here?"

"No, up north."

"That's cool. So you don't know our kids here, then."

"Not yet, no."

"Oh, you're in for a *treat*," said a teacher with curly red hair, flattening her hair to her head and then releasing it.

"If you like to eat shit for a treat, that is," said Walter Thompson. He'd just come in, stowed his lunch in the fridge, and then turned to the group, hands deep in his khakis, both elbows out wide.

"Ha-ha, yup," she said back. "We all eat shit for breakfast around here. So," she said, leaning toward me, "what have you heard?"

"Not much. I just got in, really."

"Lemme put it to you this way," said Chuck, straddling a folding metal chair across the narrow table from the one I'd just sat down in, then clapping his right hand on my left shoulder. "They used to have cages here."

"And probably still should," added Walter, who'd gone back to the fridge and was now eating a triangle of tuna fish sandwich in one hand as he spoke. With his other hand, he caressed his long, damp forehead wisped with dark wavy strands.

"Cages?" I said, feeling pranked.

"You bet. They'd drop walls of jail bars from the ceiling in the hallways when things got real bad—you know, riots, gang fights, shooting. Keep different parts of the school divided up."

I sensed the lure was rubber but bit in anyway. "What do you mean, 'real bad'?"

They looked at one another knowingly.

"So you *really* don't know anything about the Creek, do you?" said the woman with the curly red hair, which seemed to vibrate. "I'm Ronda, by the way."

"Reid," I said, nodding back. "Don't know much beyond what Mr. Johnston told me."

It sounded like someone said something nasty about the principal, but I didn't quite catch it.

"Better pay attention to us who know," said Chuck, turning back to the group.

"Tell him how you keep things in line around here, Chuck," Walter said, then slouched in his chair, continuing to caress his temple—gently at first, then increasingly digging in his fingernails.

"So if any of y'all know D'Marcus," said Chuck, "you know he's a son a bitch. Walkin' 'round my class like he's the game rooster, hittin' on all the girls. He started to get into it with a girl . . ."

As he spoke, his neck stretched his shirt collar tight like a wrapper on a two-liter Coke bottle that had been in the sun too long. He stuck a finger with a dirty nail in the collar around his Adam's apple to try to grease up some freedom.

"So I tol' him to sit his ass down. And he says, 'Whatever, bitch' outta the side of his mouth. So I say, 'What'd you say to me, boy?' And his coward ass says, 'Nothin,'" but he ain't even lookin' at me. So I say, 'What'd you say?' And he's all like, 'Man, lay offa me, cuz,' and I told him, 'We're gonna take this out in the hall right now.'" He punctuated the last two words by hitting his open hand with his closed fist twice.

"You didn't!" Ronda accused him through rose lips that matched her sunburnt freckles.

"Yeh, course I did. I ain't 'bout to take that crap from no one, specially not no D'Marcus D'Angelo on the last day a school. So I slammed the door hard and got in his face and said, 'Ain't no one here but you and me. You wanna say somethin' to me now? You think you can back that shit up, *bitch?*'"

"Oh, shit!!!!" said the surrounding teachers, our attention total.

"So, he sprints off down the hall full speed, hard as he can, an' I follow right on his heels." Chuck moved his arms back and forth and breathed as if he were running: "Whoo, whoo, whoo," with three short, fast breaths. "An' I'm yellin' after 'im, but I shouldna been yellin', cuz I got outta breath and he got a lead on me. Slams through the doors at the end of the hall." Chuck slammed his palm onto the table to imitate the sound. I jumped, then tried to pretend I hadn't been scared. "He jumps down all the stairs, an' I can't do that shit no more. Bad knees from wrestling. An' he gets out the door at the bottom."

"So you lost him?" asked Ronda.

"Yeah, but now I'm thinkin' he's gotta be comin' back next week, don' he?" said Chuck, folding his arms across his big pecs.

I felt like I'd missed something in the story. As the group was breaking up, I leaned in to Chuck and asked him, "You chased a kid down the hall?!" expecting him to reveal an inside joke or a punch line.

"What about it?" he said, my question suddenly appearing ridiculous to us both.

"That's . . . crazy," I said.

As he scanned me head to foot, I hoped I didn't sound too disrespectful, like maybe I meant crazy-cool. "Naw, gotta keep these kids on their toes. You'll learn," he said.

———

As the time to meet my students approached, I felt more and more nervous.

One of my mentors had told me back in college that being nervous is normal, good even. If you stop getting butterflies, he'd said, that's when you need to get out of teaching. Because teaching matters a lot, and you *should* care—deeply and viscerally.

Some hours, my nerves felt like butterflies. Things were aflutter, with exciting, colorful possibilities unfolding. I thought to myself, *Kids are kids and so of course they'll be great. After all, there's so much to talk about, so much to learn.*

But as I heard more from a few of the other teachers during that prep week, a sort of reverse metamorphosis started. The butterflies inside me lost their wings and began to crawl and slither like caterpillars, wriggling around inside my gut, souring and sickening.

Like when I sat through half an hour of debate in the teachers lounge about whether one of the teachers' husbands—a firefighter—should have to respond to fire emergencies in dilapidated drug dens, where laundry hampers were being used as toilets. Walter argued that if the occupants didn't put in the effort, then firefighters shouldn't have to come put out the fires. He said they had real people to protect. That a lot of these folks, and their kids who came to Battery Creek, were "just worthless shitheads."

I felt like I had when I'd seen a neighbor punch Jamie in the face—shocked, infused with adrenaline. I adamantly rejected this way of treating people, didn't want it to happen, didn't want to be around it. And I wasn't immediately sure what I should do about it. Fight? De-escalate?

I made a mental note that Walter seemed like a total shithead and, discombobulated, fled.

CHAPTER SIX

Thankfully, on the walk to my classroom, I saw another teacher on the floor of his, sitting crisscross, rummaging through books that ringed him in piles, like mounds of sand and shells around a child playing at the beach. Curious, I asked, "How's it goin' in there?"

"Who, me?"

I nodded.

"Aw, great. I think. Just trying to work my way through some of these I found around the library, the textbook storage room, and some of my own personal collection. Come on in!" he said, standing suddenly and extending his hand across the pile, then trying to step over it toward me, tripping. "I'm Michael F—whoa!"

He fell down onto one hand, then stood back up, dusted his warm hands off, and offered them both to me. "Fry. My friends call me Fry." Beneath lonely and frazzled strands of short brown hair, Michael had kind eyes tucked above ample red cheeks.

"Fry? It's good to meet you, man. I'm Reid."

We talked for hours. We both had no more than our student teaching experience and were eager to meet and talk history with our students. We worked through the various history textbooks the school had for the different grade and course levels—thousands of pages of glossy text and pictures, hardback, durable, old—and arrived together at the same conclusion.

"There's not much in here, is there?" he asked, patting the tall pile of the school's history textbooks.

"Not much. It seems to be, like, dates and names and terms. Kind of the opposite of the point of history, huh?" I scratched the top of my head.

He scratched his. "Exaaaactly. It's the kind of stuff that made me hate history for years!"

I thought of my advanced history classes, and how the teachers had taught us to analyze every source—where it came from, why it had been created, and what all that meant for what we could and couldn't learn from it.

"So, my understanding," said Fry, "is that the adoptions for these happen at the state level, and the state's got a pretty clear agenda here. And it's ridiculous to think there could be one definitive source of history."

"Yes! We need to bring in a variety of sources here, and let the students discover and bring in additional perspectives—"

"And figure out how to analyze all these sources. Primary sources. We need a lot less of the state's view of history and a lot more primary sources. So this stack over here are some of the primary sources I found in the library that could be relevant, and this stack over here—"

"Let me go get my stacks out of the car too. I'll be right back!" I said, running off excitedly.

—————

On the drives from and back to school, my mind wandered, and I wondered who my students would be. I thought about the incredible possibilities described by teachers like Fry, or Rosa Perez, my assigned mentor. She'd told me, "Never you mind all that other noise about our amazing kids" and had students coming through her classroom, even though it was the summer, just to exchange books and abrazos.

But what Chuck and Ronda and Walter had been describing was so vivid that I felt I'd been on the chase that Chuck went on. When Chuck looked at me sternly and told me I'd learn that these things were needed here, with these students, it was as if I could smell the rot of the laundry hampers.

Come next Monday, any of the teenagers I saw as I was driving around town could show up in my classroom—the one under the hood at the auto body shop, those eating shrimp cocktails in the front window of a restaurant, or the guy taking the garbage out the back. The girl coming out of Staples with a bag of supplies. The guys driving the red Ford F-150 with double Confederate flags flapping hard off the back. The kid walking the long footpath beside the highway past old slave camps. Those on the large white-columned front porch, and those on the little collapsing porch behind jalopies with grass growing through their engines. There were so many possibilities.

I pulled into the Dixie Rentals trailer park on County Shed Road. It was the nearest place to school with a "For Rent" sign.

They had a trailer available with furniture left by the previous tenant. The manager advised me at length not to "let in no prossies" or I'd get cased, and then robbed by their pimps. It seemed like she would've preferred I not teach at Battery Creek High School—"You sure you wannsta teach *dem* kids?"—but she was willing to overlook it for what remained in my savings account to cover first and last months' rent.

———

After getting a couple of panicked phone calls from me about needing to prepare four different courses in short order, Dolliver decided to fly across the country and help me get started. He worked with Fry, me, and Rosa, and we organized primary and secondary sources by "essential questions," which Dolliver described as the motivating inquiries for a field of study.

"And before you start the subject matter," Rosa advised, "you have to build the community. The relationships. The culture in these classrooms is not always the best. And that's mostly not *on* these children. I've had my culture denigrated enough to recognize when it's happening and when culture's not being respected. Many families here go back more generations than you can count. And they deeply value each other. As a language teacher, I'm biased, but I think the biggest attribute of the local culture is shown in the language. Think about being forced into isolated islands with various African peoples who didn't share a common language. They integrated those African languages and aspects of European languages together into Gullah-Geechee. And anyone who's prejudiced enough to think students' ways of speaking are dumb doesn't understand language at all. Bringing together Gullah-Geechee, African American Vernacular English, and academic English in a classroom is a sign of strength, originality. Three languages means three times the intelligence, I say."

With Rosa's guidance on the culture, Dolliver's guidance on the subject matter, and my shared enthusiasm with Fry to give it all we had as new teachers, I had a lot of support to start off the year on a good foot.

But then I realized I didn't have anything but running shoes or flip-flops to put on my feet. Then my car broke down, so I didn't have a way to go buy shoes, or even a way to get to school on the rapidly approaching first day.

Before his flight back across the country, Dolliver stayed up late into the night, underneath the car with a flashlight, installing a new solenoid and some other things I'd also never heard of, got the car running again, and handed me his brown loafers, which made me cry.

Dolliver didn't need his teaching shoes anymore because he'd been driven into retirement following feuds with administrators about his not taking enough attendance, and other such things. He said that in schools we count people more times a day than we do in prison. That the subject matter could be far more compelling than any disciplinary policy—the positive power of learning could carry the day with students—if we could just focus our energies there.

———

"OK," said Walter Thompson, once most of the social studies teachers had taken a student desk chair. Walter sat to the side, with one thigh on his teacher's desk, and one tasseled brown leather slipper on the floor.

"A few things we need to check off today."

Oh boy, I thought. *Departmental priorities, from our chair! A chance to talk with the whole team about the education stuff.*

"Attendance, end-of-course exams, and referrals. Now, let's run through these so we can get the hell out of here. But first, raise your hand if you've already picked up the set of textbooks for each of your classes from Mrs. Grunt."

About half the hands went up.

After Fry and I had combed through the textbooks and developed our essential questions and caches of primary sources, we'd decided not to check out any textbook sets for the students.

"That's what I thought," said Walter. "We need better access to these books. It's been hard to get the secretary up to the storage room on demand to get these things distributed. And we can't start Monday without them. So raise your hands if you still need at least one class set."

A few hands went up.

"Reid!" he said. "You didn't raise your hand for either one."

"I . . . don't need them," I said.

"You have a set for each class?"

"No, but that's OK. Fry and I are working together on other readings."

"OK, both of you need to get a textbook for each of your students. That's what transfers the responsibility to them."

I felt the urge to argue, but figured I'd better not. I could check out the books and keep them in the cabinet in my classroom so that the kids could access and analyze them alongside our other sources.

He pushed his reading glasses up on his nose, marked his paper, clicked his pen, and put it into his pocket. "There are a few other things here," he said. "I've been asked to review the new attendance policies with you again.

Then I'll report back that you have all been fully briefed, and the responsibility's yours from there." He pulled some handouts from his clipboard and gave each teacher a small stack.

We'd already spent most of yesterday's all-staff meeting in the auditorium talking about what was in these handouts, and Walter was repeating it. Frustrated, I doodled math in the margins. They were asking us to take four different types of attendance for each class.

"After you enter it into your gradebook, you should fill out the attendance worksheet, which will be picked up by a hall monitor each period, along with the diversity count form . . ."

I figured maybe a minute for each of the four different types of attendance. And students attended seven classes a day.

Someone asked if just entering the information in the online gradebook during class time would be sufficient.

A hundred and eighty days of school in the year . . .

"No, your hard-copy gradebook"—he patted his on its dense, textured brown cover—"is the legal record. You should start there and work your way through."

They're talking more than eighty hours of lost time—nearly three weeks of classes, just gone! That can't be what we should do.

"OK—next item on the ol' docket here," Walter said as he scratched the dark, curly hairs coming out above his third shirt button. He bounced the receded tip of his pen off his clipboard. "End-of-course exams. Those are laid out behind me," he said, pointing back with his thumb. "So come and get what you need there."

I looked around the room as we waited in line. There were ten of us, all white. What the students of Battery Creek—two-thirds of whom were Black—would learn in high school classes about all that had happened in human history, it ran through us.

Over the door hung a huge clock, which Walter pointed to once we were back in our seats. Then he tapped his wristwatch too. "Let's get through this so we can get outta here, huh, folks?"

Murmurs assented while papers shuffled.

"Now, these are last year's exams, and they are subject to change this year if agreed to by the teachers responsible for each course."

For all the debate about whether testing kids was good or bad, my view was that bad tests were bad and good tests were good. A bad test will distract from the things that matter, and mislead teachers, students, and parents about how we're doing.

And for history, what I had in my hands now was definitely a bad test that couldn't help me check our progress on meaningful learning. It was asking kids really low-level stuff, like what date something had happened, or what a vocabulary word meant, or the name of an event. So when a few hands went up around the room, I was relieved that others, too, seemed to have concerns about the test.

"What percent do they need to get right to pass the end-of-course exam?"

"Sixty percent," said Walter. "Yes, Mr. Kimball?"

"Last year, the Scantrons got backed up and it took forever to get these things all auto-graded on the last day of school. Any chance we can get some more Scantrons this year?"

"Thinking about next summer already?" said Walter, chuckling. "I don't know if we can get more Scantrons, but you're welcome to come in and use mine here. It only takes me about ten minutes to run the answer sheets through and get all my kids' final tests graded, so I'm happy to share—just within the department, of course."

"Wonderful. Thank you for that," said Mr. Kimball.

"Mr. Cutter?"

"All set. Everything's good. That answered my question too."

Everything's good? I looked over at Fry. He was squinting at something on the back of one of the packets, and I couldn't catch his attention, so I decided to jump in on my own. Our jobs were to bring these subjects to life, and explore the most important questions, so I tried to ask such a question after Walter saw that there was no one else he could call on.

"Mr. Saaris," he sighed, pulling his floor-leg up onto the teacher's desk.

"What was the Civil War fought over?" I asked.

"I'm sorry?"

In my teacher trainings over the years, I'd had more than enough of the idea that a bubble-in test is the greatest measure of a teacher's success.

"This question, number 31 on the test? 'What was the Civil War fought over?'" I asked again.

He grabbed a test and flipped it over. "Oh, OK. The answer keys. Yes! So those are on the back of the tests."

Fry raised his hand slowly and, when called on, offered, "I was just actually looking at the answer to that Civil War question myself. And I have the answer key, but it still doesn't make sense to me."

"Let me see here," said Walter.

"The test provides four options, but I don't think you'll find the answer in that key," I said. "What would you say the Civil War was fought over?"

He wasn't about to. He shook the paper flat and looked down at it through his glasses. "This could be an answer to that question," he said.

"Sure, it could," I said. "And there are so many others—so many more possibilities, so much to discuss about a question like that. Different ways it's been answered at different times, by different people, for different purposes."

"Well, maybe you should form a book club or something to talk about it," said Walter.

Isn't this the social studies department meeting? I thought. *I just want— sometime during this week of training and preparation—to discuss social studies!*

"What about this question?" asked Fry. "'Where is the US-Mexican border?' with options of four different geographic features to choose from."

"Take it up with an atlas," replied Walter, reddening. "It looks correct to me."

Building on Fry's question, and remembering advice that Dolliver had given me when he'd helped me prepare, I asked: "Shouldn't we be talking with students about *why* a border is where it is?"

"I don't know. Maybe?" said Walter, twisting his mouth up toward one of his nostrils. "For now, we've got one last agenda item between us and the end of the day here, and I, for one, don't want to be holding back the whole group to nitpick a couple end-of-course questions."

"I mean, let's make this about more than the test," I said. "What do we want to teach our students? What do we think they should learn and be able to do by the end of a year working together?"

Walter was quiet for a moment. Then, "The questions match with the textbook, and they've been tried by the teachers here who actually know our students and what they can do. OK, we've got to let other people in here too, Mr. Saaris." He squeegeed both hands back the full length of his head, as if drying off from a swim. "I'm going to give us two choices here. Who wants to stick to our agenda and get this last required item done so we can go home?"

Except for Fry and I and one other teacher, all the hands went up.

"OK, the majority has it!" said Walter. "On to in-school and out-of-school suspensions. I assume everyone has plenty of these referrals from your mailboxes downstairs?" He held up a pink slip with multiple carbon copies affixed, which reminded me of my hefty middle school demerits collection, from when I used to roam campus during class time.

"Got 'em."

"Yeah."

"Thanks for getting us more of these this year, Walter."

"You bet. I know they're in high demand this first week or two, and so I insisted that you each be provided with fifty to start. And you can request more as soon as you're low. Pull one out now, and we'll talk about the two types of suspension options we have, as well as options that could escalate to arrest and/or expulsion."

This was our chance to talk history, and we were talking *expulsion?* As I looked at Walter, I experienced a feeling that would come back to me again and again. I'd start to unknowingly seek it for comfort and solace when things weren't going well: a neurochemical cocktail we'd studied in Dolliver's class, and which I was now developing an addiction to. There was some rage that pumped adrenaline through me, accelerating my heart rate, bringing me energy, widening my eyes and dilating my pupils so I could scrutinize someone who seemed like an enemy to my cause. There was the intellectual stimulation of ticking through all the reasons I thought I was right and this person was wrong. And there was a conclusion I'd wrest from those spiteful chains of internal logic to calm and relax myself: the sense that I knew better, was better.

It didn't cross my mind that Walter might feel equally righteous, energized, stimulated, and vindicated when he scrutinized and condemned some of the students or—as things developed that year—me.

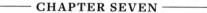

CHAPTER SEVEN

The night before the start of my teaching career, the last thing I saw through the blinds before I got into bed was the dance of orange cigarette tips a few trailers away, smoked by some Black men out barbecuing.

Tossing around for hours in my small trailer's bedroom—in that space between thinking and dreaming, when everything becomes one singular experience—I thought I knew just who the bad guys were.

My mind started all the way back with Erin's father, who'd slithered into bed with her at night and who'd left Erin alone for days when she was just a two-year-old, struggling to find food for her wailing-hungry baby brother.

But after those bad guys were gone, banished, in jail, barred from seeing Erin, in came the professionals who caged *her* behind one-way glass, despondent and crying on the floor. They seemed to think she had to be broken.

This second set of bad guys used the things that had been done by the original bad guys—*molestation, sexual abuse, drug abuse, alcoholism,* and *abandonment*—to scare us about what Erin herself might do. Erin didn't do anything worse than what I'd done, but their assumptions about what had happened to her and how that had shaped her led them to see in her *predatory behavior, defiance, remorselessness.*

They said if we didn't take swift corrective action, my little sister—who liked singing "Today is the greatest" with me—might become the most horrible thing I'd ever heard of: a pedophile sociopath.

And yet the "treatment" seemed designed to deepen the damage, prevent the recovery, hold her in hell.

Given that she'd never had the basic loving commitment of a family, why would the professionals talk my parents *out* of providing that?

Given that she'd never been able to run around and play carefree, because she'd been taking care of her baby brother and trying to avoid abuse, why was she so often locked in her room to watch through the window while I played in the woods with my friends?

Given her wondering whether she'd somehow brought her horrible past upon herself, why was each mistake she made now met with punishment instead of forgiving love?

Why did the therapists hold down someone who'd been held down so horribly before: smothering her in blankets for a forced "rebirth," and making her bottle-feed in their arms, even though she was eight and simply wanted to stop being held down?

Why would you take someone so obviously in need of love, warmth, and care, and prescribe deprivation therapy: sleeping on the ground behind lock and key, having to earn back blankets, pillows, and anything more than gruel and water?

People can and do suffer damage. But our most defining feature is our capacity to recover—to change, adapt, and grow, when decent circumstances finally arise.

I would be on the side of the professionals who create decent circumstances: an open, positive, nurturing environment, built on my unshakable belief in the incredibleness of the kids I would have the privilege to serve.

If only I could get some sleep.

———

Knocking.

Was that my door?

I listened but heard only bugs, loud in a little way.

A dream.

Three heavy knocks. The whole wall of the trailer seemed to vibrate behind my head.

Holy crap! My cellphone screen told me it was 2:37 a.m. *I've been in bed for five hours without sleeping! I need to sleep to be ready for tomorrow—for today! The trailer manager said to watch out for prostitutes, so I'll ignore—*

Knock fell after knock. More than a dozen. Then another flourish of pounding and silence.

Just sit still. Don't move. They'll go away.

"No one's here—let's bust in!" someone whispered fiercely. The words shoveled me out of bed.

I smacked the light switch. I stomped the hall floor. I opened a drawer in the kitchen and pulled out my only kitchen knife—an old one my mom had sent me in a cardboard box for my birthday—and slumped down against the door, holding it with both hands.

Sometime later, I was still on the dirty brown carpet in the living room, curled up against the wall. I was either dreaming or hallucinating about stabbing people when I heard bleating. It was a pig being slaughtered. No— it was rhythmic.

Whaaaaa. Whaaaaa. Whaaaaa.

My car alarm. In between electronic screams, I heard someone running up the dirt road, jumping over the potholes, dashing away between trailers.

I opened the door a crack and didn't see anyone, so I swung it all the way open and stepped forward, down the steps, and around to the shadowed side of the car, where I found the driver's door open, and clicked off the alarm.

My stereo face was gone, and I reached down to the red carpet on the floor to feel for it—

"Hey!" said a man just behind the driver's door. I rebounded off the seat's springs, hitting my head on the top's side beam. I flexed my arm out at full length, with the knife toward the man. He took a big step back.

"Pete!" I yelled out, relieved to see the familiar face of my neighbor. "What the hell!? I almost stabbed you, dude."

"Sorry, man. Heard the alarm."

"Yeah—someone tried to steal my stuff."

"Probably n*****s. Wouldn't be surprised if they're your students. Loud alarm you got there," he said in his New York accent, stroking stubble, his eyes magnified by thick, medium-sized spectacles.

I could hardly speak, but managed "You shouldn't say that . . . I've gotta go. First day of teachin' tomorrow—er, today."

"I'll look for you after work," he said to my sweaty back, "see if you're still alive."

As the pre-dawn shadows slid through my short-window blinds and across the sheet wadded in my lap, my mind sank lower. *What's* wrong *with him? Does he really think those awful things?*

———

All that'd been happening was starting to get me to think such things.

My imaginings that night were so vivid that I couldn't have told you, even months later, whether or not they actually happened. On the precipice of the first day of school, I dreamed of a Black student rounding the corner into my classroom, suddenly in my face with wolf eyes and skin as dark as the moonless 3:00 a.m. night. Hunkered shoulders and the explosive legs of a lion, body-checking my spine into the light switch by the door, muscles swelling the skin on his arms, face, and neck taut.

He disappeared.

I flooded my ten-thread, scratchy Walmart sheets with sweat. Burrowed into the corner where the plastic walls met my mattress on the floor.

My body buzzed. It pulsated, begged for water—no, to go to the bathroom—as I heard murmurings outside my classroom door. The murmuring began to hiss and whistle and squeak and then scream.

Students lurked, looked in, disappeared. Then, with the bell, they barreled in and talked to me using every curse word I knew and then some.

They asked me why I was there, who the hell I thought I was. But I couldn't answer them.

And then a few folks starting cursing at one another about being skanky.

And it built. A swell of noise and phrases I didn't understand, then one Black girl tackled another, taking her whole desk down in a jumble of chair legs and Black legs, and I saw her raise a long-tined comb above her head, clenched in her two Black fists—and stab her classmate full force in the head.

Blood dripping down a forehead.

A fistful of black hair pulled, one from another, in the tumult.

The immense young Black man pulling the two girls apart and escorting one into the hall.

My breathing as though I were at the end of a race, hunched over, hyperventilating, useless.

I needed to get to the phone, to call for help. To get the other girl out of there. To get *me* out. It was ringing. Bleating.

———

With a start, I realized I was listening to the blare of my phone's alarm. I unwadded myself from the corner of my bedroom, got dressed, and dashed off.

I tried to make sense of what had happened as I slammed through the potholes toward Dolphin Drive.

I touched it to be sure: it was gone—the face of my stereo had been torn off. So the robbery was real.

I checked my phone again. It was now 7:22 a.m. on August 9—minutes before the start of the first day of school.

That meant I must've eventually fallen asleep—after all my thinking about how I believed only amazing things about kids, and that people who didn't (like Walter Thompson) were the bad guys.

After the robbery, I'd fallen asleep and dreamed that horrible scene in the classroom—imagined horrible things about people I needed to believe in. I was supposed to be the responsible adult, yet that vivid, violent scene seemed more real to me than the misty fields I drove sleepily through as I tried to make the first bell. In my mind, I saw the Black fist coming down again, and almost wished for Chuck's cages.

Realizing that a bunch of the fear and bullshit and horrible things I'd heard were in my head, I shook it hard, letting my lips flap back and forth, flinging phlegm off the corners of my mouth and into the saw grass. *Out!* I told myself, nearly veering off the road.

I'm one of the adults who sees each student for who they are and all they want to become. Forget the other noise! I commanded myself, believing it was an order I could follow.

I wish I could say that this was some big moment of revelation for me, but it wasn't. Visceral images of Black violence were so common. Sometimes they blurred the faces on *Cops*, but you could tell that most of the people they showed getting arrested were Black. I'd never had a close Black friend or a Black teacher. But I had had colleagues at Battery Creek High School discuss Black gang hallway warfare with me. My parents had usually had the nightly news on when I was growing up, and I saw the 1990s "war on crime" images, and who appeared to need locking up if we were to win.

I didn't like what I'd imagined of my students, but I thought I could just push on past it. No matter how visceral the nightmare had been, I wouldn't give that kind of garbage another thought.

In psychology class, I would teach about how the patterns that our brains fire off for something real are identical to those we fire off for an imagined reality. That the pathways that get fired most—and most viscerally—build up their myelin sheath, making it much easier for those pathways to fire again and again, like a rut in a road pulling your wheel in deeper with each ride. The students and I would debate whether anyone could possibly rise above those physical realities in their brain: patterns of action and reaction, stimuli and responses. The things we're exposed to becoming the patterns that our brains practice into robust networks of neurons that can tightly connect things like "Black" with things like "violent."

Oh, how we would argue about the scholarly question of whether we're more than just those patterns—the firings in the wrinkled lump bringing images and ideas to life. How I challenged them to explain a mechanism by which anyone could possibly transcend the physical cause-and-effect reality of the brain to steer some sort of a higher course for themselves.

And how I still thought none of it applied to me. That I could enter that school, simply shed the well-worn pathways through which my bad dream had readily flowed, and magically create a whole new reality for myself and the students who were waiting inside.

I careened up the walkway on the backside of the school toward the archway entrance, popping open and chugging down an entire can of cold vegetable soup for breakfast before I opened the door.

CHAPTER EIGHT

I joined the flow around a large hall monitor who stood like a fifth pillar in the very center of the school's atrium. She greeted the students as they entered the building with comments like "Move that junk up dem stairs before gravity pulls your mess back on down, hear?" and "That new 'do ain't gonna help you none. Best put that weavin' time to what's *inside* yo' head. School time!"

In the second-story hallway, there were bright red tube tops tighter than paint on a car, fluorescent orange highlights in brown hair, yellow-bleached hair over manicured black eyebrows, green-and-blue army fatigues, indigo lipstick, and violet eye shadow.

The kids were vibrating life.

An effervescent cluster lounged outside my classroom. They parted for me to undo the thick metal bolt above the door handle. I stepped into C-223, my students quick behind, dispersing to chairs I'd arranged in a circle in the center of the room. And in an instant, there was no more time to think about this. We were straight up in it.

"What's with this circle, mane?"

"You our teacher?"

I tipped my forehead down lightly at the young man who'd asked.

"Check out teacher wit his gangsta suit!" he said to someone else in response.

I assigned myself to one of the twenty-four identical student desks in a meticulously arranged circle. I was glad they'd noticed it right away. It was meant to look and feel different. The focus wasn't to be a teacher at the front. It was meant to be an equal conversation.

But that wasn't about to happen.

The first thing they teach you about teaching is that you have to take control of the classroom, because the kids outnumber you, they out-energy you, and they will roll you if you let them. But I didn't want to try to crush them to my will. I wanted to let them help steer things. So I sat and listened.

The students took charge, lobbing questions and debating answers with one another all at once. Sometimes one of the questioners would be loud enough to volley above the rest.

"Where's Miss G?" asked a redheaded boy, rubbing his cheek.

"Seriously," said others, reinforcing the question.

I didn't know anything about her, so I shrugged while I panted and sweat through the armpits of my shirt into the suit coat, which I soon had to take off to keep breathing.

"Damn," he said, slumped.

My head turned from one to the other. I was going from zero to over a hundred kids, and their faces and quick comments blurred together. I needed to focus on what they were saying, find something to hold on to, figure out who they were.

"The circle?" I repeated, my voice squeaking a bit. Roiling hot inside, I was desperate to show up cool on the outside. To show that though I was only a few years older than some of them, I deserved to be a teacher and had something to offer. "Well, I have a different kind of class in mind—where we learn from each other. Like, through discussion. And the circle sets us up for that."

"You mean just like . . . talkin'?"

"Kind of. Yeah," I said.

"'That's tight, yo."

"Thanks," I said, thinking about how hard it'd been to arrange the perfect circle with just the right number of chair-desks.

"Where you from?"

"Around Seattle."

"Seattle? Damn—I mean, dang. All the way 'cross the country? Whatcha here fo'?" asked a large, Black young man who, for an instant, I connected mentally to the student who'd slammed into me in my dream. Disgusted by the notion, I pushed it hard from my mind and focused on his name placard. I'd designed, printed, laminated, folded, and taped a pyramid for all of the students so that we could see one another's names—and so I could quickly note which pyramids were left by the door when attendance was required.

His name was Buddy Jones.

"I don't know, Mr. Jones," I said, hoping they liked me. "I like it here?" the words sweated out of my tongue and spilled onto my desk.

I couldn't get any other words out.

We looked at each other, them at me and I at them. And then folks looked at Buddy.

He was covering his very short hair by tying what seemed to be a piece of black nylon stocking around his head like a bandanna. By the time he was done, a flap of the fabric hung off the back of his head like a curtain, shrouding his large neck. "Uh-huh?" he said, and the others looked back at me.

"I . . . uh . . . wanted to come here because I heard people sit on their porches and talk with each other. So I visited some schools, and this was my favorite."

"Say whaaaaa?"

"Nawwwwww . . . Cuz trippin'," said another boy, who was shorter and a bit rounder. I looked at his name: D'Shaun Peters. "Cuz mean," he said louder, "Creek's the only place to take him." He turned his head swiftly to the left and then the right, pursing his lips.

Most of the class was laughing.

"Ain't nowhere else wantcha?" accused a young woman behind a name card that read "Jauhntavia Prince." She slouched back in her chair, with hair that had been straightened then crimped, a short purse over her shoulder, white makeup lining black eyes.

"Oooohhhhh," said several voices, building, guffawing.

For a moment I cringed, worried that the louder sounds of the group might build to something nasty. Instead, the laughter bounced off the walls and petered out on the stained carpet.

I kept my hands folded in my lap, wondering—as I think they were—where these first minutes of class were taking us.

Some of the students tilted their heads slightly sideways, trying to get at things from a different angle.

"You go to college?" asked a pale, blond girl, who saw I didn't mind the questions. She looked away as soon as I turned to her to respond.

"Yeah, I did," I said, nodding and looking at her name card: Callie Rollins. The nodding in her peripheral vision seemed to draw her head slowly back toward me, though she didn't meet my gaze.

"Where you went?" asked Buddy.

"Thanks for asking, Mr. Jones. I actually went to three different colleges. Duke my freshman year, then I spent a semester in Washington, DC, at

George Washington University, then I spent the last few years at Harvard."
I prayed it'd impress them.

Everyone quietly brought their heads around to watch me.

A boy with glasses and a slight mustache, Juan, spoke. "Are you for real?"

"Yeah," added the girl next to him. "You serious?"

"Ain't nooooo way!" announced one of a triad of girls who'd been whispering together.

"Yes," I said proudly, hoping my degree might earn me some credibility—especially with the students who were only a few years younger than me.

"Then why are you *HERE*?" said Buddy, slowing down and patting one of his hands on his desk. "At Battery. Creek. High. School."

"This Godforsaken school," muttered a kid named Tony Massocks, who wore baggy pants with a chain wallet.

"I visited a lot of schools, and this was my favorite."

"How you mean?" asked Buddy.

"How what?" I asked politely.

"How you *mean*," said another.

"Am I mean?"

"How *do* you mean, dear sir?" said Jauhntavia in an embellished British sort of accent.

"Yo, dis man ain't from Harvard," cut in the kid next to Buddy.

"Yeah, ain't no way," echoed a girl from the triad.

Conferring with those around him, then speaking for the class, Buddy said, "You gonna hafta prove that."

Huh? "What for?" I asked. "You don't believe me?"

"*I* believe you," he said, "but some'uh these peeps ain't never gon' believe *that* till you show 'em the paper."

"Yup. Show us the paper."

"The *paper*?" I asked.

"The—how you say—uh, diploma."

"You dumb shit," said Jauhntavia. "Don't know 'diploma.'"

"I knew it!" pouted Buddy.

I cut in, saying "Come on, now," to Jauhntavia, then, "You'all want to see my diploma?"

"Yeah, show it to us," joined in Callie.

The class seemed lit up by the idea. It felt good to know I had something they were interested in—something for tomorrow.

"Sure, I'll bring it in." I added, "But since I'm gonna show you'all where

I'm coming from, you hafta tell me about where you come from—and tell me why you're here, OK?"

"Deal!" Buddy yelped gutturally, thrusting his open hand toward me. I started for an instant, as though it were a knife.

Then I shook his hand and looked to the others. "Deal?"

"Deal," they said in unison, some of them sighing the word.

I breathed deeply and smiled, glad that we agreed. Most of them seemed mildly satisfied.

"So, you were asking about why I'm here. Learning changed my life. I think it's the best thing there is. I got a real chance at it when I started the Advanced Studies program as a junior in high school. When teachers started asking meaningful questions and told us that what we thought, what we researched, mattered. And it all comes from dialogue with folks—dead and alive—but especially each other."

"Talkin' to dead people?" asked Tony. "This guy is *whacked out*, yo."

"Like through what they maybe wrote down when they were alive," I responded.

"Ahhhh," he said, snapping, then pointing at me and nodding.

"So this class isn't going to be about me lecturing. It'll be about us exploring issues together and learning from one another. That's where I'm coming from and what I'm hoping for here. What do you think?"

Dozens of people looked at me, and everyone clearly expected me to say more, to keep things going, to carry the class.

I had practiced for this. I was ready. I knew that lots of young teachers stumbled here, and some would never recover—not even over a thirty-year career. They developed the habit of talking to themselves. They answered their own questions, filling any silence with their own words so as not to be overwhelmed by the stares.

I sat there, reading their eyebrows and the twitches in their cheeks. *Say something. You're up. You're the teacher,* they said. *This is getting really awkward . . .*

". . ."

"You gonna say somethin', mister?" asked a girl whose posture required no leaning on the chairback. Her name placard said "Allie Duncan." She gently pulled a curling-ironed, hairsprayed, long black bang away from her eye.

"I already did. It's your turn," I said to her. Then I clamped my mouth down tight over what otherwise might have emerged as a nervous giggle, accidentally making a grumpy face at her before looking away toward the others.

"..."

"..."

The silence started to hurt. And then Buddy broke it.

"Yo, I getchu, Teach," he said, looking at me with a genuine, gentle tilt of his head. To the others, he said, "He's fo' real."

Thank you, I thought. *Maybe I am for real.*

"I'm witchu, Teach." Others nodded along. We were all watching Buddy now.

What will he say next?

Though I was his same height, six foot five, Buddy dwarfed me socially.

All of a sudden, after just a few words from him, I felt competent and accepted in this faraway place.

Clearly, Buddy's approval was all we needed to move forward.

"Well," said Callie, half timidly, "I'm here because I want to graduate."

"Yuh, git da hell outta Creek. Das what I be talkin' 'bout," muttered Jauhntavia seriously.

"So," I said, trying to sound thoughtful, "you want to graduate and get out of Battery Creek High School. Sounds like you don't want to be here."

"Now you gettin' it!" said Buddy. "But police say we gotta be here."

They squeezed only half the laughter out before I cut in. "I think that's pretty sad," I said, looking right then left for reactions.

"Ain't *sad*, it's just straight up," said Buddy, showing me his palms.

"I mean that I'm sorry to hear that. You'all have about a year or more of your lives still to spend in this building."

"Oh-*FIVE*, oh-*FIVE*, oh-*FIVE*," chanted Buddy.

"Oh-*FIVE*, oh-*FIVE*, oh-*FIVE*," chanted a couple of other seniors who were also retaking the graduation-required class. Buddy put his hands up and swayed side to side, leading the group like a rock star would a football stadium of followers.

"Oh-*seven*, oh-*seven*," chanted some sophomores lightly.

"I mean, if you're going to spend another *year of your life* in this building," I said, "I think it's pretty sad if you focus just on getting out and maybe miss the opportunity to learn and grow, improve yourself, enjoy yourself while you're here."

"Ain't nothin' enjoyable 'bout dis schoolhouse, Teach," said Buddy. "You ain't learned that, you ain't learned nuttin' 'bout Creek."

"What would you rather be doing?"

They gave terse answers about surfing and Xbox 360, and one I misheard as "Club Rinkin"—it turned out she'd rather be at the club drinking. Several said they wanted to be sleeping.

"OK," I said, then stopped to think, pursing my lips and looking up at the ceiling.

"I still don't get why you're here."

"You here to study us?"

"I bet he's with the FBI."

Tony's face was lax, his jaw open loosely. Then he sat up and said, "Drug investigator?"

"He's a scientist, here to experiment on us. Find out how the dumb people live."

"You got a hidden camera in yo tie, mista?" they joked. "We gon' be on Tee-V?"

"I'm not here for any of that. I'm here for you'all," I said proudly. "So, I wanna hear what you want to get out of the next 179 days so I can plan accordingly—"

"Hundred-seventy-nine days left? Hell—oh, sorry," said D'Shaun.

"What do you want from our time together?"

". . ."

". . ."

"I'll go first! I mean, can I go first?" said Callie, now fully warmed up.

"Sure," I said.

"I want a good grade so I can become a vet."

"I'd like to go to college, so gotta get past this first."

"I want to learn about history," said Juan.

"I ain't care," said one girl. A second—Allie—spoke immediately when it was her turn and said she was going to go to college in New York. The third didn't answer at all, and I said we'd come back to her, which she clearly didn't like.

I nodded to the next student in the circle.

"Just pass da class."

"Yeah, pass dis shit—I mean, pass dis stuff." said D'Shaun.

"I ain't know."

Is this a waste of time? I wondered. *Seems like most are saying nothing. Don't know, just pass, don't care.*

"Grade."

"Go to college."

"Learn."

"College."

"Nothin'."

We came back to the third girl in the triad, Tatyana, who'd shaken her head when it had been her turn before. "Ms. Crum?" I asked. "What do you want from our time together?"

"..."

"She ain't wanna talk, Mr. S.," offered a student.

Another one whispered, "She's slow."

"Naw, she's just waiting for us to listen," I said, angry at the whisperer.

In a classroom, dozens of people waiting for a minute feels like dozens of minutes waited.

Eventually, she saw we were intent on hearing her thoughts and said, "National security, with Allie."

"National security?" I coughed lightly. "You want to learn about national security?"

She didn't move to respond. She was watching me as though I were a subject in her experiment. *What're you gonna think now?* she seemed to wonder, examining my face.

"Excellent," I said. "We'll talk more about that for sure."

We'd gotten to everyone. They all stared at me.

I'm teaching nothing here, I kept thinking. *This is no help at all. And now it's quiet. Not quiet again already!*

"..."

I better say something.

"What else we doin' today, mister?" asked Allie.

Uhh . . .

"..."

"That's what I'm trying to figure out from you'all—what you want to do."

"Ain't dat yo' job? Why you tryna make us figure out what to do?" asked Allie.

"Yeah," said two of the boys at once.

"Didn't dey train you ta teach . . . *Teach?*"

The class laughed.

"What's this class all about?"

"Yeah, we're ready to learn, but seem like you might not be ready to teach?" asked Allie matter-of-factly, and I winced.

"What we gonna do?"

OK, I thought. *They're ready.*

"So, what I thought we could do today—"

The bell surprised me with a loud tone that brought everyone suddenly to their feet.

After I watched them leave, I read the words I had posted by the door. They were mostly for my psychology class—to provoke a debate about nature and nurture.

> *Give me a dozen healthy infants, well-formed, and my own specified world to bring them up in and I'll guarantee to take any one at random and train him to become any type of specialist I might select—doctor, lawyer, artist, merchant-chief and, yes, even beggar-man and thief, regardless of his talents, penchants, tendencies, abilities, vocations, and race of his ancestors.*
> *—Behavioral psychologist John Watson*

I tore the words down quickly before my second class of kids showed up. *What was I thinking? What arrogance.* I didn't run the world. The clock had run me down. I could barely hold on to my breakfast. Maybe these students could be any of those things they wanted to be, despite what Walter said. But why had I thought I could orchestrate any of it? I was completely sapped after fifty minutes of teaching.

———

After four more goes of it that day and somehow making it back to my trailer, I must've passed out on the dirty burlap couch. When I woke up, my thirst tried to make my legs move, but they wouldn't. I'd raced triathlons and biked across the country, but I'd never been responsible for leading a high-stakes conversation with a hundred people for nearly five hours. I crawled across the linoleum for a large Gatorade and a big bag of Classic Lay's potato chips, both of which I emptied while slumped against the cabinets, then sighed all the air out of my lungs.

—————— CHAPTER NINE ——————

While I waited in the circle on the second day, I cracked open a large green bell pepper, pulled out the seeds and the stem, and started crunching.

The sun was warm on my hands and strong enough to light the room through tinted glass. I got up and walked to the door to turn off the overhead fixtures.

The triad of girls came in together, looking meticulous and confident.

One of them said, "What *is* that nasty smell?"

"Think it's that man's pepper," another whispered.

I swallowed hard, and it was kind of loud. I pretended to read from my notepad, holding it up close to my face. They put their bags beneath three chairs and left. I smelled perfume they left behind.

Then I heard from the hall "Ooooooh, bitch, he schooled you!" and my breath quickened at the cursing—loud from a bass voice.

My being here makes no sense. I'm supposed to be their history teacher? I grew up in a middle-class suburb, and most of these kids are poor. I'm a Northerner in the Bible Belt. I don't really know anyone here, what they're like, what the real history is.

Then they were all seated around me. They'd come back! I swallowed a laugh and choked a bit on the ridiculous notion that I—mere months ago a student myself—could teach these folks what they needed to know.

They spoke first: "What we doin' today?"

"More talkin' 'bout stuff?" Jauhntavia asked.

"You know we need to be learnin' some history up in here, not just talkin'," said Allie.

This was my chance. I waited until they were all looking at me.

I stood up and went to the whiteboard. I breathed a hot, quick sigh, before writing the first of our essential questions: "WHAT IS HISTORY?"

They seemed a bit interested, though less so once they saw me noticing their interest.

They said nothing. For one heartbeat. Two heartbeats. Three heartbeats. Four heartbeats. Five heartbeats. Six heartbeats. Seven heartbeats. Eight heartbeats. I think I was holding my breath when Tony said, "Boring, of course."

Everyone laughed, and I turned to the board to hide my snickers, and started breathing again.

"True dat!"

José Gutierrez said, "The past."

"The past?" I said, ignoring Tony for now. "Good. Someone else?" I wrote "The Past" on the board next to the question.

"..."

I saw the light changing in the room as the sun moved up higher in the sky.

"How about you, Ms. Rollins?" I pointed to Callie.

"Yeah," she said. "It's the past, right?"

"Yeah, we already got the answer, didn't we?" asked Jauhntavia.

"So all we have to do in this class," I said, trying to draw them out, "is study the past?"

They nodded.

"All of it?" I asked.

"Yeah, all of it," said Buddy, "so we best hurry up with it, cuz we only got a hundred and seventy-eight days left after today."

"So, we've got to study what happened five minutes ago when you'all walked in here? Is that a part of history?"

"Yeah," said a girl whose nameplate read "Sandee Liu." She added, "And what Mindy said about me in the hall ten minutes ago, we should study that real close. When people say stuff that's just straight-up wrong, that's history too. A history of being *wrong*, which she definitely has a history of!"

"Wait a minute," I said. "I'm a little confused. You think we need to study everything that ever happened—but we only have, like, a hundred and fifty hours to do it? I'm not sure it'd fit." I wrote "EVERYTHING?" under the question on the board. Then I lingered, steaming up the word on the board longer than I needed to, trying to collect myself enough to turn around and face all of them.

"Well, maybe not *everything*," said Max, who'd said only "surfing" and "to pass" the day before. "We can leave out the stuff that's not important."

"Like what?" I asked, turning back toward the class.

"Everything that's not in the textbook?" asked Margaret Winslow, a girl with long, straight brown hair parted down the middle.

"Oh, well then, that's easy," I said, picking up a heavy blue textbook from my desk. "So whatever the publisher says is history is in, and everything else is out?"

"Why not?" asked D'Shaun, putting up his palms.

"Why not?" I asked him back. "Well, what if the publisher put something in that's not supposed to be there, or left something out that *is* supposed to be there?"

"They probably wouldn't do that," said Ronnie Sanders, rubbing his rough red hair with an open palm. "After all, aren't they the experts?"

"Wait," I said. "I thought I was the expert. I mean, I'm a certified history teacher—"

"From Harvard too. We know," said Tatyana.

"So, what if," I asked, "this book says something's a part of history and I say it's not?"

Everyone was with it. They were all focused and thinking. Dozens of minds igniting dozens of cylinders simultaneously, heading beyond the horizon any one of us could reach on our own. *This is what it's all about*, I thought. *This is teaching!*

"Like what?" asked Callie after no one else wanted to talk.

"Well, I don't know," I said, pausing for a second so I could think of something. I opened the book to the chapter on civil rights. I held up the book and pointed to MLK. "Like, this book talks about Martin Luther King and doesn't say much about the student movements. What if I say that Martin Luther King was a great guy, but that the students and educators are the ones who really made the civil rights movement happen with their teach-ins?"

"Well, you're the teacher," said Buddy. "What you say goes."

"So, then, it's not the publisher who decides? It's me?" I asked the class.

I wrote "TEXTBOOK" on the board. Then I wrote "TEACHER," and turned around to face the concentrated social pressure of forty-eight eyes scrutinizing my two.

"Are you going to tell us the answer or what?" asked Sandee.

"You agree that I have the answer?" I said, underlining the word "TEACHER."

"Hey," she said, "honestly, whatever you say goes because you're the one with power over our grades."

I wrote "PERSON WITH MOST POWER DECIDES" on the board. "Great," I said, sitting on the edge of my desk for a moment to catch my breath. "Then I say that history is whatever we decide in this discussion."

"That's not fair," moaned Sandee. She stuck out her lower lip in entreaty. "You're supposed to tell us, you know. That's, like, your job." She then put all of her attention into a shiny black purse, burrowing deep to find something.

There was a little lull while she did this. I thought it was important that everyone say something, so I called on Allie. "Ms. Duncan?" I asked.

"Mr. Saaris?" she replied.

"What do you think?"

"About what?" she said in the same tone I was using to ask her the question.

"About this lovely question we've got right here on the board," I said.

"I don't know," she said, also now searching in her purse.

"That's OK," I said. "We can wait for you to figure out what you think. You can just give us any idea you have about it when you're ready."

She frowned at me. "Right now?"

"We'll wait until you're ready."

She frowned harder. But it was a question I knew she could answer, so we waited.

Ten seconds later, she said, "Well, I don't think it's just what you say. That's what I think."

"Wait a minute," I said. "You disagree with the teacher? Uh-oh. Now we've got Ms. Liu saying that it's whatever I say, and Ms. Duncan saying it's not whatever I say. How are we going to have a history class if we can't even agree what history is?" I paused, pleased with the idea.

"I think," said José, raising his hand and waiting for me to look over at him before he continued, "I think that there is no right answer to the question. History can be lots of different things. Like what a book says, or what a teacher says, or what we say it is."

I responded right away. "Well, if it can be anything anyone says, then we're back to studying everything, aren't we? I just don't know how we'll have time to do that if it's what you say it is and what I say it is and what the book says it is and what Ms. Duncan says it is, and what Ms. Liu says it is." I wrote "WHATEVER ANYONE SAYS" on the board.

"Well, I don't know!" said Sandee. "Why don't you just *tell us* already? Geez."

"Why? Because Ms. Duncan thinks history is *not* whatever I say it is, so that means I can't just tell you, right, Ms. Duncan?"

"That's ri-ight," she said, donning a sarcastic smile.

"Hmm," I said, rubbing my chin for emphasis, unsure if this was getting us anywhere.

"I know," said Sandee loudly, while still looking into her purse. It didn't seem as if anything should have been able to get that lost in a purse that tiny. "I think history is not just what someone says it is. It's the facts."

"The facts?" I asked, writing it on the board. "What're those?"

"What are facts?" she asked.

I nodded, and then for a moment we all watched her abundantly apply lip gloss.

"They're what actually happened?" said Max.

"Well, how do we know what actually happened?" I asked. *I'm good at this*, I thought.

"We look at the facts!" said Sandee.

"And how do we know what the facts are?" I asked. "If we go to some people who were at a historical event, for example, they could tell you different things. Like . . ." I thought for a moment, then said, "Follow me out into the hall, please."

"What?"

"We gotta get up?"

"You serious?"

"We really gots tuh go in the hall?"

"Come on Mr. S. I *just* gettin' comfortable!"

"Yes," I said, answering several questions at once. "Let's go."

After a minute's struggle against the inertia of seat-sitting, we were all outside the door.

"OK," I said, delighted to see the students in the hall, standing by the locker bank.

Sandee, I noticed, had brought her purse and seemed to be applying some sort of second kind of lip gloss.

"So, we all attended the event in there together. Mr. Saaris's first-period US history class on August 20, 2004. And since we were all there, we should know the facts about the event. Like, how many chairs were in the room?"

They went haywire trying to come up with an answer, some people counting the students, others guessing, someone remembering there were other chairs stacked on the side, no one agreeing, while I stood right in front of the tiny window in the door to block their view.

When I brought them back into the classroom, everyone scanned, concentrating, counting chairs.

"OK," said Sandee, "so now we know there's thirty-one in here."

"But that's not the point," I said. "The point is that facts will usually be disputed, and people will have different opinions about things in the past. And this was about something that happened just a minute ago. Imagine any other type of event that happened, like, a decade ago. A hundred years ago. So where does that leave us? History as facts? We're getting a lot of these facts from people, and people are interpreting and guessing, aren't they? So if you say history is facts, what exactly does that even mean? We couldn't agree on a simple fact of how many desks there were in the room we were all *just* in!"

"OK," said Buddy, who'd looked like he'd been concentrating throughout the conversation. "Where's the dictionary?"

"That's a good idea," said José. "Let's look up the word. Where is it, Mr. S.?"

"I have one on the computer," I said.

"Can I use it?" asked José.

"Be my guest."

As José went for the computer, Tatyana, Allie, and Jauhntavia started talking about something softly, but it was building.

When José started reading the definition he had found on the computer, the girls started snickering. Soon they were laughing so loudly that no one could hear what José was saying, and everyone was looking at them.

"Ladies," I said, in my best teacher voice.

They quieted down. But something happened between that group of girls and José before he got back to his seat. I don't know what it was, but it took the color out of his face, and he didn't say a word for the rest of the day.

I repeated the definition José had read from the computer and asked, "So, what do we think about the dictionary's definition? Does Merriam-Webster have the answer you were looking for, Mr. Jones?"

He was talking energetically with Jauhntavia about an upcoming party and didn't hear me. Something about no adults and all the *stuff* folks could want to do. I got frustrated because it had felt as if we'd really been grappling with a central challenge of history—the messiness of it, the different opinions, and what we could make of all that together. And now they were off on something else. I decided to try looking at them quietly, stoically, which took a couple awfully awkward minutes to finally work.

"Oh, sorry, Teach," he said to me, turning his desk away from Jauhntavia and back toward the center of the circle. "Just had to settle some business about this weekend, is all. IF . . . you know what I'm sayin'." He swirled his head in the air in giant punctuation.

"Mr. Jones," I said, "I think you're saying that your weekend plans are more important than what we're talking about here in class."

"What?" he said, incredulously. "What is history? No, that's important too, Teach, but this is *important*. IF you know what I'm sayin'." He twirled his head again.

"Well then," I said, "let's talk about that. You want to use this class to plan your weekend? What are you going to do?" I knew better than to use this teacher tactic, but the idea of Buddy being drugged out like Jamie had been scared me.

"Well," he smiled, "I'm glad to have the opportunity to share with y'all that there will be a special party this weekend out in Yemassee."

My understanding was that some kids rode the bus hours each way every day to get from and back to the remote parts of Yemassee.

"And at this party there will be all the things any young man or woman could ever want to take part in. IF," he said, pausing for dramatic effect, "you know what I'm sayin'!"

"Oh yeah, I know," said Tony. "How do I get in on this?"

Several others wanted in too, but I cut Buddy's response off, saying, "Mr. Jones, what makes you think this is an appropriate time to give out party invitations?"

"You told me to speak freely, that's all," he said with mild petulance.

"I assumed you were going to share something worth our while." As soon as I said it, I felt bad. I'd baited him out to talk about the party, then shamed him for doing it. "Uh, why don't we get back to the question at hand here?"

Buddy said, "All right, sure," seemingly glad to have had the interlude to discuss the party, but still willing to try to follow me back. Unfortunately, there wasn't time to get back before the bell.

CHAPTER TEN

To get the stress out, I really needed to run.

So I talked to the athletic director and asked what's up with cross-country running. Because it's usually, like, a hundred degrees after school in August unless there's thunder or lightning, not much was up with cross-country running at Battery Creek High School. There were a few kids who'd asked him about it, and he told me I could coach and run with them if I wanted.

While the heat melted the tar that held the track together, I had fun with the kids, digging in fire ant hills, and listening to their school-inappropriate humor while trying to hide my laughter.

One of my runners, Jim Matthews, kept calling me goofy and said my head was too big. If I tried to get him to tone it down, he'd make a face like the abominable snowman—"Jlaalaa!"—and skip circles around me. He was tall and skinny but said he used to be really fat, and needed to run to keep the weight off.

Jim would catch us all up in arguments about anything. The hill of fire ants and how badly the bites would really hurt, and who'd dare put their hand in the middle of the mound to test it?

"What d'ya think they're thinking, Coach?" he asked one day, while we waited to see if other runners would show.

"I don't know," I said, tired and hot.

"I bet it's not *that* different from us. Don't you teach psychology? How could we know?" He was always asking the fundamental question of epistemology: *How could we know?*

That night, after I'd planned all the next day's lessons, I pulled an E. O. Wilson book I'd been meaning to read out of one of my boxes so I could try to impress Jim.

When I saw him again, I told him he was right. There were a lot of similarities—how a colony of ants working together have a similar amount of connections as a human brain does. How the synaptic gaps were larger, but just as in the human mind, the ants shot chemistry across gaps to trigger the next set of neural networks. That they had about as much biomass and geographic span on the planet as human beings did. Then he'd ask another question that would send me back to more after-hours studying so we could talk about it all the next day.

He asked how long it would take to fully get to know someone else (he had a particular girl in mind). If you had fifteen years of catching up to do, would that take fifteen years to cover, and then you'd really know each other? And we were off into questions of history, and what's important to know, and do we ever *really* know? And how could we test it?

Other runners would be trying to stop talking about heavier topics as they ran out of breath, but even without breath, Jim kept going: "Naw . . . it don't . . . seem like that'd . . . answer it. C'we figure . . . if . . ."

Since there were only four students in my advanced psychology class, when Jim stopped by my room after school, I asked him if he wanted to sign up. I'd asked the other students to bring their friends, and wanted to do my part too. I was surprised when he told me he'd been placed in the least academically intense of four levels for all his subjects. I wondered if there was something I didn't understand about why he needed to be in those classes, but I decided to tell him about how much Advanced Studies had meant to me, pitching hard like I'd tried to pitch Jamie, until, I imagine, Jim started hearing "yada, yada, yada" and cut in.

"That sounds good, but I'm not sure I got time, Saaris-man. I gotta get fit for soccer this spring. And for"—he elbowed me in the side and mugged a grin—"I'm hoping something might could happen with that Traci girl. She's quite—"

"That's quite enough of that," I said. "You can just go ahead and talk with kids your own age about that kind of thing."

"OK," he said, "but *you* know what I'm sayin'." He elbowed me again, harder.

"Oh boy," I said, walking out the door. On our way down to the track, I asked him if he was bored in his classes so far, and he said that yeah, they were pretty unbearable. And I said that good advanced learning is the opposite of boring, and didn't he owe it to himself to try it out? And then he said yeah, he really should take Advanced Studies (A.S.) classes, that I was making sense.

On the last day students could change their classes, we saw each other across the hallway. He was headed north, I south. He wore in the middle of his back one of those sneaker-sized packs with strings for straps. It was blue, and his T-shirt was huge and plain black. A lot of the kids were wearing these T-shirts as big as a dress.

He made his abominable snowman face when he saw me, a toothy, escalating roar. "Saaris!"

We navigated the energetic flow of kids like crossing a ten-lane highway, looking both ways and then making our moves toward each other as openings emerged.

On our temporary island in the flow, we clapped our hands together, thumb around thumb, pulled each other in and one-arm hugged, then back out to just our hands, fingertips on tensed fingertips to make a loud snap, then an exploding fist bump.

"You been workin' on your dap, Saaris?"

"A bit, yeah."

"That's our best one yet. Good on ya."

"You know," I said, blushing. "Anyway, you got that schedule changed yet? Cuz I haven't actually seen you in any of my advanced classes."

"Mmm," he said, frowning. "You know how it is."

"Can I see?"

"Fo' sho!" He pulled the crumpled half page out of his pack and held it out for me. As I reached, he pulled it back, pointed at me, laughed. "Heh-heh-heh! You too slow, Saaris. Got that big head slowin' you down. Try again?"

I grabbed for it and he pulled it away. I folded my arms. "OK, man, you want me to look at it or not? Cuz class is gonna start here soon."

"No need to pout, Saaris—here you go." He set it on his two hands as if it were a cup of tea he was serving me.

"Thank you very much, sir!" I said, smiling.

As I read, I put four fingers to my forehead and my thumb to my jaw.

"Hold up. This isn't for real?"

"Yeah. For real boring!" He was dapping up Bryan, who'd joined us on our little island. They did a couple flourishes I didn't know.

"What happened to signing up for the advanced classes we talked about?"

"Aww, you know," he said, looking at Bryan. "I got a lot goin' down, and I'm not sure I'm up for all that stuff. Bryan and I may be hittin' cruise control this year on the school stuff. Gettin' fit for the ladies. Doin' our thang, you know?"

When he saw in my face that I wasn't playing, he stopped talking.

"Really?" I pushed. "Because there's actually only five classes on your actual schedule here, and there's seven periods in a school day."

"Yeah, I didn't get to change it. Honest, I do wanna do the advanced ones like we talked about, and I do wanna do college and all that. And how you said—you promised me, Saaris, don't forget!—that it'd be more interesting than these boring basic classes, right?"

"Absolutely."

"Bryan, you wanna come to A.S. with me?"

"Naw, man. I'm good," he said.

"Come on—you sure?"

"Yup."

"OK, Saaris, how we gon' do this?" he said, turning away from his best friend and towards me. "You know, I talked to them 'bout this and they said to forget it, cuz of my grades—"

"Who did?" I barked.

"Ms. Barnes," he said softly.

"Paula Barnes? OK, let's go," I said. "You sure you're not coming, Bryan? You'd love it, too, and I know you'd be good at it."

"Naw."

We let him go and headed down the central hallway as long as a couple football fields. On the right, we passed Ms. Magnuson's room, where she hosted "free days" for students to play poker. For twelfth-grade English lessons, she'd do all-class games of hangman that half the kids slept through. Not twenty feet across the hall, in Mr. Maloney's advanced classes, students were reading Thoreau and debating civil disobedience and the origins of science.

The Supreme Court had deemed separate unequal in 1954. President Eisenhower's National Guard had enforced this in Arkansas in 1957. Pat Conroy taught in Beaufort's still-segregated district at the end of the 1960s and wrote that the water dividing schools and races from each other was wide, and that educational opportunities were still being determined by "fanged and implacable cycles." In the 1970s, schools finally started to get integrated here. And now it was the 2000s and Battery Creek High School's hallway was so full of gorgeous sounds, beautiful people, ideas, handshakes, hairstyles, combs, colors, sneakers, stories, Black, white, Asian, Latina, Native

American children, all together, bubbling over with the possibilities of a year of learning, making new friends, growing together to that age of becoming: beginning to vote, build a career, and start a family, and the future is now—here—as Jim and I walk down the middle of it all, smiling.

And then the old historical forces took hold around us.

The bell bleated, commanding kids to enter the room listed by #3 on their schedules. Right behind the bell, the security guards came holding out their arms and walking forward, moving waves of kids through their assigned doors. The waters parted, white from Black, and when each student was where the school had decided they belonged, hard metal latches clicked shut behind them.

All the kids were gone, except for Jim.

"Where do you need to be, son?" a guard asked him. "Show me that schedule there."

Jim, normally pretty unflappable, fumbled with the document.

"He's with me," I said, looking the guard in the eyes.

"He's with you?"

"Yes, sir."

"OK, Mr. Saaris. Have a good day." He put two fingers up to his eyebrow and made a casual salute, then walked slowly away down the hall, shifting a lot of weight from one foot to the other and back as he went, the walkie-talkie on his hip crackling, then fading in the distance: "ALL CLEAR." "All Clear. "All clear . . ."

We made it to the office of Paula Barnes.

"Who is it?" she replied to my knock.

"It's me-ee," I said in a singsong voice.

"Everyone finally where they need to be out there? I kind of like to avoid the crazy . . ." She tapered off as she saw Jim slide through the door to stand beside me, his hands crossed over each other.

"Except for this one," I said.

"Where's he supposed to be? Lemme see your schedule there, young man."

She had a hundred such documents arrayed on the desk she'd turned away from when we came in. On her big, boxy computer monitor, the cursor blinked over a scheduling database application.

As Jim handed over his document, I tried to make my case. "Paula . . . er, Ms. Barnes," I started. "I think Jim here should really be taking Advanced Studies classes. He's been really bored in his classes so far and can do so much more."

"It says here he has a 1.7 grade-point average." She tapped the screen with a long nail, then met my eyes and grimaced with a small shake of her head, as though Jim wouldn't notice.

"Yeah, well," Jim started, then stopped, looking down at the floor.

"I had the same grades when middle school didn't challenge me," I said. "I can tell you, from having spent most every day with him at practice, that he is quite capable. He just hasn't been challenged yet. He always wants to figure things out—biology, math, philosophy, history. But he's not getting any of that stuff at a high level in his classes. Advanced Studies is perfect for him."

"Are you sure?" she asked.

I looked at Jim.

"Yes, ma'am," he said.

"OK, I'll put in here 'On authority of Mr. Saaris,'" Barnes said, working her computer now. "It's on you."

Jim and I high-fived lightly so as not to make a sound.

"He can be in my first-period history, hopefully, to get ready for the advanced they start as juniors next year? And third period is English for the tenth graders in Advanced Studies, right?" I asked.

"We'll see. And yes, it is."

Jim and I strode out together. "Thank you, Ms. Barnes," I said over my shoulder. "I'll take him there."

"Thanks!" said Jim.

"Come back to get your schedule after third period."

"Will do!"

———— CHAPTER ELEVEN ————

I had the class work for the next several days on an assignment Fry and I came up with. Since it'd been hard to develop a shared definition of history in the abstract, we'd explore a concrete example, and the students would present a brief history of the United States as they currently understood it. Then we could figure out what they knew and how they thought about the subject, and build from there.

The day of the presentation, Max, Ronnie, and José—first through the door—looked from one side of the room to the other, then whispered something. Allie and Jauhntavia, coming through behind them, noticed the boys before they noticed the room.

"Y'all boys best keep dat train movin'," directed Allie.

"Standin' like fools all up in the door, and yo, Mr. S—where we sposta sit?" Jauhntavia asked.

I was sitting and watching them from a desk against the center of the classroom's back wall. Every other desk in the room was stacked by the walls to my right and left. D'Shaun reached for a desk, but before he could pull it from the pile and flip it right-side up, I said loudly, "Hey! You don't need that! What do you think you need that for, Mr. Peters?"

"What I *need* it fo'?" he asked indignantly. "Fo' sittin'!"

"Fo' sho," added Jauhntavia.

"You don't need to sit today," I said clearly, loudly enough so that everyone could hear. Only Buddy and Tatyana weren't listening.

"How you spect us to—" Jauhntavia started to say, before José cut in.

"We got that presentation today—don't y'all 'member?"

"What presentation?" about half of the class asked at once.

"The one we was workin' on these past two days," pleaded Allie. "Come on, people, now!"

"Now, you can't just go and tell us we got a presentation . . ."

"When the bell rings, you're on," I offered.

"Thas in, like, two minutes, yo!" yelped Tony.

I extricated myself from the roaring by looking down at my yellow legal pad, punching the top of my mechanical pencil twice, and beginning to write:

> *Monday, August 30, 2004*
> *A History of the United States of America Presentation*
> *Period One*

José, Max, and Sandee were conversing in loud hisses, and seemed to be very aware that I was waiting for the presentation to begin. Jim—it was his second day in my class—walked through the door wearing a huge red T-shirt, blue jeans, and bright white shoes, took a quick sweeping look around, and joined the three of them, his backpack small against the reams of fabric, layers, and folds of cotton and denim.

As I'd done when they were preparing to present, I wrote down everything I heard and saw, so that we could refer to it later as a historical record.

I wrote that Buddy asked Tatyana out, got rejected, and then asked D'Shaun what was going on, to which D'Shaun replied, "No clue." Ronnie had been looking out the window for the first minute of class. I wrote down what he said after stepping to the front of the room to represent the group: "Mr. Saaris, we ain't gon' be ready today."

"Speak for yourself," said Allie quietly, holding a small stack of three-by-five notecards.

"So I can take a nap?" I asked.

"Well, you should probably just go ahead and teach," said Ronnie.

"Teach?" I spat tersely. "That's your job, yo."

Ronnie laughed. "Seriously, though," he said after a moment, "we're not ready."

"That's cool, Teach. Imma take a nap here, then." I put my head onto my arms and began to snore loudly.

"No, Mr. Saaris!" shouted Sandee, sounding like a tantrum about to burst. "Mr. Saaris, wake up! We're going to do this! We just need another minute to get ready!"

"I'll just be sleepin', yo," I said, starting to snore again.

After some more hurried whispering, they began.

They gave the date of the first European settlement in the Americas, and the names of countries people had come from to the US. They gave the date of the Declaration of Independence, and the date George Washington took office. They gave the dates of John Adams's and Thomas Jefferson's presidencies, then asked one another, "How many of these we wanna do?"

Where were all the good thinking and discussion and ideas I'd heard while the small groups were preparing for this presentation? How had their insightful debates snapped into rote recitations? I'd been noticing in all my classes that when students were put on the spot for scrutiny by a teacher, a protective layer seemed to descend. Like teachers who'd wanted to keep the bars in the hallways where students ran the show, students in class seemed to want a protective distance between themselves and the adults with power over them.

They talked about the Civil War by saying that the South split off but then we all fought and got back together. They gave some dates. They named some more presidents. They talked about major wars by giving their names and saying who fought. The whys of these things were not discussed.

Then they got to the civil rights movement and said there was a struggle that was finally won because of Rosa Parks and MLK. They moved from there to naming and dating the Vietnam War. There was whispering that someone hadn't done their part on the 1970s, and then for the 1980s we got a list of Ronald Reagan and the Iran-Contra affair and Reaganomics, without any context about what those things meant or why they might be of interest.

And then the history of our country was over with Bill Clinton, Monica Lewinsky, and some giggles.

"Any questions?"

I looked at them with a smile. They stood at the front of the room, watching me, their eyes asking, *Was it good? Did we get a good grade?*

"There's twenty minutes left," I said.

"We're done," said Sandee.

"Part of the grade is using the whole time, remember? And part of the grade was also to have everyone equally involved in the presentation," I said, looking at the group of students who had slouched at the side of the room throughout, saying nothing.

Allie handed Jim an open textbook. He hadn't said anything yet, and he stepped forward now, holding the book with both hands, his head bent low.

"In 1970, Richard Nixon was president. And he resigned from the presidency, and then Gerald Ford took over. Jimmy Carter was the next president in 1977 until 1981." He paused for a long while, looking at the textbook, turning a page or two. "Other things that happened in the 1970s were the hostage crisis and the energy crisis. Jimmy Carter gave a speech about energy policy, which had a 'mixed reception,' whatever that means."

Tony got pushed to the front of the room as Jim stepped back. Tony didn't have a book in his hands. "OK," he said. "So, I don't know much about the progressives, but I just did a little reading about them, and apparently they were big in the early 1900s. They wanted rights for factory workers and"—he paused to look around—"and 'consumer standards,' I think they said, but I don't know what that means." He stopped there.

"What else?" hissed Margaret.

"Yeah, come on—what else?" asked Sandee loudly.

Tony crossed his eyes for a moment. He went over the book Jim was still holding, turned some pages, then ran his finger over some lines of text, reading: "The progressives became the Bull Moose Party for Teddy Roosevelt after his party wouldn't take him back when he ran for president. That's all I got."

Sandee started clapping loudly, and a few students picked up it and clapped too. She bowed. "Thank you—thank you very much."

There were still ten minutes left, during which they had nothing more they wanted to share about the history of the country. They milled about, chatting by the door with their backpacks on, watching the clock.

It was hard for me to sit there and let that time go, but I wanted to follow through on giving them the full period to show me their stuff. Maybe it wasn't their stuff so much as it was Walter's and the social studies department's stuff. They'd had these students for years. The district had had most of them for a decade. And this was the level of interest and engagement they'd created—a tooth-pullingly painful forty minutes of reading contextless names, dates, and factoids from a textbook—with the formal study of everything that'd happened in the United States so far and everything it implied for our future.

––––––

I made a really bad decision. I used the rubric I'd given them before the "brief history of the US" assignment, and I graded the crap out of their presentation. I'd told them that history could and should be interesting, engaging, grappling with big questions. They hadn't done any of that, so I gave them a zero for that heavily weighted section.

If they showed a strong ability to do the work of a historian by the end of the term, I would give them a strong grade and forget about this whole diagnostic-assignment grade. But I didn't explain that to them, and they were used to a system in which each bad grade was a mark against them that might never be undone.

I'd hoped to use this exercise, and the grading of it, to set a high bar for all that history could be and all that historians could do—all that I would work to ensure that everyone in this class could readily do. But instead, it came off as though I thought they didn't—and maybe couldn't—measure up to any of that.

And because I was desperate to appear as though I knew what I was doing (when I didn't), I stuck with my approach to grading them even when they objected, obliterating any trust I'd built. I was no longer the quirky dude from Harvard who might have something to offer through these strange open conversations in a circle. I was now the smart-ass telling them they didn't know a thing about history. And I was dangerous to them because I appeared to be wielding what authority I had to show all that I knew, at their expense.

Not that I realized any of this at the time. I thought I was valiantly fighting the good fight—attacking the bad schooling they'd gotten in order to defend and uplift them.

———

Later that week, I noticed that they no longer seemed interested in getting into the discussions with me, kept asking to go to the bathroom. "Look, guys," I tried. "I get it, all right? I get it—I really do. I went through a lot of bad classes in school myself. Classes I just walked out on to wander the halls with my friends."

"Really? They let people into Harvard who walk out of class?"

Several of my own teachers had taught me about civil disobedience and getting into "good trouble." One of them had even said the main thing she hoped I took away from her class was to question authority. I didn't yet think about how differently disobedience and questioning authority could turn out for my students.

"Some of the best learning has happened when people organized walk-outs from class . . . But the point here is that school is about finding chances to pursue your curiosity. There's so much to learn! And it—"

"Yeah, yeah, learning's great. You done tol' us."

"Hey, but I get that school's been pushing you away from this subject. Did I tell you that all five of the kids in my advanced history class only signed up because they thought they'd have a hot teacher who's not here anymore?"

"Oh yeah, Miss G . . . If only she was here, steada—I mean, you're cool too, Mr. S!" said D'Shaun.

"Yeah, yeah," I said. "But literally no one in this school is signing up to study history here by the time they're in twelfth grade. The school has managed to get all of you to dislike it."

"I'm in twelfth grade!" said Buddy.

"Yeah, but yo' dumb ass failed like me, so you *had* to come back to this basic class," countered Jauhntavia.

———

I figured that if we stepped outside typical school history topics and talked about something they knew intimately, we could get to some real historical analysis and insights that I just knew they had in there. So I asked them to tell their life histories.

Max talked about surfing, D'Shaun talked about video games, Allie said some nice things about her aunt and cousins, Sandee talked about helping out at home, and Buddy talked about football as his ticket. Jim said he used to be fat but was now into weightlifting and soccer. But most of their talks were like things had been about the US: the year they were born, the names of their parents, the number of siblings they had, the names of their schools . . . until the clock ran out.

The big exception was Callie Rollins. After mentioning she wanted to be a vet, she talked about being passed around from home to home growing up, being molested by family members, then abused, rejected, and now living with a foster family.

Everyone was supposed to ask everyone a question about their life story, and Callie's revelations were greeted with questions like "What's your favorite color?" and "Do you like to go to the beach?" It frustrated me that the kids had glossed over her pain, but I just sat there impotently—and I was the one who was supposed to be the responsible adult.

Dealing with the worst of what was happening felt too heavy, too sad, too much. I wanted to be there for her, but I was drawn into my own thoughts about Erin and what she'd been through.

Based on Rosa's advice, I was trying to develop our community, relationships within which discourse could flourish. But I didn't know how to be there for my students, or where to take the conversation. I wasn't about to admit any of that, though. I'd just try to figure out some next steps, period by period, day by day.

──────── CHAPTER TWELVE ────────

We didn't yet have the five girls and five boys needed to field our cross-country teams at the races, so I slipped a paper into the stack of announcements the secretary read on the loudspeaker each morning: "Coach Saaris challenges everyone in the school to a race for $100." Second place would be $50 and third, $25.

The game was elimination by getting lapped. For some reason, when Max and Jim found out their prize money was coming out of my pocket, they absolutely insisted I keep it, said I was doing a good thing, which made me feel a deep gratitude and peace.

Outside the classroom, community seemed to come easy. Discussions, care, consideration, humor, and seriousness, all in right relationship with one another. I wanted to bring this out in the classroom, but there were some really problematic dynamics and habits that seemed to take over in that room when I talked, which I couldn't yet figure out.

────

Several miles into a team run that was threatening thunder, I got the insight I was looking for.

The next day, I went up to the whiteboard. "OK, I figured out how we're gonna start to flip some things around here. You're gonna *love* history. It's just something you've never really had the chance to do in school yet." I started to write. "This is what you've been doing":

YROTSIH

Interest sprouted.

"Why-rots-sh?" someone asked.

They were all trying to figure it out.

"*This* is the key! *This* is what's been happening!" I tapped on the word proudly with a purple marker. "Last week, when I asked you guys what history was, you basically said it was a whole bunch of everything that'd ever happened, or whatever the publisher says it is."

"This some kinda foreign language you got up there, Saaris?"

"We gots tuh know."

"Then," I continued, glad to see their curiosity again, "when I asked you to present on the history of the United States, even though that's supposedly been a part of your schooling for, like, ten years now, you had *nothing* interesting to say about it. You gave me a handful of dates and names and stuff you just looked up.

"But that's not so much on you, because really, you've been given the subject of history backwards all these years. It doesn't start with a bunch of facts and authorities saying what it is. History starts with questions that fascinate you. That's what I finally got in eleventh grade, and it changed everything. Before that it was worksheets and what year was the War of 1812—"

"Oh, I know that one!" said Tony. "Is it 1812?"

"I assume so," I said. "I don't really know anything about it."

"How you mean, you don't know anything about it? You're the Harvard history teacher, man. You gotta know."

"No, you don't, actually. That's what I'm saying. I literally don't know anything about the War of 1812. When I got to an advanced class, the teacher told me I needed to learn some facts, sure—if they helped to understand something bigger that matters. Maybe you don't remember some dates, but you remember that these things tended to happen after those things and then you talk about why that might be."

I looked at them and wondered if we were connecting.

"So what is this why-rot thingy, exactly?" asked Margaret.

"Well, what I'm trying to say is that you guys have been studying the topic of history backwards. Starting with the notion that the textbook has all the answers and that those come in the form of facts that you need to memorize. So you've been studying yur-ot-see. The subject of *history backwards*.

"Ooooooohhhh," moaned Allie Duncan. "Y'all. It's the word 'history' backwards." She seemed most engaged—and very quick on the draw—when she could find a clear, direct answer, just like I'd been before I got into more challenging classes. If something was too complicated, it was scary, because I'd never been shown that I could do it, and I didn't want to risk looking stupid stumbling or making a mistake, so I'd disengage and say the question was stupid—like Allie had when we debated the meaning of history.

"'History,' backwards?"

"Oh yeah, I see it!"

"You sly dog, Saaris," said D'Shaun.

"That's me," I said proudly. "And it's not just a cutesy thing I came up with. This is a really big deal. I think we'll need to go at history the opposite of what you've done so far. It sounds like you'all basically have been doing dittos and problems in the back of the book, just like I had for years."

"Yup. If we do anything."

"So, let's start with ideas!" I said, really geared up.

"Ideas? Like what?"

I hadn't quite gotten that far in my planning. I had the four new courses to prep every day. I was proud that I'd assessed this group, figured out what was needed and how to explain it to them. But I'd only figured this out late at night, when I still had another class left to plan for. I thought this idea would carry us through the period, and so I'd moved on to prepare my psychology lesson.

Now they wanted examples, and we had thirty-five minutes left on the clock. *Crap.*

They were all looking at me, challenging me to show them that history could be interesting.

I got one of those sudden sweats, when you realize how high the stakes are. I thought about one of the biggest things I'd learned in my advanced history class—how to examine evidence and understand that where it came from might affect what you could and couldn't learn from it. There was this whole framework we used to critically analyze sources. We could build to that, but for now we just needed a compelling question to provoke thinking about the idea behind it.

I remembered one of the essential questions Dolliver had suggested to me and Fry, and—nervous about how it might go over in this department, in this school—warily whispered, "What's's?"

"Huh?" said Jauhntavia loudly, leaning across her desk and cupping her ear exaggeratedly.

I decided to go for it. "What. Is. B.S.?" I enunciated.

Jauhntavia threw herself back on her chair in raucous laughter and kicked her feet around giddily.

"B.S.?" smiled Buddy and D'Shaun at each other, while Tony started parroting the word over and over loudly.

"Lord, this man sposta teach me some history," muttered Allie, then something about B.S. that I couldn't hear.

Margaret, Max, and José looked confused.

With a countenance both serious and mischievousness, Jim raised his hand. "Mr. Saaris, what does 'B.S.' stand for, again?"

Hearing the question opened my mouth into a smile and got me breathing again. I thought fast and said, "Bogus stuff."

"Ohhh," he said, "is *that* it?!"

We all laughed and laughed, then launched into a conversation about the nature of truth, and how they as historians might be able to sort through conflicting accounts in order to make sense of what's really happening. The students talked about the angle of the person who says or writes something, and how that will influence what they say, how everything is seen and framed. What we as historians might interpret, based on where something came from. They knew source analysis better than my history professor in college had. I added some terms and formalized the approach we could use to link together a document's origin and purpose to think through its value and limitations, but their critical analytical skills carried the day.

———

Teaching—trying to take a leadership role in the complex human development of a lot of people—is really, really hard. For a little while at Harvard, I'd had some good support from a mentor who observed my classes, took detailed notes of everything that happened, and then asked thoughtful questions to help me reflect on what worked and what I wanted to try differently next time. It wasn't about him saying Good or Bad and making me defensive about my passionate work; it was about what had actually happened, and my intrinsic desire to improve it, to seek suggestions, to try new things, and to do better each day.

That first semester at Battery Creek, though, the janitor was the only other adult to enter my classroom. Rosa, my assigned mentor, was very helpful, but we had the same planning period, which meant she was always teaching her own classes when I was teaching mine. So she had only my interpretations to go on, and—wanting desperately to be successful—I told her about the things I thought were working, not really opening up about my fears or the possibility that I wasn't succeeding. To encourage me, she praised my ideas. And she didn't have any experience teaching social studies, so she wasn't able to help me with particular course content.

Fry was more self-aware and vulnerable than I was about his shortcomings as a teacher, which allowed him to learn more quickly and make further strides than I did. Exhausted after five incredibly intense hours, plus planning, grading, and coaching, I was not my best self, and I sought comfort in the unhelpful elitist patterns of thinking that I'd learned as a student. I was drawn back into mental ruts carved over many years, addicted to the stimulating and soothing idea that I was smart and my approach was the best. So, Fry's mistakes and reflections, which could have been a great source of learning for both of us, got twisted, in my mind, into *Oh, he's making mistakes, and he has doubts. I've got that stuff figured out already because I can see how he's messing it up, and don't have any mistakes like that to speak of.*

And I sometimes tried to further boost myself by villainizing teachers like Walter. Their put-downs of students were certainly awful, but focusing on that kept me from hearing and learning from one of their main messages to me: you don't know Creek kids yet or this context, so pay attention and try to learn.

Instead—like many of us when we're worried we might not be good at something—I paid attention to other things I thought I already knew and could do well. After our classroom conversations about how to understand the bias of different sources got derailed by kids making fun of one another and we were losing the positive, open dialogue, I sought out an old Harvard mentor and got a copy of a class contract he'd put together to help build positive culture in his classes.

I edited and developed the document, capturing all my ideas in writing, spelling out what was needed and how things would work in great detail, like a college paper. I remembered the famous advanced calculus teacher, Jaime Escalante, from *Stand and Deliver*, who said, "Students will rise to the level of expectations." The reason I wasn't yet seeing the progress I wanted to see with students in class wasn't because there was something wrong with or irredeemable about them. I figured I just needed to make my expectations clear. And, as Rosa advised, this meant not just big statements but step-by-step guidance about what it means to write a successful essay, and how to go about it. How exactly to pursue rigorous research. How to structure a compelling argument. To make those expectations visible and accessible to students so they could find their paths there.

Step by step, I created a detailed syllabus for regular and advanced history, for my economics course, for psychology. I even put together a written plan for cross-country, articulating the key techniques and milestones—as though reasoned argument were what it took to win a race.

———

In the morning before class, the copy machine jammed printing my contracts and syllabi. Secretary Edith Grunt scolded me for overusing the copier, and I said I was sorry but that I really needed to get these ready for class.

"This copy machine is for single copies. For class sets, you need to submit a request to the copy center."

"How long does that take?"

"You can ask at the copy center."

"Well, I need this for class today."

"That's not right."

After being told at the copy center that it'd be a two-day turnaround, I came back and used the copier next to Grunt, which she'd just unjammed. I left it going and ran to get to class before the bell.

"Mr. Jones," I asked, "could you go down and get the copies from the front office? They didn't finish before I had to come up here."

"Saaris, are you not coming to class prepared?" asked Allie.

"Tryin', Ms. Duncan, I'm tryin'." I slugged back about a quarter of my gallon jug of Walmart water.

Though I didn't yet have the document, I dove into concepts from the contract, telling them about how painfully shy my mom had been in school. I asked them what they thought she did when she got into a class where participation was expected, gathered all her courage to finally talk, and then heard someone snickering (even if that snickering had anything to do with her). Without knowing her, they knew that she'd clam up for the rest of the course.

We talked about how important everyone's thoughts were for building a meaningful and variegated understanding of history, and how we had to create space for everyone to join the conversation. We got goofy acting out respectful and disrespectful behavior, and I was getting off into something about how I expected folks to really show respect to one another, and anything short of that I'd take as seriously as someone disrespecting my mama, when, thankfully, Buddy showed up with copies of the class contract.

"Oh man, Saaris," he said. "Mrs. Grunt is very, lemme say, not happy with you."

"Thanks, Mr. Jones," I said, grabbing from his hand and dishing out the documents in a flurry, desk by desk.

"Look," I said. "There's a lot in here. I've been working on some of these ideas for a couple years with mentors, and they've been working on these ideas for decades, and I think you'll like it . . . eventually. I'm going to offer you some things today. And I'll expect some things in return. That's how a contract works, and this contract is going to guarantee that we respect one another. If you don't like the contract and you or your parent don't want to sign it—"

"Nuh-uh! Nuuuuh-uh! No way, Saaris. Ain't *no* way."

Tymeca looked over as Tatyana was saying her no ways. Tatyana had the contract open, her finger pointing to something. Tymeca pushed her finger aside and read what was beneath it, then said, "Oh, heck no. Man, you crazy. You cray-zee!"

"It's *very* important that you know you can choose 'yes' or 'no,' and it's up to you. If you don't like this contract and you're not willing to uphold your end, you just say it's not for you—"

"Not for me!" announced Tymeca.

I shook my head, worrying I'd lost them before I had a chance. "And I'll appreciate your knowing that. And I will help you find another US history class. But if you remain in this class, you will need to fulfill this contract. That's the deal."

"This thing's, like, eight pages long!" said Tony.

Some of the students who weren't speaking seemed to be nodding approvingly at the contract as they looked it over.

"It's the plan for the class, based on where you guys are in your history journey, and what you've shared that you want to learn about. Let's take things one at a time here. We just talked about the respect one. You respect everyone in this room, and everyone in this room—that includes me—respects you. Pretty simple, right?"

"Yep," said Max. Then he blushed a little bit because he was the only one who had said anything.

"*Right?*" I asked more loudly.

"Right," came from an unenthused smattering of voices.

We talked about how if someone did any of the disrespectful things, they'd be asked to leave the circle and sit by the window for a few minutes. Dolliver had taught that if you ran a great class that's interesting and engaging, kids would be on the edge of their seats to get *into* the discussion (instead of preferring to walk out or get kicked out).

"OK," I said, feeling in control, "we've talked about how we're going to learn from each other through conversations—what's called Socratic dialogue. Do you'all enjoy that, or do you prefer just doing the problems in the back of the book?"

I had set up the question sloppily, so I didn't get a clean response. Some mixture of the words "Socratices," "conversation," "dialogue," and "book" blended to mud.

Because I had heard someone say "book," I said, "Some of you may prefer a single textbook and think that you're not ready for this type of college discussion format. That's fine. We'll help you find another US history class. For those who stay—"

"When can we leave if we want to?" asked Tatyana.

"Don't interrupt," I said, frustrated that it looked as if I'd lose her, and maybe more. Then I added, "Please."

Keeping forward momentum and positive energy in a class full of kids can be really hard if someone keeps interrupting and saying "This sucks," bursting each bubble you blow before you can clear the wand.

Tatyana was sitting up straight, and her hair was in a tight ponytail. If she moved at all as we made our way through the rest of the contract, it was only a slight twitching of her dangling hair.

"To make Socratic dialogue work requires everyone doing their part. Because we are all counting on a good discussion for class, everyone needs to come prepared. Otherwise, we don't have all the pieces we need for the conversation. Does that make sense?"

"Yes," said a few kids.

"Let me give you an example. Say we're preparing for a conversation about student activism. And Margaret's supposed to look at teach-ins and Jauhntavia's supposed to look at what happened at Columbia University when the students took over the administration building, and Max is going to look at Barbara Johns. And I'm going to plan the lesson so that it all fits together so we can have a really good discussion about it. Then what happens if Margaret comes in without her research about teach-ins?"

"Then she's in trouble."

"Well, maybe. But what's the bigger problem?"

"We wanted to use it as part of the class, and it's missing, so it's a problem."

"Right-o! Think about when you do homework in some other classes. A teacher marks it off in the gradebook. And if you didn't do it, then you didn't learn what you were supposed to learn. And that mostly hurts . . . ?"

"The person who didn't do the work."

"Right. But if we're going to have a big discussion about student activism and it depends on everyone doing their part, and one part is missing, then who loses out?"

"Everyone?"

"Right. Exactly. So the agreement is this. We can learn in this active way, where everyone's a part of what's happening. Where the work we do matters to each other on the daily. And I'll plan it. But it will only work if you do your part—in this case your homework. Does that make sense?"

"Yes."

"Good. OK. And the last agreement is this," I said, ecstatic at how well this seemed to be going. "This is a college prep class, and so it's my job to teach you up to the college level. I'll put a lot of effort into that—into making assignments, planning our discussions, selecting readings, grading your essays—"

"Wait, hold up," said Tymeca. "Now can we ask our question?"

"Just let me finish a minute, then you can ask."

"But *essays*? Come on—you've gotta be jokin'."

"Why do you think essays are a joke?"

"I mean," said Tymeca, building momentum and indignation, which was becoming more and more visible in the hue of her cheeks and the angle of her head as she talked to the class without looking at me, "it says on here a *five-page* essay."

"What?" someone blurted.

"Oh, huh-uh."

"No, no, no, Teach," said Buddy. "See, I see your game now. You come in here talkin' all nice about how we gonna make 'greements and everyone gets to choose. I know I ain't boutsta choose no *five-page essay*. You crazy, mane."

"Hold on," I said, hoping to head off the possible mutiny I'd opened up by emphasizing their choice in this. "Raise your hand if you want to go to college."

Every hand in the room went up.

"I thought so," I said. "And what, pray tell, do you think they do in college?"

"Ain't no five-page essay," said D'Shaun.

"You better believe it is," I said, getting worked up.

"But that's college, yo! This is high school. You ain't no college professor!" exclaimed Allie.

"This is part of the deal," I said. "Cuz I'm not gonna teach a so-called college prep class and pretend you passed if you're not really gonna be ready for classes in college! You need to complete all the major assignments listed on page seven if you want to pass this class. And what I give you in exchange is—"

"Ohhhhhhhh, Saaris-man. You. Oh. Huh-uh."

"Crazy, mane."

They were all on page seven of the contract.

"Read a two-hundred-page book? Yeah, right, man!"

"Read and present on *twenty* different primary sources!"

"What's this notebook thing, Saaris?"

"We can get to it. Just let me finish explaining the bargain. If you agree to do the work that I lay out in the contract, I'll do everything I can to ensure you have one of the best learning experiences of your life. You'll think about things in ways you never thought about them, because we'll multiply our learning by everyone in this room. And I'll make sure you're actually ready for the kind of social science classes you'll be taking in college. And whatever it takes to do this work, I'll be there for you. We can figure it out together. Sound like a good bargain?"

Most of the folks in the room nodded, including Allie, after a few moments' consideration. Not her friends Tatyana or Tymeca, though.

"Right on!" I said, thrilled. "OK, so let's talk about these specifics here."

"All I want to know, Teach," said Buddy, leaping past the hands in the air around him, "is how you're gonna say we got to write five pages and read two hundred pages. That's just craaaaaazy."

"There's *four* of those five-page essays here!!"

"This is the kind of work you should be used to by now, right?" I asked.

"Nohow."

I pointed to Tony Massocks, whose hand had been up for a while.

"I ain't never gonna write five pages in my whole life," he said.

"How long of an essay have you written in your other classes?" I asked.

"One page."

"Not usually that much, though."

"One page typed?" I asked.

"Naw, double-spaced by hand."

"What?" I asked, shocked. "Is that true?" They were sixteen years old and no one had ever had them writing at even a middle school level?

"Most def, Saaris."

"What book are we supposed to read?" asked Max.

"That's up to you," I said. "I can help you choose, but it can be any book pertaining to US history. I have to look at it to make sure it fits that criteria, but you get to choose."

"OK, so I cuh choose, like, a comic book, then—that's fine," said Tony.

"Teach," said Buddy, "I ain't gonna lie, but I ain't read a book since elementary school, and back then books was small, yo."

"No joke," said D'Shaun.

"I can't believe that," I said. "You'all have English classes, right?"

"They don't make us read books."

"Nope."

"That's wrong." I meant the school system, not them, but I didn't specify. "And no, Mr. Massocks, a comic book doesn't count as an academic book."

"But you just said . . ." complained Tony.

"I said that I need to approve the book before you start with it," I said, noticing that Tony had his head back and was looking at the door upside down. He drew a finger across his throat, then cocked his hand into the shape of a gun and released the thumb-bolt with his top two fingers against his temple. He shook his head violently, then went limp.

"OK," said Tymeca. "How do we get out of the class?"

"Yeah," said Tatyana.

The bell rang, but I wasn't ready for it: "Stop!"

Everyone stopped.

"I need to tell you something. You'all said you wanna get ready for college. That's what you told me is *your* goal. I really believe you can do it and that together we can get there. That's what I'm committing to help you do. You need to read this contract at home tonight. That's your homework. Tomorrow everyone needs to have their contracts signed by you and your parent or guardian." I paused, looking at the kids, happy to have documented and laid out my plan. "Got it?"

They filed their papers and pencils in their bags and zipped them tight.

"Yep."

"Got it, Saaris."

"Sure."

"You got it, Mr. Peters?"

"Yeah."

"Mr. Matthews?"

"Yes, sir."

"Ms. Duncan?"

"Yep."

"Ms. Crum?"

"I'm probably going to leave the class, but yeah."

"That's up to you," I said, thinking, *Why you gotta mess up the momentum at the end of class?*

"Mr. Jones?"

"We'll see."

—— CHAPTER THIRTEEN ——

It hadn't been nearly enough. Only half a dozen kids got their contracts signed. Some were ready to take me up on my offer to change them out of the class. Others were more mixed, like, *Hey, I didn't get it signed yet, and I'm not so sure about things, so if you're gonna harsh on me for that, I guess I should just go to a different class.*

"Hey!" I interrupted the side conversations about getting out of class and what was happening that weekend. I must've been reddening, because everyone dropped into stone silence once they noticed me.

"I'm just getting to know you. But it seems like—I don't know how to put this—maybe some of you are really getting taken for a ride here."

I didn't see understanding, so I crunched up my forehead and wrung something else out.

"I'm saying," I said, my voice breaking a little bit with the strain of trying to get what was in my head out of my mouth and in through their ears, "you'all are so talented, so full of energy and passion and possibility. I truly and deeply believe in each one of you. But the A–number one skill I think I'm realizing is needed here is, you have to be able to sort out the wheat from the chaff."

"Whatcha talkin' 'bout, Saaris?"

I was getting mad at myself and the whole situation. "You have to know what's B.S.! Like we've been talking about. Every one of you raised your hands about wanting to graduate college. And yet you're getting told you're gonna achieve that without any academic work. You shouldn't be fooled by it."

Allie scrutinized me.

Tony pinky-fingered his earwax a little, then stopped to think.

Buddy gave me a casual bring-it-on flip of his hand to let me know I should keep going.

"Look, I'm gonna tell you what a lot of people say about schools where there's lots of poor kids or kids of color. It's, like, a whole thing for people who are getting trained as teachers. A *low-income school*. They talk as though the income level of the school determines how much kids are going to be able to learn and how much they'll succeed.

"They said the crap that happened to my sister before she was six was going to determine her life and what she could become," I said. I saw that even though they'd never heard of my sister before, they knew exactly what I was saying about her now.

I was scared I might fail these kids too, but I wasn't brave enough to tell them that. So I went off on others.

"Some of my professors told me teaching doesn't matter. That it's not life or death, that it doesn't make much difference. But you know what? This *is* your life. And what you get from your education will affect you forever—from your income to your health to the say that you have in this democracy. And you've gotta learn—no. Scratch that. It's my responsibility to teach you how to distinguish B.S. from the real meal deal." I let the cliches rip as I heated up.

"Like this textbook," I said, holding up the thing Walter had been incessantly pushing me to use as the centerpiece of the class. "I just found out the other day how they chose this thing. The companies who make these throw a party and give away boat cruises and fancy dinners and the folks who choose the textbook go have a blast of a vacation, and THEY DON'T EVEN READ IT. They just pick the salespeople they like and then they adopt the book for, like, every teenager in the state!

"You guys asked before if we should just listen to what the publisher says history should be? The folks who put this together are folks who are doing really well moneywise, and so they may write a history that talks about how everything's led to this time that they think is really great, and that everything's hunky-dory."

"Hunky-wha?"

"And that's an imporant perspective on history, but maybe you also want to learn about the history of injustice, and what works to change things and make things better. Every source has a purpose, and that should affect how we interpret what they say. These guys have a purpose to make money, and they throw big parties and kind of want things to stay as they are, because they feel like they're doing really well with things this way."

Buddy asked, "How do we get in on those parties?"

"Get in on them? They're B.S.!" I responded.

"No, no, I get it, Teach," he said. "I'm just joshin'."

"OK, good," I said, relieved. "Because how societies work, how money and power work, how our own minds work, how numbers work, how to read and share competing ideas with Frederick Douglass and Thomas Jefferson and Harriet Tubman and Mahatma Gandhi . . . this is the real stuff! To be able to develop your own ideas about these things and to build the life that you want and the society that you'all want as the upcoming generation . . ."

I didn't know where I was going, but I noticed Jauhntavia looked a bit betrayed.

And then I realized. "Look. The truth is, they try to call most of the classes 'college prep' around here—apparently even the ones where they don't teach reading or writing skills. And since you'all plan to go to college, and this syllabus I've put together is like a college-level class, you should be getting college-level credit for doing this work. I'm gonna see about switching this over to an Advanced Studies history class.

"And we're gonna figure out together what's behind this B.S. you've been getting fed," I said, holding up the big blue textbook, then setting it down on its face. "This Yrotsih! You can do *so* much more. And we're gonna figure out what's really been going on, and give you the keys to the future of your choosing."

"Wait, we gonna be in Advanced Studies?" asked D'Shaun, lips and eyes opened wide.

"I can't do no Advanced Studies after failing the lower one," said Jauhntavia.

"Says who?" I asked.

"I dunno," she said.

"Well I say y'all *can* do it," I said, blurring "you" and "all" all the way together for the first time. "We'll do it together."

"Eek!" "Yikes!" "Yowza!" said Callie, Jim, and José.

"Are we together on this?"

Excepting Tatyana and Tymeca, who did change classes, we were. At least for a bit.

———

After a busy morning teaching, I called Erin during lunch.

She said, "So, can you believe you're gonna be an uncle?"

"I . . . don't know what to say."

"Say congratulations, you doofus," she said.

Is this something we're celebrating? I thought to myself. She'd texted me a couple months ago to try to get some money to get off the street. *If you bring a kid into such instability, you might put them through some of the bad things you've had to go through . . .*

"Congratulations," I said. "How did this all happen?" I tried to end the question on a high tone.

"Hey, come on now, hey!" she laughed.

Why was she laughing?

"Cut that out!" she yelled. "You're going to lose another life!"

"Erin?"

"Come *on!* Ha-ha!"

"Erin?"

"Yeah—Janeeta and Smitty are playing Xbox. Have you ever played *Hell Cab? Death Taxi?* Whatever. *You know!*"

"Maybe—I'm not sure."

"It's friggin' crazy, you know, like—whoa!" Then there were some muffled sounds.

". . ."

". . ."

"Erin? I've been thinking about something I wanted to ask you."

"Yeah, and you wouldn't text it to me, even though I asked you, like, a hundred times last night."

"I know. I wanted us to talk on the phone. What would you think about moving to live with me for a while?"

"What do you mean? Like, *move?*"

"Yeah. I mean, you'll have to think about it, I'm sure, but I just wanted to bring up the idea. What do you think?"

"Holy shit! Whoa! Don't tickle! Can you hand me that Coke? Fine—I'll get it . . . umph. Thanks a lot, fart brain! Silly Smitty's throwin' Teddy Bear at me."

"What do you think of the idea?"

"Like, moving to North Carolina? Where is that, exactly? And wait—why?"

It's South Carolina, I thought. "Well, I was thinking it would be fun for me to be an uncle, and we could work together. And you sort of said that you're having trouble finding a place to live and that you're out on the street a lot, and this trailer's got two bedrooms, and maybe this could be a really cool solution to all that!"

"But where *is* North Carolina?"

"I'm living kinda near the Atlantic Ocean," I said. "It's really warm, and there are palm trees everywhere, and beautiful oaks. And we have a nice coffee shop," I said, running out of amenities I thought the town could offer her. "And we could sort of . . . work together, you know?"

"I don't know. I'd have to talk to Janeeta. What we could really use is, see, they make you have a car seat—ahhh! Ha-ha-ha, ohmygosh! Oh, ha. Ummm . . . you can't leave the hospital without a car seat for the baby, and so we're trying to get one of those, and a couple other things. Apparently, you need . . ."

"I don't think we'd have problems with any of that. I mean, like I said, we could work together and maybe figure all that out?"

"Yeah. I mean, I want to come to North Carolina, but you know I couldn't visit until after I give birth, right?"

"Why is that?"

"Can't fly when you're pregnant."

"Really? Well, I bet Mom and Dad would drive you, then."

"I don't know if they even want to talk to me now."

She had asked to use their credit card for a hotel room one night, but then a bunch of other charges started showing up, and they canceled the card, even reporting the number as stolen.

"Sure, they want to talk to you. Anyway, what do you say?"

"About what? The whole living thing?"

"Uh-huh."

"I mean, I don't know about Janeeta."

Who the hell is Janeeta?

"Well, obviously you don't want to decide right now. What do you think of the idea, though? I really think we could, you know, work together, raise this baby. I guess at least get started out well, you know?"

"Yeah—ha-ha, *good one*!! Ahh, umm. Sorry."

I couldn't tell if she was talking to me. "I've got to head back up to work now."

"Whoa! It's really good talking to you. I'm so glad to talk to you."

"Me too. Really. And congratulations again. I really want to be involved, if that's possible. If you have to talk to Janeeta first or whatever, just call me back about it."

Big promises of family had never gotten her much.

"Like I said, we need to get this car seat, and that's going to cost money. And I'm really trying to get together some other stuff, like baby blankets and, you know, a few things of clothes. So some money would be really helpful."

My mom had a story about Erin since she'd been sent away from our family. It went like this: Erin's not trustworthy. Erin makes bad choices. Erin doesn't take responsibility. Erin must be abusing drugs or something; her monthly checks from the state just seem to evaporate. We can't help Erin much, because Erin won't help herself.

At that point I believed that story without understanding its source and purpose. While it could make you feel bad for Erin, it didn't make you feel bad about yourself or push you to do better by her.

Erin didn't call me back about my idea to team up in South Carolina. And for a while I blamed Erin, like my mom would, thinking, *I figured out what needs to happen here. Erin just needs to listen and get with the program. I did my part, and beyond that I can't be responsible for what happens. Erin's her own woman; and if she doesn't take the opportunities I'm offering her, then that's on her.*

That's how I justified not sending any money or a car seat for my baby niece.

—— CHAPTER FOURTEEN ——

For better or for worse, I focused on the arena in which I felt I had more direct control. Students and parents signed the contracts, and we had agreed-upon rules in class now.

I kicked bunches of kids out of the circle for a few minutes at a time for showing disrespect to their classmates. I kicked kids out for not doing their part of the work. And then, if they disturbed things from the side when they were supposed to be doing their part of the preparation for class, or listening to their classmates' discussion, I kicked them out of the classroom for the rest of the period. They were so angry about it—especially the kids who weren't used to getting in trouble.

Dolliver had white hair and commanded a level of gravitas I didn't think I could. So I got some nonprescription glasses, and used the techniques from my mentor at Harvard: show students how serious you are about enforcing the things that matter. That if they want to be a part of it, they have to do their part.

Margaret and José and D'Shaun railed that it was unfair when I asked them to move their chairs five feet out of the circle, and how dare I? I told them our agreement was for them to move quietly and not add to the disturbance; when they kept trying to debate it, I asked all three of them to leave the class. We talked later that day. They were pissed, and worried.

I said, "Look, I'm literally doing exactly what I said I would do, what we agreed to after having that long conversation about the importance of respect and doing our parts and centering respectful dialogue. Every class period is like twenty-four hours' worth of time, when you multiply it across all of us. We can't waste this invaluable opportunity we have to learn from each other. And if someone's wasting it, there are consequences we've all agreed to."

Jamie had told me that the most important thing I could do as a teacher was to be consistent. "Mean what you say and do what you say. Then kids can start to count on your word know what's happening, to know what the consequences will be, and to make empowered choices. Without that, you rob them of agency, because there's no clarity about what the consequences of their choices might be."

Sometimes I overreacted—like one day when a lot of folks hadn't been paying attention for quite a while. I quietly went over to my computer and created, then printed, a new essay assignment due the next morning. I told them to think through the different perspectives that night at home, since we hadn't come together to work through those ideas in class that day. I didn't consider how a one-night essay assignment on no notice might run up against home responsibilities, computer access issues, or force them to undertake the work without the support I'd promised to make available to them.

But often, I kept us on a pretty even keel, using the syllabus and contract as our map.

After a couple weeks, no one was getting kicked out of anything. I think they started to see how each of their pieces and perspectives were important, how it wasn't paper-shuffling assignments, but rather contributions to discussions that mattered to them and their classmates. They'd each develop some expertise on a piece of the puzzle at home, and then we'd come into class and try to put it all together.

———

I taught the cross-country team the hard work of not stopping—never stopping—during a run. It's the hardest thing to shift in yourself when you get into distance running: knowing that its getting harder and hurting some doesn't mean you should stop. That's when you're getting stronger and most need to follow through on the idea you're after.

To help them with this, I took them out to a long loop run on an island that'd been marked "uninhabitable" on historic maps of the region. I told them about how horrid the mosquitoes were, and that if they stopped they'd be bitten like crazy. We were mostly through the six miles—including José, who kept calling himself fat and saying he could never do it—when a few of them got serious about stopping running. Transitioning to a walk, they said they'd just have to take the mosquito bites. I pointed out the massive banana spiders just off the trail, and the alligator ponds, and they decided to pick up the pace again.

As with all young runners, they needed to see that they could do it, and they also needed practical tactics to pull it off. So I told them that the shallow breathing they were doing when they got winded uses only half their lungs, and that they had to breathe out fully to empty the carbon dioxide at the bottom, doubling the amount of oxygen they'd be able to get in.

Some of them were leaning on the Corvair when I got back with the lingerers, who seemed to nearly limp the last few meters before falling to their hands and rolling onto their backs in the sand and gravel.

"You did it! Yes! Gotta keep on your feet, though," I said. "Walk it off. Help them up," I said to the car-leaners, who laced the most tired of the arms over the less tired shoulders.

On the way back to town, misted ocean rolled over the windshield of the convertible, then through us. We had music instead of mechanical bells, and sun, so much more powerful than fluorescent fixtures. Our walls were the horizons, which looked lazily, hazily over meandering marsh rivers, shrimp boats with masts full of nets, and Highway 21, which had taken us to the end of South Carolina to meet the ocean, and now bore us back.

Though we never won anything official, we did get a lot of dead bugs plastered to us trying, and we built up enough endurance for some really good ketchup fights after races. Then, on the bus rides home, windows all down, when I fell asleep, Max and Jim would squirt Taco Bell Fire Sauce into my mouth.

———

No matter how much academic preparation or support I provided, though, the five-page essay assignment for each unit always drew boos and hisses.

I wrote out detailed, step-by-step instructions. Reviewed drafts. We built essays together on the whiteboard so we could trace the seeds of ideas emerging from piles of evidence. So that they could turn our discussions into systematic and sophisticated documents.

When they asked to write shorter papers instead, I told them it wouldn't be fair to lower the bar and shine them on with an easier assignment, because they wanted to go to college, and this was the type of work that would really get them ready for that.

Individual kids would hit snags, and with about a hundred kids at a time to keep up with, I did my best to stay on top of it—which is to say, sometimes not very well.

When Buddy repeatedly missed the essay deadlines, I told him I could work with him one-on-one after school in between my time working with the runners. He said he had football practice. I said I thought his schoolwork was probably more important, and that I thought the football coach would agree with me.

The coach did not.

But thankfully the principal did.

Buddy was pissed, and the days of "I gotcha, Teach!" were over. Now I could hardly get a word out of the friendliest and most talkative student I knew.

As writing twenty lesson plans a week and grading all their essays dragged on me, I turned to performance enhancers.

Late one evening in the only coffee shop in town, I ordered the first cup of coffee I'd ever had. My green pen raced through the balance of the 250 pages, noting in each case the most interesting idea in the essay, the best evidence, and any concepts that were unclear or disconnected and in need of getting integrated into the big idea.

On the walk home, I heard dogs barking behind huge, swaying hedges and motionless wrought iron. I hallucinated the barkers hurtling out of the green-ery at me, and started running. Once in bed, I lay flat on my back and never descended into sleep the whole night through. But when my alarm went off at 6:30 a.m., I was still full of energy, and skipped out the door to school.

———

When I cleared my desk by handing out all the graded essays with loads of positive comments and guidance in the margins, and they submitted new and amazing drafts, I felt like they were becoming scholars and masters of history.

And other days it felt as if we were—and would always be—victims of its repetitive cycles.

Callie Rollins seemed my best chance to help someone like my sister.

She was flying on the essential question we'd taken up, called "What's for desert?"—all about what people deserve, and America's historical develop-ment of positive rights.

Callie and her team researched some of the high-water marks for positive rights—like the movement for common schools, "forty acres and a mule," the GI Bill, and modern pushes for greater government involvement in se-curing broader positive rights, like the New Deal and the Great Society.

Though she'd been the shiest at the beginning of the year, now she was passionately wielding primary sources, like an old FDR speech. She deftly argued with some of her classmates who'd taken up documents from historical proponents of freedom *from* government as the principle that they thought would better help people thrive.

Callie seemed to be thriving, taking it all in, starting to refresh—until she said she had to leave.

She came by after school to casually let me know, and said goodbye. As she made for the door, I became desperate. I asked her to walk me through things, which she patiently did, telling me about how her foster mom was taking Callie's checks and spending them on her birth son. How Callie decided she wasn't going to sign the checks over to her foster mom if she kept buying him more expensive basketball shoes while her one pair of regular shoes fell apart.

"And she kicked me out," Callie told me.

I leaned forward, my forearms to my thighs. "That's not right."

"It is what it is," she replied. "So I found a place to live, but it's too far from Creek, so gotta change schools."

"In the middle of the year? When we're just getting going? That can't be right. What if I find you a ride or something?"

She seemed to recognize an inevitably I wouldn't, but humored me, letting me walk her down to the counselor, and watching me plead with him. Couldn't *he* do something? Wasn't he the professional who could fix this? He listened compassionately, then helped her fill out the transfer paperwork because she'd decided to go.

What is the point of all this paperwork if it can't solve something like this wretched foster cycle?

What the hell kind of good is it for me to peddle books and essays to Callie and her classmates, based on some things I'd researched in college about education being the most impactful thing? What good is anything in the face of forces that seem to roll stubbornly over generations, regardless of our insights and efforts to change things?

———

And, Sandee asked me a week later during lunch, "what's the point of any of this classwork if we all just die, anyways?"

I started saying something about how I knew she could do better on her essays if she could just . . . And then I realized from her expression that this wasn't that sort of conversation.

My uncle Curt had passed away earlier that quarter, and I'd dashed out of the school so fast, trying not to let anyone see my face looking like that.

Sandee let her sobs out, asking me again what the point of any of it was, given death's inevitability.

Shocked and sad but still not wanting to show it, I said calmly that I knew what she meant, that I'd started worrying about death when I was five and my grandma died.

Sandee said that was nice, but "it's not the same as having a bunch of young friends die in car accidents in the past year! One of them, Jeremiah, worked *so* damn hard, and got such good grades. But now he's just dead!"

I wanted to be there for her, to do something—anything—to help with the tragedy of it. I didn't know if I was supposed to hug her, if I was allowed to hug her. So I sat awkwardly by with a frown until she wiped her eyes clear and said, "Well, that was embarrassing."

And I said, uselessly, "No, no . . ."

––––––

At the time, my personal answer was that the point of it all was teaching: harnessing whatever ideas and skills I'd developed to try like hell to lead my classes to something amazing.

I'd dream about essential questions at night. Argue with the office manager during the day about using the copier yet again to compile speeches and declarations and newspaper articles and diaries. Push the department chair's objections to the side when he told me Allie's aunt had complained again about Allie not having a textbook to take home and study. I didn't want the kids depending predominantly on one version of things as we wrestled with tough historical questions. But Allie wanted something more to depend on than my piles of photocopies.

Rosa and Fry and I talked about how to build classroom rapport, shared understanding. How to scaffold to college essays, and how we would focus on teaching things important enough that students might remember them in fifty years. I was trying to create an almost-sacred space in our daily circle where students could grapple with the most important social studies issues and grow their own ideas about the world they wanted to create.

Dolliver told me about the complicated idea that this work should be "taken seriously and carried lightly," which I didn't understand. Another simpler notion he shared was easier for me to glom onto: "Teach me to live, that I may fear the grave as little as my bed. Teach me to die."

I continued to arrogantly hate on folks who I felt weren't taking teaching responsibilities seriously enough. But taking it too seriously was crushing me. It turns out a savior complex is not only annoying to others, it's corrosive to those infected with it, because such a self-aggrandizing lie inevitably leads to frustration and letdown. The higher I tried to put myself and my work on pedestals, the teeteringly further I was away from the human connection I craved—the relationships I'd need if I were to have any hope of succeeding as a teacher.

Back in my own high school days in a high-strung hammock, waiting and hoping Jamie would call, I'd told myself that the books and the ideas I had must be better than the relationships I didn't. At Harvard, I'd been flatteringly misled to believe that my ideas and I were "the best." And at Battery Creek, when things weren't going well, I too often sought dangerous refuge in the false notion that I could see everything clearly from the one room I occupied on one side of a long high school hallway.

─── CHAPTER FIFTEEN ───

W hen the conversations began to touch on the topic of race, students seemed surprised I allowed us to go there. The topic was not openly discussed in most classrooms at Battery Creek High School in the 2000s, and where it was, the gist seemed to be that race was no longer a factor in people's lives. Whether or not most people believed that, it's the idea that got the most formal airtime.

The books the students had been studying for ten years told a story of a few great folks unlocking freedom, eventually for everyone, with Lincoln freeing the slaves in the 1860s, schools desegregated in the 1950s by the Supreme Court, and voting opened up for everyone in the 1960s by Congress.

At first, I heard from both Black and white students that race wasn't a big factor anymore: old news, an excuse.

Some Black students ventured the idea that maybe inequality was still a part of the story. They were met with broad rebuttals that, *Yeah, there might be differences in who was sent to jail or who was richer, but you can't blame the government for that*. And people need to stop making excuses for their own bad choices.

Enough folks would nod along that some of those who were attempting to argue that discrimination or prejudice were still factors today stopped talking, quietly staring at the woven, blue-gray carpet.

At what point does a conversation about such things go too far? And when has it not gone far enough?

I had no clue. And I was worried that as a new teacher managing such a fraught topic, I could really bungle it and cause the students harm.

However, I thought there was likely much bigger harm in *not* having these conversations. In letting one idea—the idea that poverty and incarceration among Black residents was their own damn fault—dominate and end the dialogue. So I tried to move us into historical information we could analyze and assess together.

Everyone seemed to agree that bad things had happened with slavery and Jim Crow. The disagreements were about what followed emancipation, and what, almost a hundred years later, the school desegregation orders and civil rights acts did and didn't mean.

————

Jauhntavia whispered, "One, two, three," and then said, simultaneously with Allie, "Our topic for today is the Penn Center."

"Is that that place out towards Lands End?" I asked. "On St. Helena?"

"That's right, Mr. Saaris," said Jauhntavia. "Good job!"

I beamed.

"I'm gonna talk about how it got built up," said Allie, looking at her notecards while the class sat attentively listening.

"And I'm gon' talk 'bout how they tried to keep us down and shut it down," added Jauhntavia.

"Great!" I said. This was starting to seem like a day when the contracts, and the kicking kids out of the circle, and the time we'd spent really getting to know one another, would really be worth it.

"It was the first school for freed slaves, started in the early 1860s, I think—"

"While the Civil War was on, then," Jim said from the audience.

"And a couple years before the Thirteenth Amendment."

"You'll get your turn, D'Shaun," said Allie.

"K, sorry."

"As I was sayin'," continued Allie, "we're talkin' the first schools here for folks who used to be enslaved. Right up the road. If y'all hasn't seen it, you should. Actually: Who's been? Who knows 'bout it?"

Several Black students put their hands up, but none of the other students did.

"So, the Penn Center was hummin' along, teachin' folks all sorts of good stuff. And this was a time—for those who ain't know—when lotsa good stuff was in the offin'. There was talk of forty acres and a mule for every Black family to try to repair things and give folks a fair start."

I shouldn't have cut in, but I couldn't help myself. "In an agricultural society, land was the ticket to building wealth and economic standing. Sorry:
just so excited to learn about all this with y'all . . ." I trailed off.

"And Black folk were becomin' the majority for votin'. And we won
state offices like"— she looked at her cards, shuffled a couple—"lieutenant
governor."

"Hot damn!" said Buddy. "That some real sh—stuff!"

"Yup. And majority in one of the South Carolina legislatures. And just
like any other school, Penn Center started gettin' dollars from taxes to pay
costs."

The brightness of the Carolina sun through the windows was nothing
compared with the bright smiles and electric energy among some of the students at this local story of progress.

Allie pointed at Jauhntavia.

"Now?" Jauhntavia whispered back.

Allie nodded.

"Then"—Jauhntavia did a drumroll on the desk in front of her—"with
the Penn Center cruisin' along for Black education, and Black folk writin'
laws in the legislature 'n' everything, turn out the Beaufort County School
Board done took away the money."

"How they gon' do that?" asked D'Shaun.

"Well, it turn out they wasn't *elected* by the people. They was appointed.
And they said no more money for the Black school. And so it had to shut
down. And they been puttin' schools where the white folks want 'em ever
since. And my uncle and my momma been walkin' in along the highways as
kids to get in here. Bottles thrown at em and everything. When we coulda
had our own schools workin' just fine."

I couldn't be sure, but it seemed as if Allie's perfect posture bent for a
moment, and her hands swept beneath her eyes.

Then she was back. "King and the SCLC did retreats at the Penn Center
and revived it as a center for Black excellence in the '60s. It still being there
and doing work today shows our commitment to endure and continue the
good fight for equality. To be in the club. And get the respect and resources
we deserve."

The poignancy struck me. Such a push for progress. Such gains. And
such throwbacks that—as Robert Caro described most of the century after
the Civil War—reversed progress. It was hard for me to imagine such sac-
rifices for gains that no one alive would get to see. And then for Allie and

Jauhntavia to take all this not as a reason to give up hope, but instead as a source of inspiration and strength to continue the good fight.

———

Buddy said he and his research partner had gotten stuck trying to figure out stuff that happened after the Thirteenth Amendment.

"So what *did* you find?" I asked.

"We did do it, though, Mr. S," said Buddy. "I don't wanna be outta this, you know."

"OK, so just tell me about what you did find. We'll all help put it together."

"So the amendment's all about freein' the slaves," he said, while Jauhntavia said, from the front, "Emancipation, whuuuuuut!"

"Yes," I said, "yes. Except for—"

"Well, it has this piece in the middle about . . . does it mean allowing slavery in jails?" asked Buddy.

"To this day," I said. "And then some have argued that other aspects of slavery continued under new names." I paused, waiting for the kids to remember. It was the best when we'd get a group conversation going like this. Nothing in the world like a room of people all focusing their mental energy on developing an idea together.

". . ."

". . ."

Margaret put her finger on something in her notebook, then closed it and raised her hand.

"Yes, please."

"Sharecropping."

"And you're saying this has some features of slavery because . . . ?"

"No ownership," she said.

"You still work for the man," said Buddy. "And that's connected to that other thing you had had us research—that forty acres."

"Uh-huh, and a mule!" I said.

"So the deal was they was gonna take lands 'round here that Confederates left, and give some pieces of it to former slaves. Actually, all the land we're on here now. All these sea islands, and thirty miles in. From here to Florida, it said. To own and to self-govern by Blacks only."

"And how'd that go?"

"Best I cuh tell, they shot Lincoln. And that next dude . . ."

"Johnson."

"Yup. That sumbitch."

I glared at him.

"I mean that rude . . . crude . . . dude. He, um, well, ended a lot of them programs."

"Great!" I said. "I mean, not great that it happened, but thank you for preparing and teaching us about it. So, technically, enslaved people are freed under the Emancipation Proclamation and the Thirteenth Amendment, but they're stuck deep in an agricultural society where land ownership is the strongest basis for accumulating wealth. And the government says they'll address it with 'forty acres and a mule,' but Johnson reversed it after Lincoln was shot, and by 1870, less than 1 percent of African Americans in the South owned land that they could build their futures on. Like in the twentieth century, one of the biggest ways to accumulate wealth became homeownership, but the federal mortgage programs given to white folks were regularly denied to Black families."

"Yeah, but," started Ronnie.

Everyone looked at him.

"Are you sayin' people should just get a handout of land or a mortgage or whatever? You gotta earn that."

"How you gon' say slaves didn't earn land? They done work they whole lives on it and weren't given nothin' for it!" said D'Shaun.

"I'm not sayin' that," he said. "I guess I mean with the mortgages. Don't you gotta earn that?"

Max, normally pretty shy, jumped in and loudly asked, "Are you saying Black folks didn't earn mortgages as much as white folks did?"

"I mean, they don't have as many mortgages is the problem, right? And so you have to assume that maybe they didn't qualify as much because they didn't do what they needed to be—"

Max cut Ronnie off. "Look, if I'm honest, before I got to this school, I thought some bad things about Black people. Now a lot of my friends are Black and the 'assume' stuff you're talking about is just so clearly wrong. Based on knowing actual people."

"But we need more evidence than knowing some people, right, Mr. S.?" asked Ronnie. "Like historical evidence."

"Both stories and broader data are important," I said. "With things like the federal mortgage programs—even with the Fourteenth Amendment saying people should get equal treatment under the law—a lot of benefits that built wealth for veterans after World War II didn't get distributed much to Black families who *had* earned them. And that's well documented in the historical evidence."

Ronnie wasn't so sure, and he ended up putting together a group to look into that more for class the next day. We discussed how some of the laws said things needed to be equal, and how the GI Bill didn't specifically exclude Black Americans. And we tried to understand how in many regions only about a tenth of 1 percent of the benefits ended up going to Black Americans. And when Margaret said, "Well, shouldn't they sue if it's not fair?" the students had a debate about that, and about how, if they'd never had any land to begin with, Black folks would get the money to sue, or the money for a mortgage or an education, which their military colleagues had been given for their service. And how Black folks at the time might not even know how unfair it was, because a lot of these processes happened behind the scenes.

They often pushed me to give my opinion, but I told them that wasn't as important as what they thought. My hope in these conversations wasn't to get all the students saying the same thing. It was to push us to hear one another's thoughts and ideas, and bring some rigorous historical information into the dialogue so that we could work to have a better understanding of things. Most of the information the kids brought in from their research, I honestly didn't even know myself. Because I was never drilled with a bunch of facts about history. I was taught—and tried to share with them—ideas of how to look at facts and information. How to understand and scrutinize and bring skepticism and curiosity to a wide variety of sources. How to build to insight.

But even though we were having decent, student-led conversations, and most folks were writing a decent essay at the end of each unit, what did it matter? Could these things take us anywhere worthwhile, given the really big issues in the school and in our lives?

My bias as a historian was to believe that the themes of the past were likely showing up in some new ways today, and that we should look for repeating patterns. But I failed to grasp the extent to which the hatred we read about in history was still with us in our school as we studied these things. Unfortunately, it would take me getting personally hurt about race to begin to move beyond abstract sympathy to genuine empathy.

———

It started when Pete from the trailer park—who'd rented me a room in a small house he bought on Lady's Island—told me on short notice that he was going to kick me out. He'd asked me if I'd be able to drive his friend home after they partied that afternoon, and I said I couldn't because I had too many essays to grade and was feeling a bug coming on. Pete, a nurse at the local hospital, prescribed me the treatment regime he followed when he felt like he was getting sick: a twelve-pack of Heineken and a full bottle of Nyquil.

When he checked on me that evening and saw the Nyquil and twelve-pack were still intact as I slogged through essays in bed, he told me I needed to drive Johnny home. When I refused, he said I needed to be out by the end of the week.

After he sobered up, he changed his mind and apologized. Shaken, I told him that kinda stuff wasn't cool, but that if he agreed not to lash out again while I was just trying to have a place to live, we could probably still make things work.

I'd gotten him to mostly stop using the N-word around me, and when he said hateful things, I responded with facts: that despite all the talk, I'd never actually seen any violence at Battery Creek High School. That my students were enthusiastic learners, and were starting to develop really interesting insights from firsthand sources. That Pete should trust me as a source, because I knew the students firsthand.

We rocked on the front porch and talked about psychology experiments where subjects were shown different-raced pictures before a phone conversation and ended up drawing out race-stereotypical behaviors from the other subject they were talking to. A self-fulfilling prophecy.

And what if we thought differently? Assumed the best of students at Battery Creek?

He sipped and nodded and rocked, and said that he got me.

One weekend, when I told him I was planning to have cross-country runners and families over for a Sunday spaghetti dinner at his house when he was out of town, he said no way, and I said fine. I rode to school to find everyone's phone numbers to call and change the venue, then to Walmart to buy the food, then to Max's house for the dinner. When I returned home that night, I found Pete in the dark on the couch. He'd ended his trip to New York early and drove his truck straight back to make sure none of *those kids* were in *his* house.

He was huge and seemed to have his non-Heineken hand on something in his sweatshirt pocket as he told me to get out by morning.

I showed up on Fry's steps deeply distressed, without a place to stay and sorely behind on what I'd promised to do for my students that week. Fry took me in and we talked half the night about our doubts and worries, insecurities and failures as teachers. How I wasn't sure I was doing anyone any good.

In moments of suffering, my elitist veneer would crack a bit, letting out some of my inner light. And then I could glimpse, through my cracks and the cracks in others, the power of shared illumination to cast away some of the shadows that obscure us from one another.

CHAPTER SIXTEEN

Then—because it's what I was habituated to doing: trying to prove I was worthy of all I'd been given—I hastily patched over the cracks and got back to pretending I knew what I was doing, that I wasn't scared of letting folks down.

It was on to the next unit, which would again culminate in a five-page essay. The students and I collaboratively wrote the essential question we'd explore. They wanted to talk about who gets included in American society and why, and how that's shifted over time. What folks have said about citizenship, rights, and inclusion, and what people have actually done. The students dubbed their essential question: Who's in the club?

We used some class time to debate the contours of the issue, then divvied up different parts of American history when the topic had come up. Folks researched their chosen thinkers and time periods at home, then we brought their sources together to understand the topic from a multiplicity of perspectives.

We all want to belong. And as we sought to understand declarations about "all men" and "equal treatment" alongside exclusion acts and forced migrations to and within the United States, I like to think we created a classroom space of belonging.

There's a lot of talk about regulating the content of learning materials and classroom conversations. Was the Declaration a high-minded aspirational document that opened up a path toward equality that the founders wisely knew would take time to achieve, or was it a hypocritical document because it was followed by a Constitution saying that Black men were three-fifths of a person?

The point was not to have a single answer to our big questions. The point was the multiplicity of answers, and a context in which we could discuss them with one another. Not to think one particular thing, but to engage robustly in advancing our thinking.

Fry and I debated a provocative idea that one of my mentors had shared with me in college.

The mentor had said that one of his proudest moments as a high school teacher was when a student stood up during a conversation about gender equality and said he wasn't so sure about it. That in his culture, men and women have different roles, and that he thought a woman's place was in the home.

The mentor said this was a moment of pride for him as an educator, because his student had felt comfortable speaking an opinion different than most of his peers; the peers had listened to him, and a discussion had ensued about the idea. Since the students had developed real relationships with one another, the unpopular comment was nonetheless respected as the honest opinion of a classmate, worthy of dialogue.

Only by creating a positive class culture, the mentor had said, could such opinions and ideas come out into the light and be examined critically. The student changed his opinion on the topic later, but that wasn't the point. The point is not whether someone has the "right" view so much as whether we can discuss our views with one another—essential practice for shared learning when students go on to join the "club" of adults participating in American democracy.

Fry said those types of comments about not including women could be hurtful to young women in the class and so we needed to be really careful with an idea like that. And I said that people also really do need an environment to more openly share their ideas—including some of their prejudices—so that those ideas get critically analyzed in a way that enables folks to more deeply consider and develop their beliefs.

"I mean, I really don't want to hurt anyone, but won't it hurt more if people's ideas and beliefs never get discussed in society with their peers?"

"But you gotta be careful," said Fry.

———

It turned out Black kids were getting called worthless — directly and indirectly. The state of the school conveyed a message that the students there weren't valued by their society. Amid so much talk of student criminality, I heard that the last principal had been hoarding child pornography on campus. Amid so much talk about student absences, the kids who came in often entered permanently substituted or even teacherless classes. Our portals to the "information age" would get so jammed up, I wondered if it was even worth going to the computer lab anymore.

I'd been taught by Dolliver that something was more important than any content you'd teach in your classes: the medium is the message. *How* teaching happens conveys even more than what you teach. And in our school, every day, the message that came across was that white folks were meant to lead, standing at the front of almost every classroom in our majority-Black school. And that the role of students was to sit and quietly listen to what white people had to say, to do what they said in order to have a decent chance of moving on.

Another common message was that our students weren't capable of much. Many looked at our school's test scores and drew that conclusion. Even if students didn't want to draw that conclusion, they might get pushed aggressively toward it anyway.

Like when Fry and I were trying to build some interest among the social studies teachers for updating a semester exam, and we went to see Walter Thompson. He said the exam was fine as it was, and instead of agreeing to any of our changes, he told us how he thought we should use the exam results.

"The Creek's been at the bottom for a long time, and it's just how deep we are that changes a little bit from year to year. But one year, all the numbers lined up."

He was in a pensive mood now that school was out for the week, talking slowly, savoring the words as he leaned back in his chair, as though his feet were up and he were puffing a cigar mid-sentence.

"There was a student . . . when I was teaching English . . . who just didn't do a damned thing. So, when he actually showed up . . . to my class one day, I walked him through it. I said to him, in front of everyone, 'Demetrius, do you know which state in this country . . . has the worst education of all?' When he shrugged, I told him . . . that it was South Carolina. And so I asked him if, of all the counties in this state of ours, he knew which county has," he paused to inhale, "the worst education?"

Walter's smile was growing as he watched me and Fry watch him.

"He didn't know, so I told him. 'It's Beaufort County—worst county in the state,' I said. Well, then I asked young Demetrius if he knew which . . . is the worst school in Beaufort County? 'Creek?' he guessed. Because of course . . . he didn't actually know. I told Demetrius he got that one right. And then

I asked him, of all the social studies classes in our school, did he know which was the lowest-level class? He didn't know . . . so I told him it was the tech prep social studies class—the class he was in . . . at that very moment. 'And you, Demetrius,' I told him, 'have the lowest grade in this class.'"

Mr. Walter Thompson opened up his arms slowly, like drapes on a stage, wider, and wider, and at his arms' curved pinnacle, from which his shirt-sleeves hung limply, he announced: "So, congratulations." He took his arms down to do a two-fingered drumroll on the edge of his desk. "You, Demetrius, are the dumbest student in America!'"

———

Following the worst day-to-day setbacks, any ill-conceived grand notion of coming in to save the day felt beyond ridiculous. How could I possibly do anything to meet the realities of folks leaving my class, folks leaving the school, folks hating and hurting other folks, generations living and dying while such awfulness continued on?

In hopes of catching our breaths, Fry and I set aside one day on the weekend when we said we wouldn't talk work. We lounged around on our little screened porch, and I listened to him play Schubert on an old piano that he brought from his local church, pondering the gators that might be lurking behind the grass where our road dead-ended and the marsh took over.

But we inevitably started talking about what was going on with the schoolkids. I wanted to blame Walter, Pete—anyone I could, really. *How could we ever have thought we could turn something around in a school whose foundation was backwards? But how could we not try? What could we try next?*

Other days, Rosa listened patiently when we met in her room, reminding me that there was a lot of care for kids in the building. Lots of educators working really hard. And that there were some things going on that educators' hard work might not be able to solve, but that the strength and possibilities within each of our students was immense. That despite the obstacles, they had beauty and brilliance and perseverance that could—and would—unlock unimaginable change and new possibilities.

In class, we talked about the way the history textbooks cast most people as bystanders. How the standard narrative emphasized towering figures like King instead of the millions of others who made the marches possible, declared that civil rights had been solved in the 1960s, and offered nothing about how people actually organized to get things done. Even a figure like Rosa Parks was billed in our US history book as someone who just happened to be tired in the right place at the right time. Nothing about how she tired herself out through all her intensive movement-building work. The focused, collaborative community effort it took to sustain 35,000 people traversing Montgomery in new ways for 381 days, to begin inverting some of the city's foundational principles.

———

I had about half a year left with those still in my class, and felt desperately now that we had to do something worthy of that time together. We needed to prove that the old primary sources we were looking at and the essays we were writing mattered beyond the walls of C-223—that we could make something more happen with all our hard work.

And maybe because I felt I couldn't bear the responsibility of their education alone, I passed a big part of it along to them.

I'd been putting smaller things on them for a while. When I was so exhausted that I had next to nothing to offer, I'd asked others to run the conversation, for students to teach the day's lessons. I'd tried to make it seem thought-out, like how Dolliver told me he knew that things were going well when he could leave in the middle of class to get a cup of coffee and the conversation and the learning went right along without him. But really, sometimes I was just too tired and my plans weren't working, and I had to give up on the notion of myself as a hero and fully count on them.

So I tried to put them in charge of making something bigger than essays happen next. "OK," I said first thing in the morning, "with all we've learned, now you're gonna be responsible for making something happen. The end-of-course assignment after our next couple essential questions will be to create a significant positive change."

They greeted this with guffaws. But I said I was serious, and we were going to do this, and did they have any questions?

They asked important ones, like "Can you really make us do this?" and "What if it doesn't work?" and "This is stupid and has nothing to do with history."

I hadn't thought it all out, but I desperately needed their help to try to get something real done. Instead of telling them about my fears of failure, the twisting agony I felt when I glimpsed the possibility that I would completely let them down, I told them I could assign whatever I wanted, and that they needed to make sure the projects succeeded. They were to use the lessons of history to figure out how to solve something they cared about.

I thought it was the very essence of having learned from history—being able to use it in the present, in Beaufort, South Carolina, to do something.

"Look," I said, after several more rounds of the same questions, "you're all in your late teens, and it's time you did something. There are times in life when people care about how much effort you put into something, but this isn't one of them. No, you won't get your grade on how hard you try. You'll get your grade on whether you create a significant positive change."

"You can't do that," said Allie.

"She's right," said Sandee. "This is illegal. You can't make students actually do something."

"Here we go again," said Tony. "Any chance I can switch classes now, take you up on that offer?" He leaned across the span between our desks and gave me a light elbowing.

"But," Margaret continued to ask, "what if we design a really good project and we do it all right and then it doesn't happen because of something out of our control?"

"Then control it," I said. "This is life. You should be able to do what you want with it. And hopefully you have enough skills of historical investigation to figure out how to make it happen. It won't be due until the end of the school year, so you'll have lots of time to get it right."

"But—"

"Look: do you think the principal should forgive me if I told him that I tried really hard to teach you guys history and failed miserably?"

Could I ever forgive myself if I took those two bedrooms, those advanced classes with Dolliver, Harvard, and everything else and didn't do anything meaningful with it? My having all I'd been given—all I'd taken—could only make sense morally if I used it to turn around some of the injustices that had enabled me to get here. But I can't do it alone. I need us to figure this out together.

I said, "You have to accomplish something, not just try. And it's got to be significant. End of story."

—— CHAPTER SEVENTEEN ——

I'd had what I imagined to be a similar experience with the challenging Extended Essay assignment Dolliver gave us when I was in high school. It seemed simple: Because I'd been able to do such things with Dolliver's help, couldn't my amazing students, too, with mine?

They didn't see it the same way.

When I ended my spiel explaining how I'd taken on the Extended Essay with "and that's how it worked," Allie responded, "Oh, just like that, huh? Right."

The students insisted that they couldn't do it, that I couldn't make them. That even if they tried, they wouldn't succeed.

"People, people," I said. "Didn't anyone ever tell you you can do whatever you want?"

"Like smoke up in class?" asked Tony.

"Of course you can," I said.

He reached for his bag with a big grin.

"And you know the consequences. There are consequences to actions, and you can choose whatever course you want to steer. It's up to you."

After a while Jim said, "Hold up, Saaris. Hold up a minute." We all looked over to watch him think it through. "We've been learning about big problems with how people are treated in this country, even today. More people in prison than ever before, especially Black guys. We read all sorts of this stuff. But you wanna say we can do whatever we want? How we sposta do that if there's all these things that ain't fair to begin with?"

I had no answer. So I did as I usually did in these circumstances. I sat down with the kids and said, "That's a great question. What do y'all think?"

Outside the window, the palms and the oaks never lost their leaves, a perpetual faded green. Most always sunny—like today—unless it was randomly pouring. But the rain was never enough to bring the grass much past yellow. It felt unchanging, the single season of coastal South Carolina peering in on us.

I restated the question, to get my own focus. "So, we're thinking about whether and how it might be possible to have lots of obstacles and still be able to do whatever you set your mind to."

Jim said, "I think you can't do whatever you want if you're Black."

"It's a tough question," I said, worried. Studying history abstractly was one thing, but when it came to applying its lessons to my students, I wanted all of its possibilities and none of its limits. "I guess on one hand, you're right. We're looking at all these inequities between different groups of people in this country. And they haven't all gone away. Even in the most basic opportunity—your education—things are partly driven by the public school you happen to attend, and how that school creates or blocks opportunities to learn."

"We get a little blocked up here sometimes," said José.

"Maybe you do," said Tony. "I go regularly. One in the morning, one at night before bed."

"Please," said Allie. "That's disgusting."

"Oh yeah it is!"

"That's enough of that," I said. "What do other people think about Jim's idea?"

Allie raised her hand. She said, "I think if you don't have a fair start, den they shouldn't expect so much work from you. You should take it easier on us."

"That's an interesting idea," I said, squirming. "So, like, you want easier assignments in high school if you went to a bad middle school?"

"Yeah, like maybe we don't have to do this change project?"

"Nice try."

Max raised his hand. "Fact is, no one's gonna take it easier on you if you had a tougher time of things. You can learn about the things that happened to you through history, but you're not gonna get a pass from anyone, so you hafta just do all you can."

"That's right," said Ronnie.

"Like reparations," Max continued. "We talked about that. And it sounds like people have been talking about it for a long time. It'd be nice if we could make everything even now, but the government's probably not gonna do that, and so you can recognize where you came from and just try to make things happen."

Jim waited for a chance, then cut in. "But how can you expect to get as far as everyone else if you're starting farther back?" he asked Max.

"Well, maybe you can't . . . but maybe you can. I don't know," said Max. "What I'm trying to say is you can't wait around for someone to fix things up, because that prob'ly won't happen."

"I agree with that part," said Jim.

"So you just gotta do it for yourself," said Tony.

"But can you just do it?" I asked. "If the deck's stacked against you?"

"Well, you were saying yes," said Max.

"I was," I said, "but you guys are getting me really thinking about it. That's something teachers like me just say. But Jim's saying, how do you reconcile that with the history we've been talking about all year—three-fifths of a person with no rights until 1865, then on to the Jim Crow century, when a lot of those systems were continued in new ways. And even when it finally seems like maybe it's startin' to get fair, the past's powerful pull comes back atcha! Like you guys were telling me about the Penn Center getting set up, then getting defunded, then getting a new life later. I don't know . . ."

"See, if you don't know, then we can't be expected—"

"No, no, that's not what I'm saying. I *know* how awesome and amazing you'all are. I have no doubt about that. What you've researched, what you've written, the ideas, the innovation . . . I believe in you."

"Yeah, we are pretty smokin'. But what about all the stuff standin' in our way?"

I didn't know, so I shrugged.

"Let's try to figure it out together," said Jim.

Hell yeah! I thought.

———

The next day, we got into specifics. They grabbed their assignment sheets, and we talked through how they needed to get approval from their classmates and me that their plan was significant and backed up with historical research. How they'd be evaluated on whether they accomplished the change, and on the ways in which their final paper described an approach to the problem that drew extensively on detailed historical insights.

After the kids learned that effecting the change would be a significant part of their grade, they proposed the smallest projects conceivable. That way they could be assured of succeeding with their intention. The same way many kids will take an easy class for a good grade so they can say that they're doing well in school.

"I'm going to collect ten cans of food," said Margaret.

"I'm going to plant a bush for Mr. Bush," said Tony.

"I'll recycle your ten cans!" said Jim.

I was not happy, and I tried to show my displeasure on my face, but they kept going.

"Those are the types of projects that could be successful in creating a change, but they probably wouldn't be approved as significant," I said, looking at the rubric. "So they would earn, at most ... Well, it would be tough to pass this if you completed a project that was not approved by your classmates and me as significant." I felt like, obstacles notwithstanding, we had to prove that the learning in our class wasn't just a fifty-minute blip in the day. It could change big things.

"I'm not even hopin' to pass this, ta be honest," said Jauhntavia.

"Your idealism was cute before. Now you gonna put our grades and shot at college at risk with this stuff?"

"Stuck with you when I coulda left, Saaris," said D'Shaun. "You was feeding us some bull. I hope you ain't gon' do me wrong with all this."

———

I agreed to their proposal to work in small groups instead of individually. And as the project proposal deadline neared, I managed to get them some time in the computer lab, a windowless beige box of a room with beige box monitors.

Max was in the back corner of the lab, seemingly sulking. I worked with other students awhile, making sure they had what they needed, and then finally got to Max.

I sighed down into one of those blue plastic chairs that has metal legs and a few slats in the back. "How's it goin' here in the corner?"

He held his lips tight.

"You good?" I asked.

"I'm frustrated with myself because I can't figure out these computers. Always had trouble with them. This's the third time this thing's crashed on me!"

"Class is, like, half over. You haven't gotten *anything* done yet?!"

"I can't! I'm trying!"

I pushed the start buttons on the computer nearest to me. "Why not try another one?"

"I've got three of 'em goin' here."

Yikes, I thought, getting up and walking toward the hubbub coming from Jim and D'Shaun's group.

D'Shaun was talking about a friend of his: "This dude don't gotta deal with none of this—oh, Mr. S.! How's it goin'?"

"What dude are you talkin' about, Mr. Peters?"

"My homeboy over Hilton Head ways."

I tried the classic teacher eyebrow arch.

"Seriously, Saaris," said Jim. "We were talkin' 'bout how unequal the education is between here and Hilton Head. Tryna figure out our project still."

"Yeah," said Traci. "You told us it has to be something specific, like that we can measure and see a change about. So we're talking about what specifically is different in the different schools."

"That sounds good," I said, then stopped talking so that they could keep learning.

They talked about the kids' cars here versus there. They talked about the teachers they had. They talked about the houses.

"Saaris?" Max tapped me on the shoulder. "I really can't do anything. I got, like, five computers trying to boot up, and I got nothing."

"We got the same problem here!" said Jim. "Come join us, man!"

"What kind of computers do they have at Hilton Head?" Traci asked D'Shaun.

"I dunno. I could ask my boy."

"If it's like the other stuff, prolly rocket-ship fast there," said Jim.

"Actually," said Max, "it's true. They do. I know because my aunt's a teacher and I heard her talking about their new science labs and tech stuff!"

I stood up and backed away. They seemed to be on to something.

"Mr. Saaris! Could we . . . ?"

"It's your project," I said, "but it sounds exciting."

———

By the next time we went to the lab, Jim, Traci, D'Shaun, and Max had decided they weren't waiting for the computers anymore. They said the computers had been waiting for their group—that they would get equal technology into their school.

That got some students excited, and they started coming up with ideas.

Other students said they shouldn't take on a project like that. There was no way. They'd never actually accomplish it. Sure, they could try, but they wouldn't get a good grade for that.

Everyone was up for helping them measure how big the problem was, though.

At the start of class one morning in the computer lab, D'Shaun directed: "Nobody turn on their computer yet! We want y'all to turn them on at the same time, and then yell out when you get to the internet. We're timing to see how long it takes. Y'all ready with that stopwatch?"

Jim held it up with a slightly embarrassed smile.

Traci was at the board with a marker.

Max was in the back corner again. "I'll get these six ones back here. Just tell me when."

"Go!" said D'Shaun loudly.

"Dang, yo!" said Buddy. "That's my ear!"

Then everyone was quiet.

The students cupped their hands over the mice, ready to call out when their computer returned its first search result for *Why are these computers so slow?*

It took a few minutes before the first student had the little swirly "e" come up that they could click on to open a browser.

"Whadda we do if it crashes?"

"Oh, uh, I'll make a note of it. And I guess just restart it and try again?"

We sat there for a long time, feeling the seconds tick by in a better and worse way than they had been ticking at the beginning of the year. It was better because the passing seconds showed how worthwhile fixing these computers could be. Jim nodded and smirked, waiting, counting.

Five minutes in, Max swallowed severely. Each additional second that ticked past without any computers getting online showed that what stood between us and what we wanted to accomplish was bigger—perhaps much bigger—than we might be able to handle.

———

The students were excited about the idea of getting new computers, until they found out that in school bureaucracies, forward progress that requires money does not come easily. Budgets were generally duplicated year to year because changes caused controversy. So the things that didn't work well usually continued to not work well, and those who got more than their fair share usually kept it.

"They can't get computers for more than a year—if at all. And I'll probably be graduated and gone by then," said Max.

"Yeah," said Jim. "We done everything we could think of, Saaris, and nothing works. We talked to Principal Johnston, and he sent us to Ms. Kraut— Krauss? The tech lady. And then *she* sent us to the tech person at the district, and everyone's brushin' us off with the same thing."

"What's that?" I wondered.

"They say they agree with us, but there's nothing they can do about it, that they ain't responsible!"

"There's nothing they can do about what?" I asked.

"The computers!" several folks said at once.

"Yeah, I know, but how are you talking about the problem, is what I'm asking. Because clearly this needs to change, and they *are* responsible for it, right? So how are you getting that across? Like, holding them responsible?"

Traci had been looking for an opening, and spoke up. "So, I took the meeting with Ms. Krauss. And I told her a third of the computers crashed."

"And what'd she say?"

"She said, 'I know.' And that she doesn't have the budget to fix them or get new ones or whatever needs to happen. Seemed like she maybe thought I was being ungrateful or something?" Traci shrugged.

"Johnston say he don't have the money, and if we want, we can take it up with the district," said D'Shaun.

"And the district guy say *he* don't have the money. Seemed like he didn't want to talk about it or somethin'."

"Let's go back to how we're defining the problem here," I tried.

"We got junk computers, Saaris!"

"Yeah, but the data you collected at the computer lab—"

"Oh yeah," said Max. "The average was it took, like, fifteen minutes to get to the internet?"

"That's just horrible," I said. Clearly this was wrong and someone needed to fix it. "And we talked about adding that up for all the waiting we did as a class, right?"

"Yeah, oh yeah!" said Jim. "A full schoolday's time we wasted just sitting there!"

"And the other school?" I asked.

"Not even a minute," he said, as if this were the simple, immutable fact of how fast an apple fell to the earth at a school with mostly white kids.

"And this is in the same school district. Where you guys and they share a budget."

"And they white and we're Black. Well, mosta us."

"Uh-huh."

"But we've been telling all of them, and they don't *do* anything," Max said, bags under his eyes. "They tell us it's up to someone else, and then we go meet with them, and they tell us it's up to someone else. And now the year's almost over, and you're grading us on whether we actually get something *done*."

"Look," I said to everyone, "I know this is hard. I had the Extended Essay project when I was in high school. And at first no one wanted to listen about it. But we got all our information together, and it became enough that the story eventually made the news—NBC, I got on NPR for a minute—and the governor put together a task force to try to clean up the meatpacking plants."

"Just like that, huh?" asked Sandee, crossing her arms.

Missing her point, I said, "No, it was a lot of hard work to figure out what the problem is and get to who's responsible for it, but you guys have already come a long way by documenting how bad this is and talking to folks in power about it."

"Don't nobody wanna listen 'bout Creek's computer lab. This ain't news, Saaris. Just how it is."

"Yeah, what else can we actually do?" pleaded Jim.

"Anyone?" I asked.

"We tol' y'all, ain't no way to get no new computers up in here. Shoulda chose somethin' easier," said Jauhntavia.

"Come on, now," I said. "What do y'all think they should do?"

After a long quiet, Allie whispered something that sounded like "usury."

"Huh?" I responded.

She cleared her throat. "You was askin' what we sposta do for this assignment." Looking at Jim, she said, "Use history."

"Yes. Great. That's the point of this whole project," I said, reminded. "Let's all take three minutes and write out some historical events that you think have bearing here."

"Huh?" several students asked.

"Saaris, why you comin' up with this stuff now?"

I'm not sure yet, I thought. *Gimme a minute.*

Then I asked, "How many of you are having trouble getting your projects done?" Seeing lots of hands, I said, "OK, so most of us. We're on the question of 'What's for dessert?' right now, so maybe getting back into that will help us. Let's look at some of the historical instances when people felt they deserved something but didn't get it. What happened? What did they do? Pick some historical examples and write 'em up."

Oh, fine, whatever, said their eyes as their hands started writing.

I polished a corner of the board with an eraser for a minute before remembering it's a good idea for teachers to do the assignments they give their students, to show that what they're having the kids do is worthwhile.

During the last minute, I sat down and scribbled on the back of an attendance sheet, while Jauhntavia stretched four fingers and a thumb toward the corrugated cardboard ceiling tiles, chewing gum loudly.

"OK—Ms. Prince."

"Well, we know dat when Rosa Parks didn't get the seat she deserved, she took it!"

"Excellent example," I said. "Thank you."

She turned to Allie, with a side-to-side swagger, singing, "I so gooo-ood. I so gooo-ood."

"Now let's go around to the right," I said.

"What if she took mine?"

"Then you should think of another one. Everyone needs an original here."

"Mine was original until she took it."

"But it's not anymore."

"Aw. Come back to me?"

"Sure. Let's do Mr. Peters next."

"How 'bout slave rebellions?"

"How about them?"

"How you—oh, OK. Slaves started to fight when they didn't get their freedom they deserved, right?"

"Yep," I said, recalling D'Shaun's essay on a Nat Turner book he read—his first essay that had balanced conflicting ideas (the challenge of responding justly to unjust laws) instead of saying something was all good or all horrible.

He and Jauhntavia high-fived, then did a chest-pumping dance—the one where you push your fists out in a circle, fast then slow, like you're stirring a huge pot.

While we went around the group, I wrote their examples on the board. At the end, Max said, "But we can't do any of those things. We can't just take computers or fight people for them with guns, or any of that. I'm sorry, Mr. Saaris, but this history isn't helping. I just want to join Sandee's group and plant a tree or something."

"Whuut?" I asked. I was really excited about the computer project. "You guys have something big here. You should do it!"

I opened my arms, and Max slumped his head. Jim held his chin in his palms, looking out the window.

"What about *you* doin' it?" asked D'Shaun.

"Yeah, Saaris: ain't chu always doin' what we do in class?" asked Jauhntavia, arching up penciled eyebrows. "So, what's *your* project, then?"

"Well, I don't do everything," I said.

"How you mean you don't do everything?" asked Allie, building on Jauhntavia's momentum.

"You write with us when we write," said José.

"You have to do the project too!" insisted Allie.

"Hmmm," I said, pretending to think, but knowing I wasn't feeling taking on something else. Things were finally getting a little easier after settling in with Fry. He was helping me learn some relaxing piano.

"When we were writing up our ideas, you had one about, like, Advanced Studies, didn't you?"

"Huh?" I asked.

"Oh, das right," said Jauhntavia.

"You was writin' 'bout how we almost missed dis class opportunity, and a lot more kids maybe could do Advanced Studies at Creek, right?"

"I did," I said, "but let's get back to where you'all are, cuz my project idea isn't gonna help y'all."

"What, Saaris?!"

"I thought you understood our . . . *expectations* for you," they mocked.

I decided to play along. "Well, maybe I could do it. It'd be fine if I try but don't actually change anything, right? It's the effort that counts?"

"Oh no, Saaris. You gots tuh accomplish something!"

"Something significant!"

"I don't get credit for your projects since I'm teachin' all you smart alecks?"

Sandee said something that sounded like "You already racked up too much easy credits in your life."

"You gotta do your own."

"But actually accomplishing a change is too hard," I pouted.

"How he gonna say . . ." Buddy trailed off. He'd been in and out these past several weeks, and even when he was here, he didn't seem to be.

"But it is," I persisted. "It's really hard to actually do something."

"No shit," said D'Shaun.

"Well, then, maybe I need to pick something really easy, like maybe getting new spoons for the teachers lounge or something. It's hard drinking soup out of the can, you know! Buncha pieces get stuck in there."

"Spoons? This guy bringin' spoons?" D'Shaun chortled. Repeating to himself, "Spoons?" he laughed, his eyes wet with joy.

Allie said, "From whom much is given, much is required. Much more than spoons. Puh-lees."

"Ah-ah-ah!" said Jauhntavia, matching the words with a ticktocking index finger. "As you can see here, the significance of the project's change has to clear a student panel. And I don't think you got the votes." She looked around. "Y'all think teacher spoons is significant, or Saaris should actually find more kids for Advanced Studies?"

A little confused how to answer, the kids shook their heads, then nodded, then started shouting out.

"No spoons, Saaris!"

"Gotta find dem missing kids!"

"That's right," smiled Jauhntavia.

A chant got going—"No. Spoons. Saa-ris. No. Spoons. Saa-ris"—then the bell rang.

"OK, OK, it seems like the student panel has spoken," I said, worrying. "I'll try. And you'all gotta keep goin' on yours too!"

─── **CHAPTER EIGHTEEN** ───

I shook my hand to get the condensation off my Tupperware. I walked a few doors down from my classroom and peeked through the small pane of glass in the heavy door. There was the regional superintendent. The right room.

I opened the door quietly and walked by more than a dozen students to the back corner, where I sat low in a seat.

Superintendent Moses was animated and all smiles, but one of the officials next to her seemed to sharpen his frown for me.

A student near me said, "Saaris!" and I put my finger to my lips, then pointed to the superintendent, who was speaking to the group of kids.

I looked over at Max. He had a very adult look in his eyes. His gaze was on a gum stain on the carpet but seemed to be seeing more than that. Mildly scowling as he thought, his whole body seemed to inflate and deflate with each steady breath.

The superintendent was explaining that money was a limited resource in the district. She gave some examples of trade-offs that they were facing as they decided how to spend their allotment. "We're talking about the hiring of teachers and the payment of electricity, so that you have lights on in your classrooms."

"But you got computers for Hilton Head," said D'Shaun.

Everyone looked at him, surprised he'd interrupted the principal's boss.

Superintendent Moses ignored him. She laid out options the students could pursue to try to get new computers. She talked for half the lunch period, casually telling the students how the world works, and ending with, "Believe me, I want computers for Battery Creek as much as anyone. I really

do. A lot of you are my former students. I think what you're doing is so important. We can have you apply for some grants to try to get money for computers. There's a bit of a process to these things, but with your help, maybe . . ."

Max raised his hand.

"Yes, young man."

"We've already looked into that, and they all take a long time, so that's
just not good enough. With all due respect."

"Excuse me?" the superintendent said, her face twisting and tightening
in on itself.

Max took a breath and replied, "I'm going to be a senior next year, and
this is my education we're talking about—our education, I mean. I'm trying
to earn the Advanced Studies diploma. Not very many people in the world
get it. And to have a chance, I need a computer that works—not fifteen minutes to boot up and get to the internet. I need to be able to do online research, and I need to be able to type up my ideas. And some of us don't have
computers outside of school at all. I think everyone at Hilton Head probably has a computer at home, but we don't. We don't have time to wait for all
these processes. We've been meeting with people for what seems like ever.
We brought it to your attention, and we're asking you to figure it out. This
is our project for class, and we want it to get done. If you can't help us, then
we'll have no choice but to take matters into our own hands."

She looked confused and immediately responded, "And what exactly do
you mean by that, Max? We're trying to help put it in your hands, if you want
it, to work on grant proposals, or maybe talk to the school board about it—"

"We've studied the history of education injustice in the state, and also
sit-ins and teach-ins and stuff. And we made a decision and took a vote and
everything . . ." He swallowed and snuffed a big breath in through his nose.
"If equal technology is not available to us at Battery Creek at the beginning
of next year, then we'll go to Hilton Head High and ask to be shown to their
computer lab, where they have appropriate technology. And we'll invite the
news to come with us so they can help explain our concerns to everyone."

I watched this idea make its way across the faces of the officials in the
room. It felt like we were a room full of kids holding our breath to see what
the adults were going to do.

They unslackened their faces pretty quickly, and the superintendent said,
"I think that would be a very unfortunate decision, and let me tell you why.
We're all on the same team here—"

The bell rang, ending lunch, and Jim said, "We've got to go to class, but
thanks for your time, ma'am!"

———

Security was opening up, taking their posts inside Battery Creek High School's main entrance—a half-dozen full-time guards, a few steps above everything, sitting and watching all of us, issuing commands.

Johnston had told me to report to his office at seven that morning, forty minutes before the first bell.

As a student, going to the principal's office had meant trouble—an effort to get me into compliance, seated and silent. As a teacher, it meant much the same.

What was out of compliance this time?

The superintendent had seemed pretty sore after the run-in over the computers.

Walter was still bugging me about using the state-adopted textbooks, saying he'd "take things up the food chain."

When I challenged the whole school to a race for a hundred dollars to recruit for the cross-country team, I was reprimanded for not getting advance approval.

There was my attendance-taking—always accurate and in triplicate, but seldom on time. Some days, rushing, I'd even forgotten to mark myself "present" on the teacher sign-in sheet.

There was the principal warning me that teaching evolution was controversial, and my wise-ass answer that I wasn't aware of any scientific controversy about it.

And always, always, always the copy machine. The students' interests and emerging needs kept turning up new directions, so I'd hustle off and run copies for the next day, which didn't give the secretary the forty-eight hours she wanted. She'd even established a new system, which locked me out after fifty copies a month. So sometimes I'd have to use Rosa's or Fry's code, which made her mad.

I sat in the front office, waiting for "7:00" to appear in red digits above her head, watching the secretary and wondering how I could apologize, whether I could fix things.

Vice Principal Paula Barnes skated around the corner in a maroon pantsuit, and beckoned me to follow her quickly back. Inside Principal Johnston's office, there were more people crowded around the conference table than I'd expected. Walter wore a polo tucked into khakis. Rosa was there, inside a billowy pink-orange-and-red scarf. Johnston—at the head of his well-papered conference table—wore a navy suit.

"So, you went fishing this weekend, Paula?"

"Oh, it was wonderful, let me tell you . . ."

I talked to Rosa, told her it was good to see her, and then said, "I wonder what this is all about."

She cut in with, "*No te preocupes*. We'll take care of things."

Mr. Johnston asked Walter to speak first.

He had a folder open on the table in front of him, including my syllabus and exam, and what appeared to be some typed notes.

"Thank you, Mr. Johnston. I have serious concerns to share about Mr. Saaris. This began early in the year, when we had difficulties getting Mr. Saaris to use our textbook in his classes. Parents complained that their children didn't have the proper resources for the class and Mr. Saaris was refusing to provide them."

I tried to butt in, but Barnes said, "Shoosh," sharply, and Rosa lightly placed her hand on my forearm.

"Recently," said Walter, "I was contacted yet again by parents, this time expressing the concern that students were not prepared for the exam in Mr. Saaris's course, and that he was refusing to provide a study guide for it. I've found, on multiple occasions, that Mr. Saaris has been resistant to using the approved and required resources in his class. With the textbooks, he told us he gave them out to all of his students, and then—"

"I never said that—"

"—he kept them in his cabinet, with the excuse that the textbooks were damaging to the students! It's preposterous, but he uses it as justification to ignore the rules.

"Then, after this last parent contact, I decided it would be appropriate to visit Mr. Saaris's class. Now, normally I don't go into the classrooms of colleagues. I see it as an imposition, and an issue of professional respect to allow teachers to teach without interference. But given the rules violations and my accountabilities, I felt the need to go into his class and document the situation."

His visit was the only time another educator came to any of my classes all year.

"I found the class discussing an unauthorized and inflammatory topic that has nothing to do with the curriculum. The specific question was," he said, looking at his notes, "When is it OK to blow up the White House?"

There was a synchronous mild gasp.

"The students wanted to explore this question," I hastened. "They picked up on the ideas in the Declaration of Independence as to what makes a government legit."

Walter continued: "Mr. Saaris has not met his responsibility to monitor students in the hallway between periods. He has not met his responsibility to educate students according to South Carolina's standards, and I feel it is time for administrative disciplinary action. With this many parent inquiries, no one will be able to say we didn't know what was going on. Now I've done my part to inform you of the problem, and it's up to you what to do with it."

Barnes directed, "Let's take these concerns one at a time, Mr. Thompson. So, your first concern," she said, tipping her swirl of trim gray hair forward as she looked down at her notes, "is the textbook for the course. What do you have to say about the textbook, Mr. Saaris?"

"Well," I said, "I think it's a pretty bad one."

"The department-assigned textbook for the course?"

"That's right."

"Would you care to expand," she said, slipping easily into the role of judge to Walter's prosecution.

I told them the current textbook and teaching methods had managed to extinguish students' innate drive to learn and no one wanted to study history anymore after they'd been through a couple years of it at Battery Creek High School.

Walter dangled my syllabus between his thumb and forefinger, saying, "Your class has no content. You propose to teach a history with nothing in it?"

"That's ridiculous," said Rosa.

"But it's true!" said Walter, immersing himself in his notes. "Here it is! In the middle of the wall above the board, Mr. Saaris has a banner that says 'You need know nothing!'"

I turned to Walter. "It doesn't say 'You need know nothing.' It's 'You need know *no thing*.'"

We stared at each other.

Then I lost it. This test was the only thing Walter wanted to talk about-- the only thing that seemed to matter to him. "You're always on about the importance of the textbook and your multiple-choice test. You think it works better? I know how to settle this. Let's have your students and my students take the test you've devised for the end of the class—and let's have them take it at the beginning of the next school year, after they've had a summer away from us. Then we can compare results."

I'd been teaching the psychology students about how the brain sorts through information—throwing away almost all of the massive amount of data incoming through the five senses at any given moment, holding on only to things at the concept level that the brain identifies as outstandingly significant. And that significance is determined by social meaning, which comes from things like deep conversations.

"That won't be necessary," said Mr. Johnston, trying to block off the path that seemed to me the most logical way out of this mess.

Walter was quiet.

"It makes perfect sense to me," I said. "Are we trying to cram something into someone's head that'll last as long as a test does, or are we trying to create enduring learning?"

"How is the content of your course determined, Mr. Saaris?" asked Barnes.

"We, um, use the essential questions you have there in the syllabus," I said. "I developed them with my previous mentor teacher, with Michael Fry and Rosa's guidance, and with the students."

"But this does not ensure coverage of all the major events," said Barnes.

"Which events are major?" I asked, trying to open up an opportunity to learn together about teaching, while also wondering if maybe it'd be better to shut up.

Barnes had been a history teacher, so she picked up on my question. "There are, of course," said Barnes, "the early colonies, independence, westward expansion, the major wars, the Depression, civil rights, globalization, etc."

"Those have all come up," I said.

"How?" she asked.

I hoped I was finding the space between normal administrator conversation and terrible trouble, in which rare dialogue about teaching might become possible.

"Well, we use the essential questions. So, for example, take the question Walter mentioned," I said, having trouble repeating it, not wanting to trigger another round of gasps by three of my bosses. "The kids chose this question because they were very curious about the way the 2000 election was contested and how our current president got into office. And so we started talking about what makes a government legitimate, and how the US was started by people asking that question about King George. We read the Declaration and other primary documents from when folks were considering taking up arms against the ruling British government. And how the right to take up those arms is now enshrined in the Constitution's Second Amendment, which we read. How some states decided to take up arms against President Lincoln, and tried to get to him in the White House and ended up killing him in Ford's Theatre instead. The questions that folks debated in the civil rights movement about whether the government could be fixed, or needed to be abandoned with the Back-to-Africa movement, or fought against. The decisions made to attack the US Army—including my grandfather, who was stationed with my grandmother and mother—at Pearl Harbor. To attack the government in DC on 9/11—"

Barnes saw I was sufficiently traversing the events, and cut in: "So you focus on political theory?"

"Somewhat, yes," I said, smiling.

Walter Thompson sat rigidly upright, the top of his head sparkling through brown hair.

"That's a satisfactory approach," said Barnes. "*Assuming you cover all the bases.*"

"I suggest events that might be useful to the students, but they don't have to do any particular event. They've already had a *decade* in school of exploring and drilling these events in ways that completely turned them off of the subject of history."

"Mr. Saaris, you need to provide thorough coverage as accounted for in state standards and reflected in the state-approved textbook," said Barnes. Then she moved us on.

"Your second concern: the study guide. Mr. Saaris," she said, apparently not wanting to debate this subject, "it is good practice to provide a study guide before a major exam, so that students and parents have something to use to focus their studies. And your third concern, Mr. Thompson, was the exam itself, is that right?"

"If I might . . . ?" I interjected.

Barnes had helped me out a lot these first few quarters. Now she shook her head, probably thinking she couldn't save someone who didn't want to be saved.

But I did want to be saved. I'd had previous experience with these types of stakes and wanted desperately to figure out how to make things work—for me and my students. "I think the study guide is a good idea, and Walter, your comments about making sure that kids have something to study from prompted me to have each student keep a notebook, so that they can study and look back on all the conversations and key documents and things we've been working on during the year. So, thank you for helping me figure that out."

Seeming to find my comment outside the parameters he'd planned for the discussion, Walter went on, as if I hadn't said it. "That's right, Ms. Barnes. The exam is the third concern. We have the same problem there as we have in the course in general: no content." With his pointer finger, he slid my exam away from him to the middle of the table.

"Mr. Saaris"—Barnes looked at the single sheet, turning it over, clearly disappointed not to find more on the back—"how did you devise this exam?"

"Well," I said, "I took the advanced history tests given for college credit and pulled from those. And I'll grade them using the guidelines for grading those advanced tests."

"For the students not in the advanced class?" Walter said, looking as if he'd just pointed out a critical mistake in my scheme.

"You may recall," I said, "that when I found out all my students were wanting to go to college, I worked to convert all my classes to Advanced Studies."

"What about the difference in preparation, Mr. Saaris?" asked Principal Johnston.

"Well, actually," I said, "they're not getting different preparation. I think that all my students can perform at this level, and so I teach them all to that standard."

"In the basic-level courses?!" asked Walter. When I nodded, he screeched, "Even the basic students?"

"There's no such thing as a 'basic class.' Most of them are called 'college prep,' even though they don't usually seem to be preparing kids for college, with almost no reading or writing happening. And there's certainly no such thing as a 'basic student,'" I said.

Walter put his tongue in his cheek and widened his eyes at me.

Rosa said, "Reid's right. His students know that they are amazing. They don't question that, because he shows it with their assignments, with his approach to letting them share their ideas. We need to support this a little more than to criticize it in our school, and then you'll see the results for yourself."

It was starting to work in my class and Fry's, like I'd seen it working in hers. Some of our lessons were getting kids who skipped all their other classes to come into school, fully prepared, just to attend ours.

To develop our teaching, we read Postman and hooks and Kozol and King writing about equal education as a moral issue that required our taking moral stands. So Rosa and I pushed further. This was about pushing beyond the department as Walter ran it, beyond the boundaries he'd drawn for "basic" students. I didn't want to lose my job. And I didn't want to be a jerk to authorities like Walter, but I refused to be one to my students by letting a low estimation of them block their opportunities to learn.

When we were making these points, Walter raised his hands and said, "This is beyond me! I register my disapproval." He turned his head toward Barnes and Johnston. "If you allow this to continue, it's on you. I've done my job."

Barnes appeared more curious than upset. She asked about the Advanced Studies exam I'd said I was administering to my students. "Have you given this type of exam before, Mr. Saaris? Like, earlier in the year?"

"Yeah."

"How did it go?"

"Fine," I said. Some of the kids had been pretty far below where I wanted them. But we looked closely at where their ideas needed development and clearer evidence, how sentences and paragraphs and pages work together toward something worth discussing. I had them redo the early essays, further developing them until they got it.

"I'd like to see those results," said Barnes, making a note in her folio. "And you'll continue to support him, señora?"

"Absolutely."

"Thank you very much," said Johnston. "And then you'll follow up, Ms. Barnes."

Leaving any other action to come uncertain, the five-minute bell dismissed us out into the company of the students.

CHAPTER NINETEEN

As we came out of Johnston's office into the central foyer, our two campus police officers were conferring with the security guards. The female officer rested her hand casually on her holstered Glock. The male officer held the chain connecting the two cuffed wrists of a young Black man I didn't recognize.

Johnston moved quickly past me, through a river of a hundred students fresh-dressed and ready for the school day, put his hand on the officer's shoulder, and whispered in his ear. Then they shook hands.

If Johnston saw me as threatening, I imagine I'd also have been shown out by this point. I'd gotten away with so much here—and back when I was a kid too.

But how would my rebelliousness have been handled by the school system if I'd looked "basic" to them? What if I'd come up in a school like Battery Creek High, where the path from playing around to prison was precariously short: running through in-school suspension days spent in windowless, teacher-less trailers, and disparate and abundant out-of-school suspensions. Would I have been that kid in cuffs?

. . . If my mom hadn't been inside the system, working it on my behalf, pointing me to the good stuff?

In high school, when Jamie was off seeking chemical stimulation because school wasn't providing him the mental stimulation it should've, I was spending my days with my friend Kahn. We'd do the same things, but he seemed to get in way more trouble—he'd get kicked out of class, got us both kicked in the shins by a teacher—much more readily categorized by our white teaching force as a problem.

If I were him, I probably wouldn't have trusted the folks running our schools to make things right. So I wouldn't have given up the cowboy boots I'd used in elementary school to defend myself against bullying. I would've kept swinging the chain that we skaters strung between our wallets and our belts, the way Kahn swung his sometimes, figuring someone at least had to try to make things right.

I might not have viewed the police officer shoving me down the stairs at a protest as an aberration. And when he told me I'd better "watch out, because we're hurting people today," I might've stood up to him, indignant and feeling that the only someone to stop his hurting folks would have to be me.

Instead, I'd seen again and again that the system would take care of me. They'd let me off for streaking down to the beach at night with friends, for being caught in the park at night with my girlfriend, for shoplifting. One officer wanted to file a report and let me go, saying he just needed my eye color. But I refused to answer him or let him see my eyes, so he called my parents to ask if they wanted to come get me or if he should take me in. Frazzled by my misbehavior, my mom asked him to take me in and put me in a cell. My parents picked me up a couple hours later. The judge-type person assigned me to counseling.

Teenagers are designed to push against boundaries, expanding the horizons of possibility. Psychologist Alison Gopnik says they're the "creative department" of the human species, built to rebel against authority as they begin to push out on their own. I'd learned it was OK to push hard. Having never faced any severe repercussions, I was still pushing hard today, while others were being taken away.

Schools that use heavy walls of punishment to try to contain the expansive nature of children's minds are liable to explode. Not because the kids are inherently volatile, but because they're made for expansiveness. And so unfair containment creates more rebellion, revolutions even. Because being a young adult means beginning to have the chance—fighting, if necessary, for it—to build your own life and pen the next chapter of history with your generation.

I imagine that if I'd been subjected to the type of authority that tried to take away my pen and lock me in a cage in school, I would've unleashed the very nightmare those authorities were trying to prevent. If things tightened around me every time I pushed back, I might well have taken up the pen they were after, used it as a dagger, and been shot in return.

Eyeing Principal Johnston and the flank of security guards behind him, I hoped he understood what should be done, and how his authority gave him a unique opportunity to do it. Perhaps he'd whispered to the officer that he didn't want kids constrained by cuffs anymore. That they should be delivered with haste to classes that opened new horizons by challenging and growing their incredible intellect.

————

Then the students' op-ed came out in the *Beaufort Gazette*.

Battery Creek High also needs computers

I am a senior at Battery Creek High School, and a group of the students here have been unsatisfied with the technology at our school. We have met with school officials, and I believe that now is the time to tell the media.

It is insulting that students at other area public schools have superior technology to our school. We have been told that it is because they are newer schools, so they get the new stuff. So we are to believe that because of the school we attend, we are to get an inferior education? We need better technology now, and our school is suffering because of it. We are demanding equal technology to other high schools in our district.

The superintendent called Principal Johnston to ask what the hell was going on over there, and also: Would the student team like to help unpack and set up brand-new computers that were on their way to replace the old ones?

————

The day the boxes arrived, Jim, Traci, Max, and D'Shaun stopped by to see me.

Jim said, "Mr. Saaris?" and waited for me to look up from my papers before passing through the door frame.

"Yes, Mr. Matthews? Come right in. You get those new computers going?"

"Yes," he said. "Just finished." He looked very serious, and then confided, "We need to talk to you. You know we were having a really hard time with this project, right?"

"Yes, it seemed like that sometimes." I put the bottoms of my feet on the side of the desk and pushed back a little bit. My chair tipped more than expected. My eyes widened, and I opened my mouth to yell, but then the cabinets behind caught me. "Sorry. Yes. Yes, I remember."

"You OK?" they snickered, and Jim seemed happier for a moment.

I used to get in trouble a lot for leaning back in my chair in school. I hadn't realized it at the time, but school chairs were too small for me, so leaning back was the only way I could get enough room for my long legs. The teachers would tell me to knock it off, and I didn't know how to explain the need I had.

Leaning against the wall comfortably now, I asked, "You were saying, Mr. Matthews?"

"Well, I was struggling because I didn't think I could do it. And even when we got to talk to the superintendent, I saw the way she was looking at me. She'd been my principal in elementary school and told me I was special needs. And I just knew, when she was looking at us in that meeting, she was like, *Who the hell do you think you are, you little shit?*—or . . . sorry."

I nodded.

"And I actually ran into her in the hall after and overheard her talking with the other administrators, and they were laughing and saying we were asking way too much. And the thing is, I think I believed that. About everything. So I never really *done* nothin'."

"Whaddya mean?"

"I'm saying, like, in my life, I never done nothin' real. Like, I guess, I mean, we've all done stuff, like played video games or whatever, but I'd never done nothin' real in the world, like *for* the world. And I wasn't sure I ever would actually be able to do anything."

He was squinting and unsquinting to really focus in, trying to see if I could see.

"Do you get it?"

"I think so," I said, thinking.

"Good, cuz we want you to understand. Until you pushed us to take responsibility for making this change, I'd never done nothin'. And now we just unpacked brand-new computers for Battery Creek. And it's not just the computers that matter in what you got us to do. You got me to see that I can really actually do things in this—in my life."

I was tired from a big bike ride to work, feeling a bit hollowed out, worried about Allie Duncan's incomplete "significant positive change" project and how mad she and her aunt were about the grade. But what Jim was saying started opening up a deep energy in me.

"I want you to know that because of what you did for us—and what you're doing for a lot of other kids here—I know that I can actually do things in my life now. Do you get how big a deal that is?"

I swallowed hard, reached for my water bottle, exhaled to still myself. "Thank you, guys. I really appreciate your saying that."

"Well, we really want you to know we appreciate you," Traci said, as the others nodded heartily. Then they all headed out into the hallway and the hot day beyond.

I knew they wanted me to feel appreciated, and it seemed as if they'd prepared key points to make sure that got across. And I smiled, though I felt deeply unhappy.

The team's success had revealed the awful power of the lie that'd held sway until now, and still choked off possibilities in so many others. A lie that had worked for sixteen years: that they couldn't do anything significant. The lie that they couldn't read humanity's ideas in books, or write their own ideas about why the world was this way and what we could do about it.

The now-plain truth—that they could do amazing things that not even their teacher's boss's boss's boss's boss, a superintendent of schools, could stop—spoke not only to their incredible power but also simultaneously to a tragedy: that the forces arrayed against them had been strong enough to bind their power for sixteen years. Strong enough to bind lots of others who'd told me of similar feelings of impossibility and hopelessness.

The Scientist in the Crib lay open on my desk. Gopnik made it clear that we're all born incredibly capable, built for ideas and creativity. Babies can do statistics. So how is it that high schoolers so often come to believe they can't?

Because we're all wired to do great thinking, incredible forces are required to *stop* kids from this deep natural tendency to explore and do interesting, meaningful things. Forces like security guards telling you to quiet down, not deviate, never run. The force of a state-adopted textbook chosen based on which company gives the best junket, a textbook written to not get sideways of anyone in the Texas legislature, because that's the standard used to qualify for so many other markets. The mind-constraining force of terribly boring multiple-choice questions at the end of each chapter, instantly graded by a little machine in the teachers lounge. The status quo force of a system in which all the incentives for staff and administrators were to keep things chill: No bad newspaper stories. Check the boxes. CYA, as a lot of emails from my department chair said. The longer you could make it without anything out of the norm happening, the more money you got, and the more likely you could get promoted to an administrator's job. Do as you're told. Fill in the Scantron of your job with light pencil. Erase and change any answers that prove at all controversial.

By keeping on keeping on in this way, our school was consistently failing to provide great learning opportunities to many of our students, consistently dampening their innate love of learning and our shared drive for innovative doing.

It was great that Max and D'Shaun and Traci and Jim had had good experiences—that education had loosened some of the bindings that had held them back. But it was irredeemably bad that it'd taken sixteen years, and inexcusable that they were rare exceptions to the rules of our school, which still bound a thousand more kids daily.

———

I thought about all Jim had accomplished over the past year: the computers that the team said they never would've gotten without him, his personal sense of having really *done* something, and his now being on track to earn a full Advanced Studies diploma worth a year's college credit. He'd told me none of that would have happened if we hadn't run into each other that last day of the add-drop period. A moment's encounter, a handful of keystrokes, and suddenly a new and better direction. He said that not many people get the chance to move up and I'd given him the chance of a lifetime.

I know that he moved me and the others in our class up. I think we all get the idea that it could be good to try to help other people—for them. The part of the story that's often missed is what greater inclusion means for those who had the opportunities to begin with: I needed the relationship with Jim and the help he gave at least as much as the other way around.

There is so much loneliness and, often, an overwhelming sense of fragmentation and incompletion today. We are hungry for learning—yes, that's a part of it. The sustained work of thinking things through, knitting together different sources and ideas as we run down the most important questions. But for all those, myself included, who have had long stretches of a racially or economically segregated education, we are missing the most fundamental source of creativity, inspiration, and human possibility: those who, with their differences, can help us see and think and become different ourselves.

This is the very essence of learning: the incorporation of external differences into changes in our minds. Learning is fundamentally social—we care about things that those around us care about. And if those around us are quite similar to us, our learning will be severely stunted: there won't be enough difference to deeply learn and expand our thinking to broader horizons of human potential.

That first year, in my toughest moments as an educator—being kicked out of Pete's house; being hounded by Walter to the point where I was worried I'd lose my job; being tired out, out of copies, behind on grading essays; losing my uncle, my temper, my way—I had counted on my time with Jim after school to get me through. In the presence of his energy and insight and intelligence and kindness, that was where the heavy stakes of teaching, of trying to do amazing things as a bumbling novice, of arguments with the department chair, and all of my other troubles gave way to something higher: conversations about animal and human nature, our own dreams and the American dream, and our complex experiences of here and now—sometimes with a Fire Sauce fight to spice it all up.

CHAPTER TWENTY

When Johnston saw that my students had done OK on the Advanced Studies exams—and in spite of some of my failures to collaborate with a few of my colleagues—he seemed to feel we were on to something, and decided to promote me to assistant Advanced Studies coordinator, which he said could help me continue to expand the program.

I got to work with a coordinator named Margey, who was new to the area after an incredible career in Virginia boosting student access to advanced classes. I learned so much from her. When she saw that most of the seniors were enrolled in only half a day's worth of classes, she called every single one of the families, offering them additional classes, detailing the preparation their kids needed for college, and offering to help them get there.

I started to see how we might take things beyond bumping into Jim in the hall and asking the four students who showed up to advanced psychology to recruit their friends. We needed a system that worked to ensure that each student was matched with the opportunities they needed.

Margey ended every conversation with me and the other teachers on her team by asking, "Is there anything else I can do for you?" And she would work most all the things I asked for into being before I had time to even think about them again. She showed me how leaders can serve those they work for by consistently following through and resourcing and empowering their efforts toward progress.

Under her leadership, Advanced Studies started to grow. We had our first student in many years earn an Advanced Studies diploma, in addition to the regular high school diploma. Margey ensured that everyone was trained to teach their subject, that we all had the materials we needed, and that the school and district made additional investments in the work.

That second year, I coached cross-country running and soccer, taught new intro and advanced psychology and history classes, and got trained by Margey to run the Advanced Studies program. The day I got the news from her and Johnston that I'd be taking over her job at the start of my third year at the school, I stayed at work late, poring over the program data, trying to figure out just what I was about to be responsible for and how far we might be able to take things.

Past dinnertime, I scribbled percentages, numbers, slashes, and then started to droop. I thought I had all I needed on the legal pad to figure out the rest at home.

I drove by Taco Bell while the sun colored the sky. Orange reflections turned the opal-white paint on my hood purple as I eased off the clutch and rolled up to the drive-through.

Buddy stuck his head out of the window and said, "Yo, Saaris! What it is?" and handed me a plastic bag of burritos. Quietly, he leaned out the tiny window, his stomach holding him up on the exterior steel counter, the sunset's magentas shimmering in his eyes. "I snuck you some extras, yo," he said. "Shhhhh."

He winked, and I grabbed for his hand as he heaved himself back through the window. But he didn't see me, flipping a switch by his ear and saying, "Welcome to Taco Bell," as he closed the window. I slowly roared off.

I didn't want an extra Seven-Layer Burrito, Crunchwrap, and Caramel Apple Empanada so much as I wanted Buddy to recommit to finishing school. I couldn't bear to think that my pushing too hard might've driven him away before he got those last credits he needed from my class.

Back home, the sugar met the tingle in my head, and I fell asleep before it was dark.

———

At home in the morning, I picked up the pad of paper and found a bunch of messy numbers. I got out a calculator and a pencil and a fresh sheet of paper. I spread them neatly on my wobbly wooden desk, then watched two squirrels make rings around the base of the oak tree on the other side of the window. A beautiful swing, just a plank with two heavy ropes, swaying from a big bough, empty.

In college, I'd spent months looking over data tables and charts, percentages, algorithms, and computer code. What I came up with was usually more boring than I wanted it to be, and so my adviser gave me an idea. He told me there is no intimacy in numbers. He said that percentages are cold, and they never started a war.

"What are you trying to say with these numbers?" he'd ask. "What do they *actually* mean?"

I began to turn the mess of math about race and income and course enrollments into people. The empty swing outside the window became an empty chair in a classroom. Assuming that kids of all backgrounds are equally talented, gaps in participation rates actually mean this: *In advanced classes, we are missing lots of students of color. We are missing poor students. How many*, I wondered, *are we missing from each advanced class?*

The pencil's graphite made ripping sounds, though the paper held. At the bottom of the page, under heading B, for "Black," I pulled my pencil over and down, then crossed the seven in the middle for good measure, looked at it, underlined it. Seven more Black kids—like Jim, like his friend Bryan, who we'd walked away from last year—would be in each Advanced Studies class if Black kids were equally included. Under P, for "poor," I slashed and twisted out "1," and then "2." I underlined the twelve with a light mark and stopped, still. Twelve kids like Jamie missing from each advanced class at Battery Creek High School.

My tears came down onto the page. Sad and furious, I looked out the window at our unmoving old oak tree. I'd finally found the answer to the kids' question from a year before. *This is the significant change I need to make. I need to try to find the kids who belong in Advanced Studies but have been over-looked. To use my new position running the Advanced Studies program to try to get them the learning opportunities they need and deserve.*

———

I drafted a report on the data and the history, incorporated feedback from my students, and worked up possible plans for all the people who could find the missing students at Battery Creek—parents, teachers, counselors, other students, staff, and administrators.

Johnston said that if I thought more kids could do Advanced Studies, he was all for it. And given that Superintendent Moses was the one who ulti-mately made the computers happen, I thought it would be important to have her support too.

Included in my report was the latest psychological science, along with some of the history, during which researchers had rigged "measures" of in-telligence to get the racist results they wanted.

The notion that Black kids and poor kids were less capable of handling the work had been used to severely limit the opportunities they had to prove their capabilities. We should ensure that students of every background had an equal opportunity to succeed at the highest levels and let their brilliance shine. I wrote:

> With some million billion synaptic connections in every healthy human brain—that's 10,000 times the number of stars in the Milky Way—an individual's intellectual potential spans far beyond even the limits of the sky.

With printouts fresh from the copy machine with urgency, I got on my bike after school while kids revved out of the parking lot, testing their cylinders, sucking on sun and cigarettes.

I rode past estuaries and strip malls and the military base, across a bridge, feeling the sweep of the idea that we as educators were missing students who were more than ready to succeed. The power of the possibility that we would find them.

The superintendent was standing on a small porch behind the school district office building. My palm was sweaty despite my best wiping, but she didn't say anything about it as we shook hands. She snubbed out the butt of her cigarette, and we went inside.

She quickly confirmed with me that folks at Battery Creek had liked the computers she'd sent us, and said, "Today's really busy, but what can I do for you? Actually, I'm going to have to check something on the email here real quick before . . ." Her white hair billowed from the air conditioning vent overhead as she focused on her monitor.

I interlaced my fingers over the two copies of the report I had brought, then unfolded them, worrying that I might get the pages wet.

She hit some keys, pausing a couple times to say things like "It's this damn . . ." or "It doesn't make sense for . . ."

When she turned back to me, I handed her the document my mom had stayed up late the previous night to proofread. "I'd like to go through this with you for a few minutes and talk about what I've found, and then maybe we can talk about what we can do about it."

She thumbed through the report quickly, licking fingers and whipping pages nearly off the staple, as though the calming effect of her cigarette had already dissipated. She pulled her glasses down from her forehead and brought the graphs closer for scrutiny.

They showed that the lowest-level classes had the most Black students and the most poor students. And the highest-level ones had the fewest.

"OK," she said, "OK. This is an access paper."

I wasn't sure what that meant.

"And why're you bringing this up to me?"

"Well," I said, "Dr. Moses, I'd like us to solve the problem and find all the missing students. And I think we can do it this year. But I wanted to be sure of your support first."

It felt like the right thing to say. But I was probably more naive about the district leaders' fixing this problem than Jim's team had been about the computers.

"And what are your plans for this report?" asked Dr. Moses, looking at me from above her glasses.

"I've been thinking," I said, "that the best way to start may be to share a version of this report with students, and a different version with parents, and a different version with teachers, and one for the school board. Each version could suggest specific steps that that group of folks could be taking, and we could all come together . . ."

"I'll tell you what," she said, opening her file cabinet, the loud roll of the metal plucking me out of my thought. "You can share this report with whomever you'd like *if*, like you say, you can solve the problem. In the meantime, I'm going to take the report"—she took my copy from my hands and moved it to the filing drawer—"and put it here. And a year from now, if you've solved the problem, then we can pull it out and talk about it with the school board and whomever you want." She rolled the drawer closed.

"And in the meantime?"

"You can work on the problem."

"But how can we get these gaps closed if I can't talk about the problem or explain it to people?"

"Look," she said distractedly, reluctant to pull her eyes from the computer screen, where an electronic warble had brought a new email to her attention, "folks already know we have this problem, but . . . we can't talk about it."

If people know, then what's the problem talking about it?

"This type of report is not going to be good news for our advanced programs. As it is, the school board isn't sure whether to keep funding them. And if you come marching in telling people that those programs aren't serving Black kids, then—"

"Or poor kids," I said.

She frowned at being interrupted. "Then the board will have another excuse to shut down the program altogether."

"But—"

"Since the program's already in jeopardy, there's no benefit going to come from bringing this up." She lifted her wedding band with her right thumb and forefinger, then let it drop a few times onto a knuckle. "We need good news. This is bad news."

"But the good news is that we're going to fix it!"

"Then we'll talk about that. When you've done it—"

"To do that, I need to share the report!"

I got another frown. She inclined her forehead toward mine, looking straight into my eyes and said, "That can't happen."

Reluctantly letting go of the idea of sharing this information with the community so that we could build a plan together to find the missing students, I said, "Oh."

Dr. Moses leaned back and went on. "Until further notice, you may not give this data to anyone outside of the staff at your school unless you have explicit authorization from Mr. Johnston to do so."

I looked away.

"Is that understood."

"I don't see how I could—"

"You're responsible now."

I twitched.

"You wanted a chance to do something about this? Go do it. I have to get to this email. The budget's stalled, and what we're facing is loss of the money needed to make payroll if these damn bureaucrats don't get their heads out of their asses and allocate the funds—"

I stood up and left. Not recognizing that the feeling in my gut was a deep and disorienting fear at having sole responsibility assigned to me, I rushed to the restroom, completely forgetting to say goodbye.

————

Johnston said he supported the idea of closing the race and income access gaps to Advanced Studies classes but asked if we could call it something other than finding "missing students"—like maybe "reflecting the diversity of the school at the highest levels"—so that it wouldn't sound accusatory. Then he said maybe I should meet with the teachers, and "Good luck."

I sat on a stool in front of the dozen Advanced Studies teachers and told them about how much it'd meant to me to do the Extended Essay project. I told them about Jim, who'd come from tech-prep classes to advanced psychology and ended up settling a big debate over religion versus science by applying the "Coke can" idea that a circle and a rectangle can be one and the same—a bigger whole, seen from different perspectives.

Rosa and Fry and some of the other teachers were excited about the effort, but I couldn't stop looking at the newspapers that a couple teachers held up between me and their faces the whole meeting. I didn't understand at the time how many initiatives they'd seen come and go. How many people they'd had question their judgment. How tired they were from decades of taking attendance a hundred times a week.

So I fumed, imagining the worst: *What the hell is their problem? Do they not care about kids at all? Is there no way to meaningfully engage them? They won't even look up!*

Being pissed off raised my blood pressure, injecting energizing adrenaline into my tired body. I fed my internal furnace with the idea that *I* knew what was right.

Rosa suggested getting all the tenth grade teaching teams to go through rosters and nominate their students for Advanced Studies participation. I said I thought that was a fantastic idea, then glowered at the newspaper hiding Walter.

We put together lists of students who weren't signed up for advanced classes and asked the tenth grade teachers to put a check next to the name of each of their students they thought should be given the challenge of advanced coursework. "Where do you see hidden potential?" I wrote at the top of the instructions sheet I photocopied.

Ms. Beacon and Ms. Walters taught different subjects to the same kids. Ms. Beacon thought none of the students were ready for Advanced Studies, but Ms. Walters thought all of them were. Mr. Mast, Ms. Campbell, and Mr. Smalls didn't even look at their lists until I followed up four times, then finally had the principal tell them they needed to get it done. Arthur Duvall got marked "yes!" by Priscilla Jones and "never" by Ronald MacFarland.

With conflicting ideas coming in from teachers, I went to Paula Barnes for advice. "There's a good number of kids being recommended, but overall, teachers seem really unsure about which kids we should talk with. What do you think?"

"I suppose we could look at kids who have an A average, *maybe* a B-plus?" she offered.

"That sounds good," I said, adding, "And how could we find more kids like Jim too? He and my best friend growing up both had D averages."

This had been Barnes's career for decades. And here I was, just a couple years into the profession, arrogant enough to ask her to help me find kids who basically had the opposite record of what she'd just recommended. Her eyes widened, fluorescent-blue eye-shadow wings spreading.

Because she'd been involved in the Advanced Studies efforts since the beginning, I imagine she might've felt as if my approach accused her of missing students. Barnes could write Jim off as an anomaly. He'd passed a full load of Advanced Studies classes last year with a much higher GPA than he'd had previously. *Good for him,* she might've thought. *He's special, an exception to the rule.* But in order for the way she'd run her long career to make sense, the rule must stand.

When I asked her about bringing more kids with Bs, Cs, or Ds into the program, she told me it would be bad for the kids, that they would fail, drop out, drag everyone else down with them. Or was it that she couldn't bear to consider that such students could succeed because that would mean that she herself had failed, having already turned away thousands of sixteen-year-olds? Just as I wouldn't consider the possibility that I could've improved my approach and gotten Buddy through to graduation, because it was too much to bear.

She rendered her verdict: "If students like that have been recommended by *all* their tenth grade teachers, then you could invite them."

I had already explained to her that several teachers said they wouldn't recommend any of their students for Advanced Studies. So, under Barnes's proposal, any student who had a single one of those teachers would be disqualified from consideration. A ninth grade English teacher who taught half a dozen thirty-student sections had recommended none of his students, so all of those 180 kids would be out, except for the few who had As in every class. The handful of kids who were in A.S. when I got to Battery Creek were all identified as a good type of special by third grade, around the time Erin been wrongly told she was a bad kind.

Hoping this might get her to think differently, I told her about a *Time* Magazine article claiming that 20 percent of dropouts were academically gifted.

We argued for a while longer—like we were playing tug of war, with the middle of the rope knotted around a flagpole—then both went home.

—— CHAPTER TWENTY-ONE ——

The mantra of our Advanced Studies program was to help students understand that "others, with their differences, can also be right." I thought I knew how to teach that, but I didn't realize how far behind the curve I was in practicing it.

I assumed that Barnes's choices were segregating Battery Creek's classes, and that she must therefore be a racist. But I leaped for the power button to turn off the computer after an Implicit Association Test I took with my students revealed a preference for my own race.

I seethed at Callie's foster parents for what they'd done to her, and increasingly at my own parents for what they'd done to Erin. Then Erin texted, saying she had nowhere to sleep that night and asking for money for a motel room. It's easy to say from the outside what others should do—to label them, or their actions, as wrong. But when it comes to actually giving up your own resources to help others, it's easy to find a "good" reason to hold back.

According to my mom, Erin's child had just been taken away from her after they'd been found staying in a one-bedroom apartment with ten other people, cocaine in Erin's blood. Isn't it time she took responsibility for her own actions? Hey, I tried! I invited her to move out here and do it the right way. And now she wants a motel stay to get back on her feet?

Though I'd later learn I was horribly wrong, I thought I could find a better use for those $60. I texted back: "I don't think I can send money now. But I'd be happy to help you finish up high school, like you said you wanted to do." I tucked the phone away and smiled to myself.

While I was decrying the alienation of Black students in the school, I'd alienated Allie Duncan to the point where she said she'd never forgive me.

During the original change project, Allie had developed a plan to distribute leaflets about the negative impacts of abortion. I thought I'd been clear that raising awareness—on any topic—was not enough to count as a significant positive change, that the students needed to go beyond learning to other types of change that benefited people. But Allie said I was wrong and stuck with her initial plan.

When I told her that her evidence of impact—the leaflets she handed out—didn't show that anything had actually changed, she told me, "Fine, whatever. Just give me whatever grade you hafta. I'm sick of this sh . . ."

"I can't give you a grade for it," I'd said. "It's not complete."

I reminded her that the contract for the class required completing all major assignments, and that this one was not yet complete to the standard I'd laid out. "So, until you complete it, I'm going to have to give you an Incomplete grade for the course."

She was furious. She said I was putting her college plans at risk, her chance to go to school in New York and be with her mother. We had fraught meetings with Barnes, and then Johnston. I kept telling Allie I would change her grade—as soon as she completed the project.

Over the summer, she wrote an incredible paper about a new plan, focused on the history and power of student voice, and using student surveys to set specific priorities for the school to implement on a regular basis.

To get more students involved in advanced classes, I was trying to make sure I understood their current experiences and perceptions, and what mattered to them. I pulled out Allie's paper from my file cabinet drawer, and started rereading it. She cited student Kiri Davis's work replicating the doll studies. I watched the video she'd referenced in her paper: Davis's *A Girl Like Me*, in which she interviews young Black girls in Harlem.

Davis asks the five-year-olds, "Can you show me the doll that you like best, or that you'd like to play with? Can you show me the doll that is the nice doll? Why is that the nice doll?" and the kids say it's because "she's white." Then she asks, "Can you show me the doll that's bad? OK. Why does that look bad?" and the kids say, "Because it's Black."

A half century earlier, the original studies of the same sort had helped Linda Brown, Dorothy Davis, Barbara Johns, and a couple hundred other students win their combined case in the US Supreme Court against a bunch of boards of education (including a South Carolina school superintendent named Roderick Elliott, who had told Black families that the Black community didn't bring in enough tax money to warrant equal educational resources, like a bus to take them the sixteen-mile round trip some students walked to school).

The results of Davis's replication were the same as they'd been more than fifty years ago, and I started to cry. The feeling that the worst of our problems may inevitably become our children's too—because of our failure to solve them—devastated me more than anything. The point of our struggles, of the gifts and resources we're given—it had to be to make some movement, some progress. To get somewhere further on down the road. Not to come to nothing.

Allie's paper had compelled me to spend a lot more time developing the social psychology unit I'd planned on the topic of prejudice and discrimination. And she'd developed the student survey so that students' insights could better guide what happened in the school.

Though she'd used the survey idea to make real changes, and gotten the grade she wanted, she still said I'd put her bigger plans at risk. That I just didn't understand her, and that she wouldn't trust me again.

She let me share her paper with other students as an exemplar, though. She also signed up for more of my classes because I was the only advanced social studies teacher that year, and she needed more social studies to earn the advanced diploma. She said, "Don't mean I like you though, Saaris. Gotta just get through this."

Now I wanted to see if she'd let me include some questions about Advanced Studies, college plans, and the like in her next school-wide survey. I described the project to her, explained how Jim was helping, and asked if she could help with the survey, saying I thought she could make a big difference if she were willing to get involved. She shrugged lightly and said, "K, fine, whatev," and walked out.

I was ecstatic, thinking things would be better between Allie and me, and that we were going to find the other students who should be in A.S. too.

Though I wasn't right about the first part, not only did Allie get information from current students about their experiences, we also created an alumni survey collecting thoughts from some of the students Margey had previously recruited. We were able to share their experiences with students who were currently considering taking on the challenge:

My A.S. experience helped out tremendously when I got into college. I was much better prepared for the type of work my college courses set, I was better at allotting my time to make sure everything was done properly, especially when it came to research, instead of just trying to wing it through projects to get them completed by due dates or letting myself get too overwhelmed. Also, much of the material covered in my A.S. courses was the same as the material covered in my freshman year college courses, so I had a lot of information to look back on to help me out in those classes.

Considering my A.S. experience at Battery Creek, I feel as if signing up with the A.S. program was one of the best decisions I could have made, academically and personally. The coursework involved with the A.S. classes requires the best of your mental abilities, to comprehend the material, analyze it in-depth, and to be able to apply it to other things. I definitely grew as a person intellectually because I was driven to push my limits in order to be able to achieve the goals the coursework set for its students.

I have definitely grown as a person because of the things I learned and experienced, and my views were somewhat changed as well. Before I would have just skimmed the surface or taken the easy way out, but now I really enjoy and prefer getting in-depth, looking at the bigger picture from different angles. I continually push myself to be the best that I can be instead of just sitting back and letting good opportunities pass me by.

———

Later, there'd be lots of questions—and we'd do a ton of anecdotal and systematic research—about whether Advanced Studies programs should exist, which ones were best, whether they should be for a select few, many, or everyone, and which factors most predicted success in A.S. All I knew at that point was that Black kids and poor kids were not being enrolled in these classes as often as other kids. I had a hunch that many of them could be successful if given a chance, and I had a principal who thought it was worth trying. We had recommendations from tenth grade teachers, some of Allie's survey results, and some folks, like Rosa and Fry, who would join me in talking with non-A.S. students about what school was like for them, what their goals were, whether they wanted to try more-challenging classes.

———

"Mister, uh, Sore-iss?"

"Yes—come in. Tiffany, yeah?"

"Yeah, wus this 'bout?" She came in, but barely. Standing just inside the door, she held her hands behind her back.

"Well, I wanted to talk to you about your course requests for next year. Come on in!" I gestured big, with my whole arm.

She sighed in resignation, made her way to the chair in front of me, and sat down, crossing her arms over her chest. "What I do now?"

"I don't know," I said, curious. "What did you do?"

"I ain't tellin' you nothin' 'bout nothin' till you tell me what this's all about."

"How're your classes going?"

"Fiiiiine," she said, examining me, appearing to scroll through recent incidents in her mind's eye, filtering quickly through ones that had taken place in class.

"Like, are they tough, easy, boring, or what?"

"Boring as shi—I mean, boring as some *stuff*."

When schools bore kids with shitty classes, tangled vines of "incidents" can grow from the shit. If the day's academic schedule is guessing a couple hangman words and grabbing a couple words out of a book to fill in on a ditto, then kids will pursue things outside the ditto, beyond the rows their chairs are arranged in, inversions of the ten rules behind the teacher.

"I don't care what you may or may not have done before," I told Tiffany. "If you're bored in the classes you're taking now, let's get you into some interesting ones like Advanced Studies, where you can thrive. What's your favorite subject?"

"Hold up! A.S.? I mean, I jes tol' you school stuff is *boring*. How you gonna say I should do Advanced Studies? I hear it's a lot. And I don't like the little that I gots now."

I puzzled to myself for a moment.

"What did you like to play as a kid? Like, a thing you got really into?"

"Mmm . . . let's see. Legos, fo' sho'."

"OK, great. So there's different levels of Legos, right?"

"Uh-huh. So?"

"So, they have those really big ones for young kids, right?"
She nodded.

"And when you got older, you probably got some more complicated Legos, like with the smaller pieces, and maybe those instructions to build with?"

"Yuh, I got the set with the Flash."

"OK, so when you were building your Flash set, you probably would've been bored going back to those big Legos for young kids all day long, right?

I'm not saying"—I leaned toward her—"that you should build more of those big Legos, which are boring. I'm saying you need to get the next level of stuff, which is *actually* interesting. If school was better stuff, like with the next level of Legos, do you think you might be more engaged? Like, willing to put in more effort, and then maybe you'd have a better time with it?"

"I dunno . . . I mean, it sounds a'ight. You sayin' I need some better Legos or, like, better classes and then school would be more fun."

"How about we give it a try with your favorite subject? I didn't see you mark one on your survey," I said, looking back at my spreadsheet.

"Oh, well, yeah. I don't really have one cuz they's all boring."

"And for career interest, you put 'comic books.' Like, you want to make them?"

"Yeah. I mean, I'd like to."

"What do you like about them? The stories? Drawing?"

"I'm not so good with the drawing, but I would like to learn that. But definitely the stories, yeah."

"OK, so we do have a new visual arts advanced class. But it sounds to me like you might really enjoy the literature class too, where they spend a lot of time on stories from all around the world: Asia, Africa, Latin America, Europe."

"OK, yeah. I mean, I guess I could try it. But . . . um." And suddenly this was a very different Tiffany from the one Mr. MacFarland had warned me was a terrible troublemaker. She said quietly, "I'm not sure if I'd be good enough?"

"Of course you would be," I said, and she budded. "Your English teacher even told me so, made a recommendation."

She blossomed. Seen as a criminal in the making by one teacher, Tiffany left my office smiling about how she was going to read and write about international literature with another teacher, who saw great potential in her.

———

Jayleen and Samantha came into my office together. They looked enough alike that you could tell they were best friends and had been shaping each other's clothing choices, hairdos, makeup routines, language, facial expressions, and laughs for years.

They closed ranks against me about halfway through the conversation. They looked at each other when I first said the words "Advanced Studies," and shook their heads simultaneously.

"Look: here's some quotes from some of the folks who make the decisions on who to let into college, talking about how taking tough classes and challenging yourself is the most important thing."

"No, thank you."

Remembering the trial period we'd offered back when I used to sell subscriptions for the *Seattle Times*, I asked them what the harm was in trying it out.

Jayleen said, "This isn't the only way to be able to go to college or get a good job, you know." I said I knew, and she said they were going to do it their own way. They started to head out, and I tried to say something to bring them back, but they disappeared around the corner.

———

Fry and I talked late over Miller High Lifes, sitting in old, unvarnished rockers behind the screen that kept the no-see-ums out.

We were deep into the period of Friday night to Sunday morning, a time we'd do our best to avoid work-related topics in an attempt not to get totally taken over by teaching.

"I'm not sure we're doing the right thing here. What do you think?" I asked, not liking the way the uncertain words tasted, chasing them with High Life.

"No doubt. These are good. Banquet is good, the Silver Bullet too, but this was right for tonight."

"Yeah, well, naw . . . I mean with all these conversations we're having with students."

"Ah, I see how it is! Before, I tried talkin' about work and you said we should change the subject. Now you wanna come back to work!"

"You know . . ."

"I think you should be proud of what you're doing. That you're trying to close these gaps that've been around for a *long* time."

"Honestly man, I don't know WHAT the hell I'm doing. I talked to a girl today about Legos and signed her up for advanced literature? What the hell do I know?"

He puffed his cheeks. The bug symphony beyond swelled into the lull of the conversation.

"I had purple hair and was going to rock concerts in Seattle and found a couple teachers I really liked. And that's supposed to mean I know *anything* about a whole bunch of kids in South Carolina? Some days it feels like the perfect job, in the perfect place, with no friends—except you. I mean, you know folks here. You are clearly making a big difference with your kids."

"Me? I'm tryna. But it's hard, man," said Fry. "They're all so good. But there's so much swirlin' around 'em, in school and out. We're just tryna say they all deserve to be challenged at some level, to have the chance to think about stuff—like, for real."

"Yeah, man. Yeah!"

"And what I like about what we're doin' on this is it's not about blaming anyone or comin' in tryna be the hero or somethin'."

I swallowed.

"Teachers are teaching what they're asked to teach," said Fry. "And I think what we're sayin' is let's open up some more of the classes where the teachers have higher-level curriculum and training to teach that higher-level stuff. And then we're just askin' kids if they might be into that. Can't hurt, right?"

"I mean, Allie doesn't even look at me anymore because she thought I graded her too hard and put her college plans in jeopardy. So she thinks it can hurt." I looked down at Dolliver's old loose loafers on the cement slab.

Fry flipped his hand down over his wrist at me. "She'll get over that, man. You keep doin' what you're doin'. Just keep listenin' to them students and learnin' from them."

"What about these teachers I pissed off? Like Walter?"

"Remember that time we were at that birthday at Outback?"

"Sure."

"How you thought it was weird he wedged himself into that corner kind of off from other folks? He told me later he has to have a view of the door and assess the threats in the room, keep an eye on things. Know who he could take out, if need be. He might see the world a bit different than you. But he's on a mission and tryna keep things safe and orderly, in a sense. And you're tryna do something that maybe pushes that sense of safety a bit. They're both important. And a bit in conflict."

"And so just be OK with it?"

"I mean, it's like that Parker Palmer thing about teaching in general. You've gotta take it seriously; and you've got to carry it lightly. Seriously because it does really matter. And lightly because this is life and if you take it all too seriously and heavy, you're gonna get crushed. We'll figure it out."

"Ridiculous that I'm tryna figure anything out for anyone else. I don't know WHAT I'm doin'. I'm, like, twenty-three."

"Well, when you show up in that suit, it at least looks like you know what you're doin'!"

"At least I got someone fooled, then."

— CHAPTER TWENTY-TWO —

One student lurked outside my propped-open door, looking side to side, then behind him, before looking in again.

"Jonathan?"

"Umm . . . yes. That's me."

"Great. Thanks for coming." I smiled, and beckoned.

"I, uh, wasn't sure I was in the right place. I've never been . . ."

"You're in the right place. I asked a hall monitor to bring you a pass so we could talk."

"Why?"

Jonathan Albert lowered himself cautiously into the chair I pointed to, as though he weren't sure it was for him and worried it might not bear him.

He said, "Is everything OK?"

No, not yet, I thought.

"Jonathan," I said, looking at him, "how are your classes going?"

"Fine," his voice cracked. "I mean, I think?"

"Are they hard? Easy?" Lots of the kids were reluctant to criticize authority, so I had learned to work my way up to things.

"I guess pretty easy."

"Uh-huh," I noted, ticking a box on the spreadsheet I'd put together. "And your favorite subject is science?"

"Yeah. How'd you know?"

"From the survey we did. A student of mine, Allie Duncan, put it together."

"Oh yeah, I remember that." Jonathan, perched on the front of his blue-plastic chair, looked around.

"And you're still wanting to go to college, is that right?" I asked.

"Yeah, I'd like to, but I don't know if I can? Like, how it works, or whether they'd take me?"

"OK. Well, one of the most important things you can do to get ready for college is to take challenging classes, to start pushing towards the college level during the second half of high school. And a few of your teachers think you'd do really well and are recommending you for some advanced classes. We think you'd do great. How do you feel about it? Maybe the advanced course in biology, or chemistry, or . . . ?" Seeing his reaction, I stopped talking, then looked down to make sure I'd gotten his information right. Yep, on the survey he'd said he was interested in medicine, so biology should be a good match for him.

Jonathan had been swallowing repeatedly. His eyes rapidly moved back and forth, not focusing on anything, the way we do when we need to get some air flow to the front of our brain, to try to cool things down.

Then he looked up and a bit to his left, his pupils steady behind a coating of tears.

I started to sweat. "What's wrong, Jonathan?"

He stuck out his lower lip and used the arm of his sweatshirt to wipe both eyes, then the wet desk in front of him. He scooted gently back into the full cradle of the chair and said, "No one ever told me I could do anything like this before."

"Don't they tell kids these days that they can do anything?"

"I mean, sometimes they do, I guess. But we all know they don't mean it."

"How's that?"

He cleared his throat. "Like, maybe they tell every kid they can be an astronaut if they really want, but that's not true because maybe there's only going to be, like, five astronauts, you know? Not everyone can be one."

I realized he was right.

"OK, but we *can* open more advanced classes, and we can get you in with some great learning and opportunities—"

"You brought me down here to tell me that my teachers think I can do advanced bio and that'll actually help me get to college and maybe be a doctor?"

"Yes, sir," I said.

Seeing his expression, I was hooked, ready for more.

————

A handful of students didn't want to go to college at all, which was fine. Some planned to sign up for the Marines with Mr. Fitzgerald, who brought students down to the library on their eighteenth birthday to fill out the paperwork to formally enroll. Lots weren't really sure what was going to happen. And most seemed grateful to have been asked about their hopes, their plans—saying no one had ever talked to them about life after high school. I didn't know what each of these kids should do with their lives, but figured a class that asked them to think deeply about a topic could be useful, wherever that—and all the other things going on—might lead them.

———

"Hi. I'm Joaquin," said Joaquin Jimenez, who stood in front of my desk, his thumbs tucked under the straps of his black backpack. His hair was pulled back loosely into a short ponytail. Below patchy facial hair, he had a strand of black suede with a silver-and-turquoise emblem around his neck.

I hadn't noticed him come in. I'd been reading a draft syllabus for the Advanced Studies English course. It was light on writing requirements, and I was thinking about how social studies, English, and other departments might get together and develop some consistent approaches to writing. It was an important skill in most A.S. classes, and some of the kids needed better guidance. I had asked the English teacher to take the lead, but what she came up with still needed something. Maybe she'd support using the "essay guidelines" document I'd come up with for history class . . .

"Hi, Joaquin. I'm Reid Saaris."

"Nice to meet you."

I was torn about pushing my approach to writing with the head of the English department. But what she had here just didn't seem quite right yet . . .

Joaquin stuck his chin out expectantly.

"Hi. Sorry," I said. "I was just thinking about how we learn about writing."

"Interesting. What were you thinking?"

"Oh, I . . . thanks for asking. Like, writing takes a lot of practice, but some students haven't had much yet. So should we teach them more basic writing stuff, or should we ask them to do essays with interesting ideas, kind of like in college?"

"You mean basic stuff like punctuation and grammar?"

"Yeah, like, should we mostly teach that, or mostly teach about writing ideas, even if the punctuation and grammar isn't great yet?"

"Well, is the point to spell things right?"

"No. The point is to share ideas, for sure."

"Well, then, don't you have to do that?"

"Uh-huh. And we can still correct spelling and grammar and stuff and help people learn that along the way. But yeah, you're right. Thanks. The ideas just *have* to be at the heart of it. That's the whole point of writing. Ideas first, grammar and punctuation supporting." I clapped the done-and-done motion.

Joaquin smiled, not saying anything else.

"Anyways," I said. "Here you are, helping me, and I asked you here because I wanted to see if I could help *you* out. So why don't you take a seat?"

"Sure." He swung his backpack off his shoulder and nearly lay down in the chair in his torn black jeans. "So," he said, "my sources tell me you're talking to kids about taking advanced classes."

I nodded.

"I mean, I'm not, like, *super* into it, but if you think it's worth callin' me all the way down here to ask me to take it, then I prolly should give it a try."

"That sounds pretty good to me. But you do have a D average now."

"Yes. Yes, I do."

"I used to have Ds in middle school after I figured out the grades there didn't count for high school. And one of my awesome advanced students here had a D average before he joined the program."

"I see."

"So, what're your classes like now?"

With both hands, Joaquin pulled his hair back across his head, plucking off the rubber band at the back and then redoing it swiftly. "I think you know what these classes I'm in are like—otherwise you wouldn't be doing all this, right?"

I said, "So, maybe like I was, you're in there watching the clock? Maybe you have better things you wanna do, like reading, or . . ."

"Yep. And music too. I play bass."

"So how about we start off with at least advanced math, English, and music?"

He paused for a moment. "What took you so long to call me down here, anyways?"

I blushed. "I mean, I must be meeting with, like, twenty kids a day now, then I have the parent calls and letters, and on top of that, I'm teaching—"

"No, no, you're good. I mean, I'm in, like, tenth grade. With preschool and kindergarten, I've had, what, twelve years of school here? And you're just now calling me down about advanced classes."

"Yeah. I'm real sorry about that."

"Not your fault. Better late than never." He popped both arms through his backpack straps simultaneously as he headed out.

"Have a good one!" I said.

"You as well." He turned and gave me a little two-finger salute from his unruly brow.

I lifted up the spreadsheet to take a closer look.

In the "Joaquin Jimenez" row, I could see that all of his teachers had marked "yes" for the question "Would you recommend for Advanced Studies?" And that he had marked "no" for the question "Has anyone talked to you about taking Advanced Studies?"

His course request form for next year was at the top of the stack.

I crossed out the standard "English 11" and circled "Advanced English I."

I crossed out "Math Concepts" and circled "Advanced Math I."

We didn't yet have enough students to run the Advanced Music class, so I wrote the course onto the form, pulled out my legal pad and wrote the course name there too, with Joaquin at the top of the roster, next to "#1." I numbered the other lines through 25 and made a commitment to myself that I'd fill the class.

I wanted to be happy about the new opportunities I was helping put together for Joaquin. But I was pissed about the time he'd asked me about—the years he'd already lost. And I was scared. Any future lost time seemed like it was all on me now. I was probably taking it too seriously, like Fry had warned me against, but I couldn't help it.

I reorganized the three hundred papers I was working from, turning them, smoothing out dog-eared corners, finding them almost too heavy to lift off the desk.

———

In came Vice Principal Paula Barnes. On their way out, behind Barnes's back, Max and Jim made O-mouths at me. *Oh, you're in trouble again, Saaris!*

"How's it goin'?" I asked her.

"Another day, another dollar."

"Ha."

"The lead counselor and I have concerns about some of the students you're signing up for Advanced Studies for next year. Mind if I grab a seat?"

"Please."

"What exactly are the criteria you're using to make sure students are prepared for advanced coursework? That they won't fail? That this little experiment of yours won't be a disaster for all concerned?"

My breathing quickened. I'd easily had more than a half-dozen conversations with Walter, the lead guidance counselor, and Barnes about this in the past week alone—folks who never talked with me about their plans to change things, only attacked mine. Folks who didn't seem at all disturbed that we had less than half the Black students in Advanced Studies as should be there if we had equal participation. They didn't seem interested in my points about the science and nature of intelligence, and about academic capability being equal across groups. They also didn't seem interested in my argument that an equitable program would be better for all of us—that as the US became more inclusive, expanding freedom, voting rights, and education access, it became richer, stronger, and more creative, not the opposite.

Now the founder of the Advanced Studies program at Battery Creek High sat there, hands folded in her lap, examining me, attacking yet again the progress I was starting to think the kids couldn't wait any longer for.

"You want to know the criteria," I asked her, "that I'm using to allow kids into advanced courses?" I didn't know exactly. "Can we start with the criteria you all have been using to keep people *out* of Advanced Studies? What are those criteria?"

"Excuse me?" She tightened, and it looked as though her follicles were sucking each strand of hair deep into her scalp, her spine slowly torquing straight, the wrinkles on her lips disappearing.

I was a bit scared, but I kept going, desperate to get Joaquin's question off my shoulders. "Mr. Johnston says we can close the gap in A.S. enrollment, but a lot of the kids are confused about how things have been done here in the past and who's allowed in Advanced Studies. So I'm asking, what were the criteria you used that kept so many kids out?"

She blinked three, four, five times.

I was tired of the explanation that "systems" were responsible for what was happening. Talking about "all the things" that the kids had to deal with. Or my parents and the caseworkers talking about "all that Erin had been through." What about us here now? What about our responsibility?

I was also frightened of Barnes's question, defensive. I had no idea what the right criteria were, or whether Joaquin or anyone else would be successful following my recommendations. It was all speculation. But did she have anything better?

"You were the lead administrator over Advanced Studies since the start, right?" *An adult caring for a child means taking responsibility. Getting it done. For Erin. For Jamie. There* are *times in life when we each have the chance to be heroic and stand up for the right thing and make a real difference.*

"Let me tell you about Joaquin," I continued. "*Every* single one of his teachers recommends him for Advanced Studies, but no adult in this building has ever told *him* this, and so he's been bored out of his mind for *twelve years*. And he asks me what took so long to get him into better classes. So I'm asking you! This kid is clearly incredibly talented. And twelve years got wasted?"

Barnes unclasped her pale hands and they rushed upward, her wrists jumping out of her faux-gold-buttoned navy suit-cuffs. Her palms collided with her octagonal glasses. She took in a desperately sharp breath, her wrists naked as her fingers worked around her eyes.

What is she doing? Is she crying under there?

She rubbed her eyes roughly with her palms as her glasses dropped into her lap for a moment. Then Paula Barnes picked them up and put them back on as she walked hastily out the open door.

———

I had a feeling I'd made a bad mistake, treating a colleague that way. I knew from psychology—and from plenty of personal experience getting made fun of—that the open, reflective, learning parts of the brain tend to shut down under critical attacks. One's energy focuses not on the message but rather the messenger: resisting them to protect yourself.

Eventually, I stood up and walked slowly out of my office at the back corner of the library, through a gate of metal bars that scanned to make sure kids didn't take off with books.

Jim and Max were hanging out in the sun, and I asked them if they could help me talk to students, and which ones on my list they knew. They each took a dozen names and went off to find their friends. After that, Jim was unstoppable. He came back to my office to get more and more lists. He ended up recruiting a huge number of missing students, because he said everyone should get a chance like that.

When time was running out, I enlisted Rosa and Fry too, and we all put together key conversation points to work through with the remaining students.

We got one student who threw his hands up and named everyone he wanted to thank; then another, who said school just wasn't for her. Someone who wanted to open a business and make enough money to ensure his family's heat never went out on them again (he decided to study economics). Another, who liked the idea of reading and analyzing pictures the way people read and analyze poems (she decided to take advanced visual arts). Then another, who said he just didn't have the time, but maybe could've done it last year—sorry.

We marked form after form and, just a couple of days before everything was due to Paula Barnes, pushed forward with the last hundred. The meetings got shorter and more to the point, and the kids' stories and all that might become of them washed over us like the intracoastal tide, quenching and then drying us out.

— CHAPTER TWENTY-THREE —

Where I grew up, the rain didn't fly in like a slingshot from the sea. It didn't hit us like tarps of water inverted. It was gentle, predictable, consistent, even tender.

In Beaufort, when it rains, it pours. This was the fourth or fifth time I'd had to dash for the school exit after rain had come out of nowhere trying to wash everything away, and I wasn't ready.

My car top was down. My students' papers, my 1963 seats, my rugs, and all my CDs, in a fabric case, were exposed.

I pushed open the door of the school and leaned into the turn, sprinting up the empty sidewalk to the far edge of the parking lot, where my car was filling with yet another storm's water. I pulled the top up, leaned heavily into the antique mechanism to clasp it to the windshield, and sat, wet and panting, watching drips of rain spill through the old fabric's seams onto me.

As I walked slowly back to my meeting, I held the bag of student papers over my head, trying to calm down.

My reentry into Johnston's conference room felt like a tightening toward suffocation. I looked at Vice Principal Barnes and said, "This makes no sense! I met with hundreds of students—hundreds—and you're telling us that we only have forty-five more students in Advanced Studies? I can probably list more than that off the top of my head."

"Well, if you want to give me that list off the top of your head," she parried, "we can check each of the names."

Principal Johnston watched us to see if there was any way we could make peace without him having to insert himself.

"And if I come up with more names of new Advanced Studies students than you have in your system, then you'll admit you made a mistake?"

"No. I'll admit *you* made a mistake!"

"Look, I brought you—what do you think?—two hundred course-request change forms on Friday?"

She folded her hands on the table.

"How many sheets did I bring you?" I gasped. "Did you count them? Or do you have a guess?"

She glanced down to the left, then met my eyes and said, "None."

"None? What? There were at least two hundred. I'm talking about Friday, when I came by your office to meet your deadline for submitting changes. That big stack I brought you . . ." I resigned myself to sitting deep in my chair and pulled at the back of my scalp.

"You didn't bring me any course-request changes Friday," she said, not moving for a few beats until she scratched the side of her nose with a long, pink pinky nail.

"Maybe I have the day wrong, then . . . But no, I'm pretty sure it was Friday. When do *you* think I brought by that big stack from this last couple weeks' push?"

"I haven't had any forms from you these past couple weeks. You gave me a handful early in the month that I entered right away."

She's lying.

She saw me realize it, but must've known I couldn't prove it.

I couldn't remember the last time someone had looked me in the eyes and lied. She simply, steadily held her own hands.

"So you're saying that I didn't give you *any* course changes these last few weeks?"

"You did not," she said.

"That's not true. She's lying. She's actually lying!" I said.

"Whoa, now, Mr. Saaris," said Principal Johnston, holding up both hands as if he were a traffic cop. "We'll not have any of that, please."

"You know I did those forms. I've been working nonstop on it with Mike and Rosa. Let's get *them* down here!"

"No one is saying you didn't do the forms," said Barnes. "Just that I don't have them. You should look again to see if you can find them, or copies of them, Mr. Saaris. That can be your next step. Now, though, we need to transition to discussing the concerns about possible student misbehavior on the College Fair field trip. Please review this document," she said, spinning a paper on the table toward me.

I couldn't read it, and my eyes blurred. *Copies?* Suddenly I remembered. When I'd dropped off those hundreds of forms, and Barnes had asked about whether I had copies, I'd told her my copy machine allocation was all used up.

———

The AC was on, but the morning sun coming through the off-white, dirty aluminum blinds wouldn't yield to it. Nor would my internal thermostat.

How silly to think I could "save" these kids, when I can't even save myself. I'm sweating the bed here, dehydrated. Headache. Used up. But due at school soon.

It was all heat now. Heat for the gnats to hatch. The heat put on three of my Black students by a campus police officer trying to crack the case of the after-hours shenanigans at the Atlanta International College Fair I'd organized.

"Nope," Johnston had told me when I tried to go into the room with one of the students and the two officers. "They're eighteen. Their parents are not required, nor are you, Mr. Saaris."

Heat through a magnifying glass on our planned end-of-year Advanced Studies retreat to Hunting Island.

Heat evaporating the effort to find all the missing kids, with no permission to add any from the disappeared papers now that Barnes's deadline was over.

Heat in my head.

Burning through any notion I'd had of coming into a backwards school in the swamp and turning it around.

In peak moments, I thought we'd been pulling it off—me and the kids and some of the teachers and administrators. That our many hands could make the work light. Stiff as a board, light as a feather, our many arms as forklifts, upending sandstone and concrete, and turning the whole thing in a new direction.

But I hadn't done the work to really engage all the teachers. And after I'd made the mistake of chewing out Barnes, the tilt of things was never the same again. Like being on a playing field angled toward one goal. And while, for most of my life, it'd been my goal things tipped toward, suddenly it wasn't.

I felt spent, lived through, a hollowed-out, throbbing reminder that things should've gone differently.

———

But when it came to reflecting on *why* things should've gone differently, it was as though I were wired to direct the current of blame only outward— away from myself.

I blamed Walter and Barnes. Johnston, too, for not standing up to them.

I studied Barnes's psychology, marveling that she couldn't see her own faulty, self-serving logic—all the mental gymnastics I imagined she must be going through to delude herself into thinking that what she was doing was right. The backwards logic that the students couldn't really be "missing" because then she would've missed them. That she couldn't have missed them because she was good. Basic self-serving biases.

But as I'd tried to teach my students, and as Dolliver had failed to get through to me—these biases are not about other people. As comfortable and habitual as it is for us to see only in others the greatest flaws of humanity, doing so means we overlook integral parts of ourselves.

I would love to be able to say that at this low point—after I'd tried to make it all about my stepping up to "take responsibility" and "right the wrong" that had been done to the missing students, then failing to deliver for so many of them—I saw myself and my actions clearly. That I recognized my mistakes and committed to a new, more honest, and sustainable way of collaborating with others to achieve lasting change without getting tangled up in twisted logic and painting myself as a hero.

Instead—like my parents had with Erin—I walked away.

I'd told Principal Johnston that in order to serve the kids the way we should next year, we'd need him to approve the resources we'd been discussing for Advanced Studies. Our kids wanted after-school opportunities to work together and with teachers, and that required transportation money. They deserved a program handbook that made sure what we were asking of them throughout Advanced Studies was clear, consistent, and accessible, and producing that would require significant time for collaboration during staff meetings. When I pushed to convert the security office inside the main entrance to a space of academic celebration and Advanced Studies, he laughed and said that would not be possible. I told him I needed more time to support kids and teachers, not the additional classes he was assigning me to teach next year. We needed to give teachers more of the Advanced Studies training they were asking for, which would require time and money.

We needed these things, I told the principal, in order to do right by the kids.

We can't do those things, he told me.

Without them, I said, I didn't feel I could do the job.

I didn't say anything about the fact that I couldn't bear the idea of walking the hallway next year, knowing how many students would be sent through the wrong doors every time the bell rang. And that I couldn't bear the responsibility I'd failed to meet.

By the time I got back from my summer vacation, he'd given the job back to Margey. If things didn't go well from there, I thought, it'd have to be someone else's fault.

———

Not only was I able to just walk away, I was able to walk away with much more than I had even a year prior, when I'd applied to and been rejected by Stanford University.

I had a story to tell, in which my students ended up scoring above the global average for all Advanced Studies kids on the independently evaluated assessments—writing at a level that some said Creek kids could never achieve because of parenting, genes, earlier teachers, and more.

In my second application to Stanford, I wrote that in one year the advanced programs had more than doubled; we'd tripled the number of Black students, closed the race-access gap, and become the largest provider of the International Baccalaureate Advanced Studies program in the state of South Carolina.

Though Battery Creek started out with a low pass rate of 15 percent on the college-aligned, externally graded tests, when we grew by fifty students in one year, our pass rate went up to 36 percent, and continued to climb in subsequent years. Suddenly, Creek students were passing about as many college-level IB exams as students were at the wealthiest school in the county. And many more students gained proficiency in those classes—great preparation to tackle college.

I also asked students about their experiences and shared some choice quotes:

I've accomplished things this year that I never thought I could.

You are the . . . only teacher that showed me that I am capable of more than is expected of me.

It sometimes scares me to think where I would be if you and I had never met.

With these testimonials, and the intention I stated in my essays to use what I would learn at Stanford to build a nonprofit organization to find all of America's missing students, I applied to their graduate schools of business and education.

I didn't tell them about Paula Barnes or the students who were still missing, or the interviews my former students conducted with school staff the year after I left in which some said, "What progress? There were too many unprepared kids in those classes, and now that he's gone, we're cutting way back."

Though I hadn't communicated it effectively to folks at Battery Creek, in my application I had analyses of all the grades and testing data from Principal Johnston, and it showed that the kids *had* been pretty successful. We'd closed gaps while raising performance on the exams, and explaining this part of the story won me a double-admission letter.

I took what I needed, then cut and ran like a foster educator. I signed up for Facebook and friended all my former students to try to keep in touch. I set up a couple of meetups at the old coffee shop where we used to have study sessions. When Jim struggled to get his college application in, I couldn't reach him. I never talked to Joaquin or Buddy again.

Though I had no idea then, I was just like Barnes: I couldn't bear the idea of letting down the children I was trying to serve as an educator. I couldn't stand to acknowledge—and therefore couldn't correct—my own mistakes. I stopped being able to really learn because the consequences of my mistakes felt like too much to bear.

The hero's history I'd spun up would find a welcoming home at the nation's number-one business school, where they would teach me to perfect the art of spin so that I could undertake an effort to repeat the flawed Battery Creek initiative in schools all around the country as quickly as possible.

Little did I know I was walking away from the very people, diversity, and insights I'd need if I were to have any hope of realizing some of my aspirations for learning and teaching. It'd be more than a decade before Johnston and I would have the chance to sit down together again and I'd begin to understand how much of him and his story I'd missed, and how much more we could have accomplished together if I'd asked more questions, listened more, and followed Margey's guidance about leading with teamwork, service to others, and doing the follow-through needed to sustain work that could make a lasting significant positive change.

PART THREE

— CHAPTER TWENTY-FOUR —

I would have completely lost the thread of broad-minded and real learning at Stanford if it hadn't been for Natalie.

At age six, Natalie moved across the ocean to a one-bedroom apartment in Chicago with her mother and grandmother, who raised her and kept their household running, while also raising other people's children and cleaning other people's houses to make money.

When Natalie and I first met and started dating, she was teaching Spanish at another high school in Beaufort, and when I went to Stanford, she started her PhD on the East Coast in her fourth language: French.

The more impressive thing about Natalie was that as she achieved things academically—and later professionally—she somehow didn't become a narrower person.

Brain work can dull the heart with ideas distant from people. And focusing on one thing deeply can blur understanding of everything else, which becomes peripheral. With her multiplicity of languages and cultures and relationships, though, Natalie seemed to be keeping so many neural pathways active that she retained a childlike ability to see everything as possible, all at once—the world glowing with connections.

It was as though she had multiple amazing minds. She had her Polish brain, from her native country and her parents; and she had another brain, developed with her US friends and teachers (who themselves came from several different cultures). She took on more languages over time (picking up Latin one summer, and studying Portuguese for a trip), and seemed to have the ability to see things from multiple angles through her single pair of eyes!

Erin had that same ability—to see things from several vantages all at once—maybe the result of having navigated so many different family cultures. I'd learned so much when I was with her, but had mostly shut her and the harder lessons out after she didn't follow my ideas about how her life should go.

I preferred the way I'd come to see things—that I was where I was and Erin was where she was largely because we deserved it. That was the patterned, rutted map of the world in my brain.

Learning requires you to observe something not already mapped in your brain. The very essence of learning is interaction with difference: the difference between what's in your head and what's beyond it, perhaps in someone else's. And if you come into contact with difference and your brain really engages with it, over time your brain will change, integrating that difference into a new pattern—a learning.

Natalie, with her many ways of seeing the world, changed my mind so often that I sometimes couldn't remember which mind was hers and which was mine. On our first date, on Halloween in a dusty old bar in Beaufort, we debated whether humans were fundamentally good or fundamentally bad. A couple weeks later, we realized we'd both been convinced by the other's argument, and now held opposite views of the topic. This happened a lot: on free will and determinism, which book was better, whether to live on a boat—and eventually, what to do about graduate school.

Though she chose Harvard, thousands of miles away from where I'd be in California, and we at first thought it wouldn't make sense to try to keep dating on opposite sides of the country, we later convinced each other it made no sense to break up. Which was lucky for me, because I'd need a real, deep relationship with a strongly broad-minded partner who had different perspectives if I had any chance of escaping the superiority notions I'd been taught since elementary school.

Every day of my formal education since I was first assigned to "gifted" classes, I parted ways from my friends who lived in smaller apartments. From those with darker skin. And no educator ever said a thing to me about it—not once.

And no matter what teachers taught about justice or equality, the 16,180 bells that marked the beginnings and ends of their classes taught us racism and snobbery. For in entering and departing these classrooms, we saw who they thought deserved the labels bestowed on me and my classmates: smart, gifted, talented, brightest, best.

"Best" literally means better than everyone else: superior, supreme.

It was flattering, the highest honor bestowed by the institutions that ran much of our lives. It felt like love during adolescence, when we're all eager for that from folks outside our family. So I cozied up to the fuzzy label.

In the Stanford auditorium that greeted our incoming class, for perhaps the 16,181st time, I was not only told that I was one of the "best"—better than everyone else, rightly and competitively chosen to be at the top school for education, and for business—but was also shown yet again what the "best" supposedly look like: far lighter skin than the overall population.

Men who looked like me instructed classes of students who looked like me to maximize personal and private benefits—and how exactly to go about doing that. To get their points across, they used the stories of others who looked like us: Steve Jobs, Bill Gates, and Mark Zuckerberg.

When Natalie visited, she offered a different story, by way of a game. She said, "Let's play Spot the Minority!"

We were at some sort of wine event for me and my classmates in the palm-treed, white-sanded courtyard of our fancy dorm.

I said, "Shhhh! You can't say that," and got defensive. "What are you *talking* about?"

"Your class: where are the people of color? And come to think of it, the women? Wait, I see a couple women . . ."

I had literally come to Stanford to build a plan to help educators notice and act on a lack of diversity, but—as Dolliver had warned—I had a lot of trouble seeing what I might be implicated in myself.

I said, "There are lots of Latino folks here, from all over the Americas."

"Where? Do you see one? Show me."

"Shhhh! You can't talk like that."

She leaned in and whispered, "Do you really see someone Latino?"

I sighed. I'd actually been pushing a school principal earlier that day, asking if she really thought that a third of the participation rate for Latino students in Advanced Studies was enough. I didn't want to deal with any of my own hypocrisy after a long day. "Those three students over there, by the fountain," I indicated with my head.

"They're white," she said, and I about fell into the lemon tree we'd been peering around.

"Come on, man!"

"I'm just sayin' . . ."

"You're gonna get me in trouble here. You don't know *what* you're sayin'. Let's go."

"Like hell I don't. Those men are definitely white."

I interlaced my fingers in hers, and we left through a Spanish adobe-style arch and into the night. As we fled the building where I now lived, I felt so at home with Natalie.

————

With Natalie's push, I started to apply the idea of "missing students" to Stanford, penciling out that there would be more than twice as many American students of color at the business school if those students were accepted as often as their white peers. Similarly, several dozen more women would have been there with us had admissions equally included women in our small class.

But I also came to identify with my education, so I defended it when Natalie and others criticized the way it worked. The school helped make me me. I didn't just go there; I would become there. Become a Stanford graduate with new insights and opportunities. And attacks on my school felt a bit like attacks on me. My adviser at the education school there taught about this: the overwhelming, status quo–preserving force of people identifying with and defining school as what they themselves experienced—making them want schools to continue to be largely as they have been in our past.

Using all the incredible math Stanford taught me, I'd worked with my first school district partner during my time there, and we identified and addressed many flaws in their process of identifying students for Advanced Studies. And I did this while proudly attending a relatively segregated graduate school that should have had ten times as many admits from historically Black colleges and universities.

I accepted $7,000 from Stanford for summer research I conducted on every high school in the US, finding that there were nearly 700,000 students missing every year from Advanced Studies programs.

They taught me public speaking, marketing, how to read and use numbers, and how to read and use emotion too. They paid about half my tuition, and paid me more than the other half in a postgraduate fellowship, which made it possible for me to launch a new nonprofit—Equal Opportunity Schools—with a mission to find all of America's "missing" A.S. students and move them up to the educational opportunities they need and deserve.

Stanford's imprimatur helped me tremendously, as did the introductions my professors made to wealthy donors, cabinet officials, and superintendents. My hope was that embracing prestige and power could help me make changes toward the greater good. I didn't understand that prestige and power are like a wild stallion—dangerous, but ridable to a destination of your choosing only if you are lucky and vigilantly forceful in harnessing a huge animal with a mind of its own.

———

After graduation, I started to get lonely launching Equal Opportunity Schools (EOS) out of a basement. I felt giddy to meet someone deeply passionate about missing students—someone who had way more experience than me too.

Zendaya Mayfield and I sat in a bright coffee shop in downtown Fenton, California. The sun was just topping a nearby building and streamed in through old, open, paint-chipped French doors, illuminating the steam off her dirty chai. In that new light, sitting across from her, anything felt possible.

After we introduced ourselves and I told her why I wanted to launch Equal Opportunity Schools, I said that I'd learned in graduate school about other education reformers throughout American history who'd come along every couple of decades and tried to change things, and that every reform effort had failed—except for one.

"The common school movement! Yes! I took that class too. Was Labaree still the professor when you got to Stanford?"

"Yep, totally. And he didn't like any of the highfalutin ideas about how people're gonna totally change education, because he said the only thing that's really taken hold in American history is common schooling. Basically, taking what's working in schools and expanding access. Expanding from just people who owned property to include others. From just white folks in schools to folks of other races, from men to women. Expanding access from primary school education to secondary education, too. And now," I said, filled with possibility, "we need to expand that access to the highest levels of our secondary schools: to Advanced Studies."

"Yes. To me, equal access to a great education is what it's all about. We know what can work. We have good programs serving kids well every day."

"Yup. Ninety percent of high school kids are in a school with an Advanced Studies program."

"So, this company you're trying to build would be about making sure that kids of every background get equal access to Advanced Studies, right?"

I nodded excitedly and she beamed.

I leaned in and said, "Though I don't often use the word, the race and income gaps in access really amount to—"

"Segregation."

"Exactly! Segregation within a school."

"And separate is inherently unequal."

"Great minds think alike."

She thought for a moment, then asked, "I wonder if this is an issue in, like, Little Rock?"

I jumped in, wanting to seem really on top of it: "Yes! I looked them up, and they have nearly five hundred missing Black students who belong in advanced classes."

"Wow. That makes sense, though. So"—she pulled off her glasses to look at me—"the president and the National Guard brought the Little Rock Nine in through the front door on national television to desegregate the school. But that really public approach didn't solve it. Because for the most part, the principals over the years have kept things separate and unequal by putting those Black kids who came into the school into the lowest-level classes."

"Yup. And so it's still separate!"

"And then, maybe like the superintendent you were telling me about who put your report in a drawer, Equal Opportunity Schools could come in more quietly—brought in by principals who believe that kids of every background are equally capable—and just solve the problem, and *then* show everyone the strong results."

I felt I just had to work with Zendaya, to be together with greatness.

"That makes a ton of sense," I said. "I was mad at the superintendent for putting my report away and saying I couldn't talk about it. But maybe she had a point that if you simply show that kids can do the work in the classes, then you don't have to deal so much with all the fearful imaginings that maybe they couldn't. Just get it done and then people can judge for themselves how amazing it is."

"A lot rides on how it goes once the kids get into the classes."

"I've seen it go pretty well," I said. "We *just* finished creating an original data set to count how separate and unequal things are nationally right now. And I'm putting out a paper with the Education Trust about it: the gap is 640,000 missing students each year who belong in their schools' advanced classes, but are being overlooked."

As a former math teacher and an award-winning school district leader with a decade of experience on me, she got it immediately. I saw her register the horror of that number and an appreciation for its bottom-line clarity.

I continued: "I did a bunch of math to figure out that we can close that gap pretty much completely by focusing on about four thousand diverse schools that already have Advanced Studies classes. Those schools just need to find the missing students in their buildings. The idea of an achievement gap seems abstract, impossible, something an educator or a parent can't really act on. Caused by, like, state budgets or our culture or something. But this is solvable, ready for action. The students are missing. They're in the building. Let's find them!"

"And my understanding," she said, taking a sip of chai, "is that these courses are one of the best ways to help kids to and through college."

I was having fun rallying the conversational ball back and forth across the table with Zendaya.

"Yes! I've read every study on the topic, and it seems like the impact could be huge: something like one in three kids that we help succeed in Advanced Studies wouldn't have graduated from college, but will now because of our program." I was glad I'd done so much research on this over the years, because I really wanted to impress Zendaya. It was fine that these universities had told me I was awesome. But I was out of school now, all alone and trying to solve a huge problem. And if I could get Zendaya involved, then maybe there was a chance we could do something really big.

"Then that means we could have a very large impact per dollar," she replied. "Because lifetime earnings are almost a million dollars higher for college graduates. And that means GDP goes up significantly too." Having both completed Stanford's MBA and master's in education programs, we were very interested in how much good each educational dollar could do.

I told her I thought we could have as much impact on college outcomes as most anything out there. "For my thesis in college, I researched the impact of education on people's voice in their democracy. It turns out that, more than any other factor, education connects people to voting, volunteering, advocacy, and ultimately the influence that they should get to have in society."

"And health too," said Zendaya. "People's access to health care and health outcomes are tied to educational opportunities and attainment."

"Health, wealth . . . and then your children's educational opportunities."

"That was true with my parents and the opportunities they helped me get."

"Same here," I said.

We decided to go for a walk and ended up in the bleachers outside her old high school, and she told me what had happened to her as a student there, back when I would've been starting elementary school.

"I told my counselor I wanted to take advanced English, but she looked at me and said I wouldn't be able to handle it. I tried to change her mind, but she wouldn't listen to me. I talked to my parents about it, and they came into the school and asked the counselor to change my schedule and put me in advanced English. But still she refused, said I couldn't do it.

"None of my friends had the advantages I had of having a mom who worked in the schools and a dad who was a civil rights attorney," she continued. "So, bringing together their understanding of schools and civil rights, they were able to meet with the principal and insist. And finally the principal overruled the counselor and told her to put me in the class."

"That's amazing," I said, thinking about what I might say to get Zendaya to understand that we were meant to work together.

"But when I showed up to the class, the teacher was the counselor who'd said I couldn't handle it."

Nothing like that had ever happened to me. "Oh my gosh, that's horrible! Wow," I sighed, and frowned. "That's so wrong."

"Well, it is what it is."

Though I didn't ask any follow-up questions to better understand what she was describing, I thought, *This is just the type of thing that school leaders need to understand, so they'll get committed to finding missing students.* "Well, you say it is what it is, but I think that, you and me, we could actually solve it once and for all."

I swallowed, nervous to suggest our working together. Knowing she'd done everything that I'd done so far, plus an additional decade of incredible professional accomplishments, she could've made a great board member to oversee my work, a great funder to push me for strong results and advise me about the best paths to getting there, a district leader hiring me to work in her district.

"Really?" she asked. "Does that mean you're offering me the job?"

I flashed through my doubts. *Zendaya seems to want this job, launching EOS with me, but how does that make any sense? Why isn't she the CEO, bringing me in to work for her, given both her greater professional accomplishments, and the fact that this issue affected her even more personally than it did me?*

I picked up on the comforting script I'd learned in school. *Well, I am uniquely awesome, I suppose. The founder type. So, I guess I'm supposed to be on this side of the table, offering the job. After all, I was the one who was just given yet another fellowship, this one by a startup guru who said he had confidence in me as an entrepreneur, lent me his brand, and gave me lots of money to hire folks like Zendaya. I guess this is how it's supposed to be!*

"I'd be honored to work together on this, yes. Very much," I said.

We both smiled, and reached out and shook hands, her alma mater behind us, seemingly ready for the two of us to come in and fix what needed fixing.

Looking back now, I hope Zendaya doesn't regret working with me, even though my cluelessness about how things should've gone would cause us problems. Instead of figuring any of that out then, I clung to the funder's vote of confidence in me (and the other, mostly white male fellows they supported) and unconsciously accepted what that suggested about the relative position that people like me should hold, compared with people like Zendaya.

And even while that suggestion held some sway over me, Zendaya and I were spending a great deal of time traveling all over the country trying to discourage others from listening to or making such suggestions.

—— CHAPTER TWENTY-FIVE ——

I t can be very difficult to get in the room with school district leaders.
A typical medium-sized district deploys hundreds of millions of dollars a year, and manages more land, facilities, and people than anyone else in the region. So principals and superintendents are highly sought after, and necessarily vigilant about who they'll meet with, and for how long.

Trying to get to them, I'd had dozens of strikeouts. I'd met Susan Jones, the chief academic officer of the Morgan School District, at a conference, complimenting her presentation and connecting her success in closing gaps in high school graduation rates with my initiative to close gaps in college-prep classes. She'd been interested for a moment, until she realized I wanted more than just a casual conversation. At that point, she began scanning the room. Waving to a friend, she quickly excused herself.

A mentor of mine knew her boss, the superintendent. That mentor's vouching for me was the only thing that worked during almost a year of my initial efforts to partner with a district. It was someone the superintendent trusted telling her that I was worth a meeting. She said her team felt like they'd already addressed this issue, but she responded positively to my analysis counting their missing students along with a plan to find them, and decided to give me another chance to meet with Chief Jones. At the superintendent's urging, Jones and I met a few times, then she had principals administer the student survey I'd designed. After that, she reviewed all the data analysis and slides I'd created before I was finally allowed into the room with her principals.

The three principals were laughing and joking about their track teams when I walked into the room—a windowless place where the biggest of decisions are made about who'll get which opportunities to learn.

"There's a lot in these," the chief told her principals as they grabbed the custom ten-page reports from me and leafed through them. "I recommend you read yours in detail back at your buildings. I learned a lot here."

"Mm-hmm," they nodded, scanning hungrily to see how their schools stacked up.

Here was a chance at a new opportunity, one of the first I'd had since leaving Battery Creek: at my suggestion, the three principals in front of me were possibly, fleetingly willing to make changes that I believed would lead to breakthroughs at their schools.

The report distilled what my team had learned from hundreds of thousands of data points we'd collected in the district in order to understand why Black and Latino students were about a third as likely as other students to be enrolled in advanced classes in Morgan.

We found that underenrollment wasn't caused by poverty, because it held for upper-income Black and Latino students too. It seemed to come back to the fact that those students who were encouraged by an adult to participate in Advanced Studies were four times as likely to sign up; our data also showed that Black and Latino students were not being encouraged as often. This held even if you looked at a set of Black and Latino students with the same grades and test scores as a set of white students. Less encouragement toward Advanced Studies meant that these students reported less understanding about how A.S. worked and were less likely to feel as if they belonged in those classes.

I waited to hear the principals' thoughts.

"These stick figures are quite something," said one of them, deflecting.

I blushed, knowing my bad drawings to illustrate the causes of the gaps looked silly. "Oh, thanks. I'm quite the artist."

While I was distracted, another principal probed, "You're saying 90 percent of parents at our school expect their kids to go to college? But that's not really possible to know, is it, because we didn't survey the parents at our school."

"Ours neither," his colleague backed him up.

"That's from a survey question we asked of the students. We asked them what level of education their parents expect them to get."

"Reid told me these findings are pretty consistent across the other schools he's worked with," said Chief Jones. "So we're not out of the norm here."

"Yep," I confirmed. "And you guys are doing a bit better with Latino students than my last district."

They seemed to love that, and their faces relaxed.

Then I said, "But you have more to do on the gaps for Black students." Expressions tightened again. "That's where a lot of the focus should be, ensuring that those students are just as informed and encouraged to participate in advanced courses."

Principals have one of the toughest jobs in the world. They don't control the resources—money, teachers, time, regulations—but they're supposed to make sure it all works for their bosses, their staff, parents, graduation rates, achievement, the budget, the law, the newspapers . . . and problems are coming at them from all sides, all the time.

"OK—what do you want us to do with this?" asked one of the principals, who I'd learned was especially active in his efforts to ensure college opportunities for Black students.

Looks like just the opening we need here: a chance at change for specific kids.

The chief and I had prepared lists of hundreds of kids, generated with survey and academic record data, and we quickly handed those to the principals, asking them to have their teams start meeting with missing students as soon as possible.

———

All the preparation I'd done before, during, and after graduate school. A year of tracking these leaders down. Zendaya coming on board. The hundreds of thousands of dollars that philanthropists had put into the effort, based on my word that we could find the missing students. The time for learning, for mistakes, was over. Now I needed to show I could get it done.

The chief and her three principals probably had a century's more combined experience than I did. But as nervous as I was, I knew the contours of defensiveness and ego. I'd navigated—and been told I belonged in—rooms like these. Four of the five of us were men, and four of the five of us were white. And I had fancy degrees and training from schools that inflated my head unduly.

So, when we met again a few weeks later, I mustered my confidence and tried to keep them focused on the changes I thought were needed—changes that might belie any claims they could make to have never overlooked a capable Black or Latino student.

"OK, so you gave us this list of students, and my team looked through it, and honestly, it's bullshit," one of the principals started in. "Excuse the expression, but come on here! You have kids on there who have special-education designations who you're telling us to put in Advanced Studies!"

Just as I still refused to own any responsibility for kids going missing on my watch at Battery Creek, he didn't seem to want to own his. By impeaching the list of possibly missing students, you can impeach the idea that kids are missing at all.

I'd anticipated this, and took a breath before replying. "When Karen and I talked, we decided to do a quick data run to get some lists started, but we didn't pull everything, including special-education status. You know your kids best," I said. "This is just a starting point. We put kids on the list who have the factors that *your teachers* said were most important for success in Advanced Studies."

"Sure, but there are kids on here who don't belong in Advanced Studies. So it seems like this whole idea—"

I cut in: "So take 'em off if you think they need to come off. I didn't say that this was a definitive list. This is about getting more information into your hands quickly so you can look at it and make calls based on all that you know about your kids, OK?"

They looked dubious, until their chief addressed them.

Jones said, "You're right. There shouldn't be kids on here with special-ed designations. We can go back through and remove those kids." And apparently she thought I had enough points to keep going down the path I'd set in motion with the superintendent: "Are there any other things you want us to look for or adjust before we turn the lists over to you to use with your teams as you see fit?"

I tried to imitate her calm exterior—saying to myself, *I know exactly what I'm doing and I cannot be flapped*—but inside I was roiling, torrents of energy building pressure, ready to tear through blockers and create a fresh path.

They listed some acronyms I didn't recognize.

"Yep. Let's filter the data for those too," Jones said, taking note.

"The data shows," I said, "that kids who were encouraged by adults to participate in Advanced Studies were four times as likely to sign up. So after we make these changes to the list and you make any other needed adjustments, you'll talk to the kids?"

They pushed, prodded, tried to delay, beg off, and I responded with the data I'd been studying so hard. It's not that they didn't want to serve the kids. It's just a lot to deal with if someone, say, approaches you as a parent and tells you you're really botching some important aspects of your parenting, and have been for a while. We defend ourselves.

I did my best to keep calm, specific, and direct with each question and concern, and eventually, the chief raised her eyebrows at the principals and asked, "So you'll talk to the kids, guys?"

They looked at one another, then nodded. It seemed to me they were a step closer to finding their kids, but what did I know?

————

It took me a while to realize that things were off in my collaboration with Zendaya during the Fenton partnership she was leading. I was busy trying to make up for the students who hadn't been found on my watch, and increasingly tearing into people with my malignant sense of superiority: we needed a better result for kids now, there would be no excuses, and I would be the one to make sure it happened. I'd use the data, but if those moves didn't ultimately work, I needed to use all the power of the moral high ground.

It was in this frame of mind that I—a twenty-eight-year-old just out of grad school—had met with the chief academic officer of the Fenton Public School District, and with Zendaya, who'd lived and worked in Fenton most of her life.

Having learned from Zendaya that the district said they were done enrolling missing students for next year, I assumed that this chief, Dr. Alison McGregor, was like the superintendent in Beaufort who'd backed Vice Principal Barnes. That she was a shameless bureaucrat blocking Fenton's eight hundred missing students from their right to learn.

And each of those missing students was like a Jamie, a Carl, a Joaquin, an Erin.

This wasn't all supposition or analogy. It came from comprehensive surveys of teachers and students, as well as a deep review of academic records and enrollment patterns, which we'd already shared at length with Dr. McGregor and her team.

I didn't know how common it would become for district leaders to tell us in the spring, "We're done," when they hadn't enrolled many missing students. Later, showing that you could effectively respond to this became a key part of the interview process Equal Opportunity Schools would use to hire dozens of talented leaders who proved capable of handling it deftly.

I was not brought in by such a process, however, and I was far from deft during that Fenton meeting.

When Dr. McGregor began explaining to me why her schools had enrolled only about a quarter of the missing students, I listened, quietly rearing. She talked about a couple of vocal teachers who weren't sure that the missing students could do the work, the fact that the time for signing up for classes had ended, that they didn't have a plan in place to train more teachers to teach Advanced Studies for the fall. They enjoyed our work together, she told us, but there wasn't much more that could be done for the fall. She said it'd make sense to focus on how to support those students we had found for now, and then try to find more next year.

Having prepared with Zendaya, I addressed Dr. McGregor's points with her over the phone—me in Seattle, she and Zendaya in Fenton. I cited our survey data showing that the vast majority of teachers wanted to enroll more missing students, telling her how she could extend the deadline for class sign-ups, and mentioning that there was an A.S. teacher training nearby that summer that should work fine. I tried to get right into the narrow opening, wedge things open for the kids. I leveraged myself against what I thought was firm moral ground, asking her what she was gonna do about it.

"Because, right," I said, nodding into the phone, "our commitment in this partnership was to close these gaps this year. And students, of course, deserve these opportunities this fall. Those who are going to be seniors will never have this chance again, right? And," I added, "you're the only one with the authority to fix this. And we need you to keep enrollment open to do that, to add the additional students. To tell the schools how important this is for the students, right? Because *you* are the leader who's responsible here, responsible for making sure each of these students gets the education they deserve. You're in charge of academics in this district, overseeing these high schools, and if it doesn't work out, that's your responsibility . . ."

I went on for a while, and then noticed there was silence on the other end.

I asked a prosecutor's leading questions. "Doesn't that make sense? Is there anyone else who can be responsible for these students there? This is what we're here for. This is why we get into education. This is your chance to make a big difference, right?"

". . ."

"Hello?" I asked the phone.

". . ."

"She . . . uh, she left the room, Reid," said Zendaya.

"She what?"

"She's gone."

"Gone?"

"Yup."

"..."

"I should go try to find her. I'll talk to you later." Zendaya hung up, and I started trembling.

———

I hadn't told Zendaya that Morgan was in jeopardy of getting the same type of results we were seeing in Fenton. I hadn't even admitted it to myself.

After the seventeen meetings I'd taken with different folks in the district, the Morgan principals said they needed to set their schedules for next year and, though we'd been able to add some students on short notice, we'd have to wait until next year to enroll any more.

I can see how that makes some sense: work on stuff and make it a bit better, feel pretty good about it. Appreciate the progress instead of growing desperate at the remaining injustice. Get comfortable because it's a long haul and change takes time.

On the other hand, the Morgan principals had responsibility for the education of the 242 teenagers on the latest list—all of whom had told us they wanted to go to college but that they weren't being challenged by their classes, and had teachers recommending them for advanced classes.

I couldn't sleep and drafted an email for the superintendent at three in the morning. I tried to pull together what they'd taught us in business school about winning people over, what I'd taught in psychology about how much change people can take, what the world's leading relationship expert said about giving people five positives for every negative to keep relationships in balance.

Mostly, though, I wrote about the kids, that I knew we all agreed they deserved amazing learning this year. We, I wrote, were the only ones who could still get it for them.

I tried compromising without losing the morally important parts, suggesting we find half the missing students—those who were going into their senior year. That way, we wouldn't actually let the younger students go permanently missing—we'd get to them a year from now, when they were about to become seniors. It was a way to lessen the load for the schools, given how busy they were this time of year, while affirming these students' rights to access advanced courses in high school, to get college-level experiences before being thrown fully into college. Perfect!

I pounded this new solution into the lighted screen, telling the superintendent that I was up in the middle of the night worried over this, about these students slipping beyond our reach. I articulated the deep data case for her district:

- That 96 percent of her students aspired to go to college, but only 30 percent achieved it, meaning five hundred graduates a year left the district unprepared for their college goals.

- That being academically challenged in high school was the most important factor in getting ready for college, but that not even 20 percent of the district's high school students said their classes challenged them.

- That the students we upgraded to advanced courses during the pilot district work had been really successful.

- That the principals had lists of students recommended by teachers and by their own comments on the survey.

- That other district superintendents in the area were starting to take a stand and push for transformed access, even though it's hard, because it can make such a big difference.

- That I believed she cared so much for them and that she'd done so much to help already. Now her district could be the first in the state to find all their missing students. They were doing it. We could do it.

The fervor I felt at sending my message off into the darkness popped me out of my chair and over the edge of the houseboat into the cold water below with a little scream.

—— **CHAPTER TWENTY-SIX** ——

As I had advised in my email, the Morgan superintendent told her team not to give up on finding the missing kids.

On top of the superintendent's support, I'd also landed a helpful grant from the Gates Foundation. Things were looking up.

The superintendent asked me to spend some time with the principals to discuss the grant and how things were going. "Really listen," she coached me, "to what they need, and figure out how you can support them."

I met with each of the principals for coffee over the summer, when they'd changed into their shorts.

Really listen, I told myself, *to where they're coming from.* It was hard, because I really just wanted them to find their missing kids. Didn't think *I* was missing anything.

They were a little cheesed that I'd gone to the superintendent and delayed their scheduling plans. So I tried to bring us back to the heart of things. *Tell me about your passion. What got you into education, into this work?* I listened. Listened for commonalities that might allow us to see the same side of things.

The first principal kept looking at his watch as we talked at Starbucks. From the get-go, he had given the project to one of his assistant principals. His school was seen as relatively high performing (despite its ongoing failure to serve low-income students and students of color well), so I imagined the idea of making any changes felt risky to him. He told me his team would talk to some of the kids and then quickly left.

The second principal was more open. He talked about how graduation had gone that year, and how each year, as he handed kids their diplomas, he was less convinced that the documents meant anything. He said that if he didn't make a change, employers and colleges would eventually find out that his graduates weren't ready for what came next. He said parents were excited about their children's graduation, but he had a pit in his stomach the whole time, wondering if he was setting them up to fail. I felt conflicted, recognizing that what he was describing was bad, but also excited to have him open up to me, because this was something I thought I might be able to help him solve.

I told him that if we moved more of his students up to the highest-quality college-level courses, then the quality of the preparation the students received would improve. He was into it.

But not nearly as much as the third principal was.

The principal of Morgan High School talked about his own experience being underestimated and how he was pushing forward on all fronts at once—bringing in colleges from all over the state to meet with his kids, building them an even more advanced academic program, despite some people's doubts that the students could handle it. His whole thing seemed to be that kids could do it, and that it was his job to fix things so they had the chance.

Then he wanted to talk about the Gates grant, and how he and his team could use it to build a support plan for kids.

I always paid close attention when someone used the word "support"; I'd frequently heard the word from educators who seemed to believe that all these so-called missing students were not *actually* ready for Advanced Studies and would need unrealistic levels of resources.

I pulled out a packet the team and I had put together with a wide variety of options, saying, "We try not to talk about missing students as needing any sort of special support, because that kind of suggests they're not ready or couldn't handle advanced courses. Kind of a deficit focus, you know?"

Something flashed in his eyes, but I wasn't sure what.

I handed him the small packet. "But these are some student success strategies here that could be useful."

"And how much will we have from the grant to invest in these strategies?" he asked, leafing through the pages.

I couldn't believe I was about to lay out my grant requirements to a high school principal. Just a few months ago, I hadn't even been able to get in front of any of these folks, and now I was setting terms. I could've taken this sudden power coming to me—so young and inexperienced—as a sign that something was wrong; instead, I snuggled into the idea I'd been taught:

I get to set these terms for this experienced, passionate, successful Black leader because I am amazing, my ideas about this stuff are the best, and I'm right about what should happen here.

"So," I said, "that's going to depend on a couple things. First, you need to find *all* your missing students. Then, we'll give the funds out based on how many students have been added at each campus that has fully closed its gap." I folded my hands on the wobbly coffee table.

He took a moment to get started on his response. "Are you saying that we might not get any of the funds?"

"Well, I sure hope you will. We've all agreed to find all of the missing students, so it shouldn't be a problem, right? It's just that doing that is the first step. Following through on what we've committed to there. Then we'll allocate resources."

To me, it was so important to find all the missing students in one year. For decades, people had been trying to chip away at the gap, with little to show for it in the national data (less than 1 percent of schools nationally had closed their gaps). In my view, it was about a responsible leader committing to a breakthrough this year—and following through on it. That could create a significant-enough shift in the school that kids who'd previously told us that "students like me are not welcome in advanced classes" would feel things really changing.

A little progress could actually be worse than no progress at all. If only a few Black and brown kids get into advanced studies classes, they can feel isolated. Feelings of isolation can lower performance, and lower performance could be used to justify the stereotype that Black and brown kids had never belonged in advanced classes. Adults might feel as if they'd responded to the data and the moral urgency, but that ultimately our idea about closing these gaps just didn't work. The window for change that we'd worked so hard to pry open could slam shut, all the energy and effort backfiring—reinforcing the barriers more than ever before, with folks saying, "We tried that. Those kids couldn't do it. We don't need to change anything else about access to Advanced Studies again." And the segregation cements.

"Well," said the principal, "these issues go hand in hand for me. We need to be able to address support—"

"Student success," I interjected.

"OK, we need to address student success in order to put more kids into these classes. Otherwise, there's no understanding of what they're actually getting into. My teachers have been eager for that part of the plan since you met with them in June. They want to know what's next there."

"What's next," I said, clicking my stack of papers on the table, "is the outreach and enrollment for the other missing students we've all identified here. Making sure they get that college-level opportunity they need and deserve. And then we can finalize a student success plan. Look, the missing students can handle the work of Advanced Studies if we focus on giving them that chance. That's what this step is all about. We have to believe in their ability to succeed at the highest levels."

He looked at me askance, and I hastened, "Which I know we do," and smiled a bit. "OK?"

Anyone else in the coffee shop probably could see that what was happening was not OK with him.

But what I focused on was the check signed by the Gates Foundation that enabled me to try to set some terms with these principals. When it arrived in the mail, Zendaya, our new analyst, and a couple of volunteers celebrated with a cheap bottle of champagne—because the check gave us resources to support missing students, and also because it implied the richest man in the world's affirmation that our way of doing things was the best.

———

Zendaya started to tell me why she thought Fenton's partnership wouldn't achieve the goals we'd set out for it, but I cut in.

"Wait, what? Are you serious?"

"Yes, I'm serious," she said, and then we were silent on the phone for a bit.

I was kicking some horsetail plants growing out of the cracked asphalt next to the marina office that housed our tiny Equal Opportunity Schools operation.

"So, there were about eight hundred students missing when we started. How many are missing now?" I asked.

"There's about 650."

I switched to rocks, watching them move the water out of their way, whipping down into the seaweeds and then the nothing beyond, saying nothing.

"Are you still there?" Zendaya asked after a minute.

"I'm trying," I replied through closed lips.

"OK."

". . ."

"Here's what I think happened," said Zendaya. "I think we started too late."

"High school's too late?!" I thought about a common hypothesis we'd heard, that students missing from advanced courses might never succeed in those courses because they'd likely been through elementary and middle schools that were in need of improvement.

"No, I mean too late in the year."

"Fenton started, like, six months ago!"

"But maybe it really does take a full year, like Dr. McGregor was suggesting."

"People build whole schools and hire whole staffs in that kind of time. We're trying to find a couple hundred missing students at a few schools and change their schedules. It shouldn't be that hard."

"Well, we might've had another opportunity if that last meeting had gone . . . a little differently."

"What? What was wrong with it?" I started walking quickly down the waterfront.

"Well, I mean, you came on a little strong."

"I came on strong? This is *your* job. To figure out however you want to come on in order to actually serve each of those missing students. You asked me to come in because you said you were stuck and we needed to figure something out."

"I did."

"So what're you saying?"

"Reid, I don't know if you know this, but McGregor left the room because she was crying."

"Oh no, I didn't know that," I said, flashing back to Paula Barnes and how bad everything had gotten after she'd left the room in tears. "Oh no. That's really bad."

"Uh, yeah. It's pretty bad."

"But you said you wanted me to push—"

"Yeah, but we're not tryna have folks break down. And I've talked to her—a couple times now. But she's adamant that they're not going to continue to work with us."

"Are you serious?" I asked again, struggling to understand. "Look, you brought me in before when things were stuck, and you said I got things unstuck, right?"

"It did that one time, but not last time."

"But this time, what—she didn't want to think about the consequences of her decisions or something?"

"You were really putting it all on her, and she can't just—"

"Well, who's responsible for those kids?" I interrupted.

"I mean, I agree with you that as chief academic officer, she really should be responsible for them getting the opportunities they need."

"And you're responsible for making sure she understands that and does the right thing. And you asked me to come in and push, and I did what *you* asked."

"Kind of," she said.

"OK—we're gonna have to talk about this more later," I said, feeling the need to try to burn off this horrible feeling on the rolling grass hills in front of me. "You're getting into town on Wednesday?"

"Yeah."

"Let's talk in person about stuff then," I said, then hung up and ran hard.

———

I asked one of my board members for advice about the Fenton partnership. I talked about how many students might go permanently lost, about how Zendaya was in charge of the partnership. I asked what I should do.

They told me that it was important to hold people responsible for doing their jobs, and that they'd heard me say—before they decided to give me hundreds of thousands of dollars—that I wanted to have the people running our partnerships take final responsibility for finding all their missing students, that I'd establish a culture of accountability and responsibility at Equal Opportunity Schools.

"I will," I said. "I want to."

"Then," they advised me, "you need to hold Zendaya responsible, and make it clear to her how seriously you take this."

"OK," I told them. "I will."

So I practiced. And I got ready for my walk with Zendaya. The plan was to let her know that firing was on the table, that she needed to take this seriously. We were both learning, and she seemed like an incredible person and a talented professional. But we needed to get better results for the kids next year, or else . . .

The day of our walk arrived, and we set off along a shaded bike path. After some awkward small talk, we built up to talking about Fenton, and I said, "Zendaya, I want you to know that this is a big deal. This is serious. The job that I brought you on to do is finding missing students and getting the gaps closed in Advanced Studies programs. And I hear you talking about what *I* did and what *I* said. But I got involved at your request, using your guidance. The partnership with Fenton was *your* partnership to lead. And now we don't have the results for kids that we committed to serve."

I felt shaky inside, but looked over, trying to make steady eye contact. She was looking away.

"Does that make sense? You understand that the job—your responsibil-ity—is to find all the missing students in the partnerships that you run?"

"I understand," she said, but nothing more.

Venturing further, I asked, "Do you want to continue with this job?"

She examined me for a moment, clearly shocked, and then nodded.

"Do you think you can meet the responsibilities of it going forward?"

"I . . . I think so," she said.

"Good," I said. "I'd like that. Shall we turn around and head back?"

She said "OK," but didn't look at me for the rest of the walk. She was looking beyond me, at something I couldn't make out.

— CHAPTER TWENTY-SEVEN —

Weeks later, I tucked a letter away at the back of my little file cabinet in the EOS office, looking around me and hoping no one had seen me do it. It was from the Morgan School District. And though it included words like "laudable" and "really appreciate," I couldn't stop thinking about the phrase at the bottom, couldn't keep it from flooding my face hot and red: "end the relationship."

I couldn't think. I could only flee. I walked out of the old marina building and across the tumultuous stretch of asphalt, warped by years of the pier moving beneath it.

How dare they! Don't they understand that there are kids going missing right now? Stuck—right now—in classes that lead to sleep, boredom, drugs, dropping out, giving up on schools that seem to have given up on them a long time ago, not being able to support their families with good jobs, depression, suicide? It's all connected. Why can't they see it?!

I had pushed yet again when the Morgan schools' data came back. They'd doubled participation by Black, Latino, and low-income students. But they needed to triple it to close the gaps: the goal we'd committed to. The principals told me they'd done their best with such limited time, and that they wanted to do more next year. I told them they were risking losing the grant, and alerted the superintendent about where things stood.

The towering gasworks at the park were beautiful, round, tall, backed by an enchantedly sparkling lake. The ground beneath had been tainted with arsenic, sulfur and coal tar—some of the most toxic dirt in the state.

I'd glimpsed a packet in the far back of the file cabinet when I deposited the letter there. Thinking of it made my breath quicken and I stopped for a moment and rested.

The packet had been given to me by the head of a local foundation. Though they weren't ending our partnership, they suggested I step down from my role leading Equal Opportunity Schools—that we find someone with more experience, more understanding of how nonprofits should be run.

Someone was ringing my phone. Zendaya. It was time for our weekly check-in.

I took the call, trying to sound confident and energetic, asking how she was doing, talking about things that were going well lately: a new opportunity coming up to maybe work with Google; a chance to present to a big group of superintendents in the Midwest, to meet with the state superintendent in Delaware.

"Reid," she said, after I'd run out of positive things to say, "I know you want me to work with this new district in Delaware for next year, but I'm not sure it's a good match."

"Why? What's wrong with the district?"

"Not the district. I mean you and me, working together. You know, going forward. Fenton's officially out now, and I was excited about working with them, but it just didn't work."

I sank to the grass. *No, no, no* . . . I thought, *this can't be happening*, as the mud soaked through.

Morgan's letter today. Fenton gone. Zendaya leaving? The funder who'd suggested I step down as CEO must be right. We needed someone experienced enough, responsible enough, to find the missing students. What I was doing wasn't working. We had money for only six more months. We'd left 600 students missing in Fenton. We'd added 129 students to advanced studies in Morgan, but had 200 more still missing.

There was something in between the story I'd been telling everyone about all that I could do and what was actually happening. And—despite all my defenses—that something menaced me.

Had I deserved to grow up with an empty bedroom next door to me—emptied out *for* me—so that I wouldn't have to worry about Erin's traumatic therapies and treatments, so that I could quietly write my Extended Essay, without the added drag of her burdens?

With no violence in my kitchen. No sexual crimes in my bed.

The debt I'd incurred would come due. All that I'd accumulated—education, power, money—hadn't been mine to take. But I acted as though it were mine to keep.

I don't know how Erin could ever forgive me for refusing to give her sixty bucks, out of the thousands of dollars I had, after she'd asked me to get her a motel room because she had nowhere else to stay.

I'd told myself I deserved to keep that money. That she didn't deserve it because she didn't know how to manage it. Why was she homeless anyway? Wasn't it because of her personal failings?

That story offered me a sham excuse. She was homeless because she'd never been given a home in her whole life. Because she'd been taken away from mine when she was nine, so that I could have it all to myself.

One of those nights, in one of those motels, while my money sat in a bank, unmoved, a motel manager gave Erin a room, and took from her what he felt was owed in return.

What was owed should have been my sixty bucks. But instead, he took fatherhood—and Erin's sworn secrecy that she would never return to claim it. That she, alone, would carry the responsibility of being a mother again.

Without a home.

Without a family.

And yet she decided, somehow, to forgive me. Which adds even more to the debt that I owe.

And now here I was, trying to run this organization, trying—and apparently failing—to implement a repayment plan.

I dropped my righteous stance, and my shoulders fell forward.

"Zendaya," I stuttered.

"I'm still here," she said.

"I'm sorry."

". . ."

"I need you. I can't do this alone."

". . ."

"And I . . . I was wrong to try to blame it all on you."

". . ."

"What I said to you on our walk was my fault, my responsibility, and it wasn't right. I went in there and pushed way too hard. I didn't listen to all you'd told me about how the partnership was going, how McGregor was already on the brink. I just wanted to get it done for—well, no, we *both* really want to get it done for kids." Thinking of Erin and her daughter, I whispered, "I think I just couldn't face the idea of my letting kids down, you know? They're *kids*. Sometimes it's too much. I don't think I could handle this without you. I'll do better. I promise."

"I'm glad you're realizing some of this," she said, then paused. "That really hurt, how you tried to put everything on me—even your part. This work is hard, and it takes teamwork. And I don't know if I can trust you, honestly."

"I'm trying to learn here. You're right—it is hard. And we need to be in this together. What if we do a full debrief on what's happened this year, and redesign our overall approach, together, so we can get done what we both came here to do, and find all these missing students?"

She was quiet for a while. Then, even though I'd wrecked her chance in the Fenton School District, she graciously gave me a second one: "I'm not going to say things are all good between us, but I guess let's give it another try."

And the fracture in my world started to heal a bit. In the following months, I tried to listen more. To really learn. I tried to remember to open myself up to mistakes, to learning, to a more collaborative, trusting, and effective path toward redemption. But a lonely and false notion still held sway: that I'd risen in life without strings, and that without strings I could somehow weave together a life worth living.

———

I asked Zendaya to lead the team in reflecting on lessons so far, and planning how we might get better results in upcoming school district partnerships. She wrote a couple-dozen-page case study on the Fenton work that deftly brought the ideas and data we'd been working with into the specific context of the people we were collaborating with.

One morning, we were in our windowless little $200-a-month office, where I'd hung Facebook profile photos of found students from Beaufort, and also a big, brown bear blanket to cover some old pipes. We were taking notes on butcher paper, with + for things that had gone well, and △ for things that needed changing.

"Maybe you can think of it like you think of students," she said to me. "I've heard you say that families and students want to do well but they don't always know how to navigate a system that throws up a lot of roadblocks. A lot of the educators, they want to be successful too; they're just worried they won't be, and they need help with how to get there."

"So, what do you think we need to change most?"

"Timeline is a big problem I saw this year."

She let me sputter about how urgent it was to find kids and how the educators should've stepped up, even with little time left in the year.

"And," she responded, "it's just really hard for them to add kids when they're already building their schedule and their staffing and everything. So, it'd be good if we could line up with their calendar, you know, remove any roadblocks we can."

She let me sputter again about how hard it was to get districts to sign up to work with us at all, let alone get them to sign up faster so that we could start earlier in the school year. That we needed to work with whatever we had, to get it done for the students—

Then she said, "I get it. We want to find the kids wherever we can this year. They're like my friends from growing up too. And I get that it's hard to get districts to sign up. I guess I'm just saying that whenever it's *feasible*, it'd be better to begin our work earlier."

"If it's doable, sure." I rushed on: "But it might not be. I can try to get them signed up earlier, but it's hard. You want to help me with that?"

Sales and fundraising were my jobs. Zendaya had told me she really didn't like doing those things; when we were negotiating her contract, she'd made clear that she wasn't signing up to sell our service or raise money.

"Nope," she said simply. "That's not my job, remember?"

"OK," I said, feeling unhappy and unclear about why she insisted on leaving me with that responsibility. "Maybe you can make a detailed calendar, then, for how you think the timing of our work with them should ideally go, once they're signed up?"

"Sure," she said, adding a note to her purple spiral binder. "I'd also say we need to do a better job responding to their concern about having good support for students."

"But we've talked about this. Do the students really need some sort of special support? That's kind of an assumption, and one that we've disproven in Beaufort, and in the pilot district I worked with during grad school—"

"You're talking about whether the students need support. I'm talking about the fact that the *educators* have a concern about this that we need to do a better job of addressing. They won't sign students up if they don't think that they as educators have it set up well enough for success."

"OK," I nodded. "So we don't have to agree with the idea that students need lots of extra supports to somehow help them with supports?"

Feeling a little stung that the △ column was filling up, I said, "Actually, let's talk about what worked well."

She humored me on that. We talked again about our shared passion, our urgency, and also some of our data and surveys.

"And the whole 'missing students' thing is good. I think it brings focus for people. It's not just some general thing—it's specific. Right?" I asked.

"Yeah—I definitely agree with that."

"'Missing students' lets us make a strong moral case. And we probably need to be making it to the superintendents—bringing them on board early and strong in every district. Because it's a systemic problem and they're the leader of the system who has ultimate responsibility for fixing it." *And*, I thought, *they can make the principals and chief academic officers get it done for kids.* "OK—is there anything else we should be changing?"

"I'd say we shouldn't make them cry."

"Obviously!" I huffed. "What *should* we do, then?"

"I'd say there's maybe room for us to develop more empathy in our model. Like, be more understanding of what they're going through, all the competing pressures they're facing, so that we can address the full context with them."

"But *how*?" I asked, worried she was implying that I didn't understand what I needed to understand to do my job. "Like, what should we actually *do* about that?"

Zendaya had her hands folded on the table. I was akilter on an old backless knee-chair I'd gotten from my dad's office.

"Good question. I think it comes back to things like the timeline and responding better to their concerns about supports, but also understanding that closing a gap that's been around for decades is a big mind shift for folks. You've seen it happen, but very few people have. And that's not the way school systems usually think about things. They're trying to get thousands of things done for thousands of kids, and check a lot of boxes and requirements and—"

"I think they need to pick the most important things and get those done first. Things like this."

"Yep," said Zendaya. "But in terms of the way *they* see the world: it may take them a bit to work up to the idea that they can close this big gap—like in Fenton, eight hundred students—in the course of a few months. We need to help them see each step, and how it can fit into all they're doing and the deadlines they face. They've got changing school boards and funding and new policies and initiatives coming at them all the time. And their job is to absorb it all and somehow deliver a consistent result to tens of thousands of children who need the daily bus, meal, teacher, lesson, and everything else to work. And they're supposed to make lots of progress, but the public kind of always expects schools to stay the same too, like they experienced when they were kids."

"Sounds complicated," I said. "You really understand this a lot better than I do, so I want to defer to you more on how we build our approach."

"And I think even if there are bad apples, we should maybe start with the assumption that they're doing their best, and they really want the best for kids, just like we do. We're there to provide new ways for them to solve the specific problems and roadblocks that they face to getting this work done. That means like helping them build a plan for how to administer the survey to thousands of kids and teachers: who'll be in charge of administering it, which days and class periods, how much time it'll take—a plan they can bring to schools. Then talking points they can use to share the results, and slides. And detailed lists of kids that meet their specifications, detailed options for outreach to kids, and detailed options for student success plans, along with costs and next steps. Making it as smooth and easy as possible."

"That sounds really good," I said. "I look forward to seeing more of those details in the plan you're putting together. And I'd add that we need to be careful with their egos, like if they're fragile."

"That's one way of putting it, yeah," she said.

I wrote "Tend to Egos" in orange marker and said, "I think that's really important."

"For some folks, sure," she said, smiling.

———

I didn't understand some of the most important things Zendaya was trying to teach me. What I did understand was that Equal Opportunity Schools had to do better if it was to survive.

Natalie and I were just back from South Carolina, where we'd gotten married with the help of friends, family, and former students and colleagues. Now she was focused on her doctoral dissertation about French novelists' response to modern technology, and on bringing a baby boy into the world. Meanwhile, I was responsible for most of the mortgage on our little houseboat, in addition to raising the money for EOS to be able to cut paychecks for me, Zendaya, and the other eight folks we were bringing on to help lead select district partnerships, analyze data, and develop internal and external reports.

Because the educators we worked with wanted to know first and foremost that their students would be OK in larger and more diverse Advanced Studies programs, we did some deep dives on the results so far.

Though we hadn't yet closed the gap in Morgan, we did add about 150 students to advanced courses in the first year. As Zendaya and I anticipated—and as had proven to be the case in Beaufort, as well as in the grad school pilot—the students added performed comparably to students the prior year. This meant that in the schools we worked with, more students than ever before were succeeding in advanced classes and on the exams that could be used for college credit. And qualitative interviews with students conducted by folks at the University of Washington confirmed that the new students generally appreciated their experiences in Advanced Studies.

Following Zendaya's advice and focusing this time on what they would find most valuable, we had a lighter partnership with Morgan the second year. And they went from a doubling to a tripling of Black and Latino student participation in A.S., with continued strong success data. Thanks to its passionate principal, Morgan High became one of the first schools in the state to fully close race and income access gaps for Advanced Studies.

Despite my having screwed things up in Fenton, Zendaya found her way back into a partnership there. Over time, A.S. classrooms in the district opened their doors to thousands more students of color.

Every bar we cleared seemed to result in our facing a higher one.

One day I got a call from a fast-talking guy in Silicon Valley who said he heard about us from one of my classmates. He told me to dream big, and asked what I would do if resources weren't an issue.

I told him we would want to run a competition for schools to sign up six thousand missing students, and we'd use what we'd learned to measure the impact, showing that this approach gave a bigger boost to kids' college prospects than anything else he could put his grant money into.

He asked me a handful of questions, had me write up the answers in a five-page Google Doc, and did a splashy release announcing that we'd been given the Google Global Impact Award.

As hard as it had been to get our first six partners, I'd just signed up to find *sixty* to work with over the next few years.

— CHAPTER TWENTY-EIGHT —

Most efforts to make change in the American school system fall apart trying to figure out how to get the attention of fourteen thousand independent school district superintendents, each of whom is bombarded daily with hundreds of pitches that they have to mostly ignore if they want to get anything done.

We focused on the thousand districts with the four thousand high schools that were mostly responsible for the national gap. And then we used several signals to try to break through the noise. To try to show that we were innovative, we put together an event at Google's campus. To show that we were credible, in the invitation we mentioned our partnership with a researcher at Harvard, and that the former assistant US secretary of education for civil rights would be joining us. And to show that we were serious about connecting with the leaders of the district, I had supporters and districts who were happy with our work introduce me to county superintendents—who oversee groups of district superintendents—willing to recruit enough districts to make their region a focus for the Global Impact Award project.

After almost everyone was seated in our big, glass conference room and our host had introduced us, I faced the superintendents, keeping my back to the slides that appeared to be projected without a projector. Following the Stanford public speaking training, I stood to the left of the images (because people read from left to right) with feet firmly planted, arms unfurled and ready to gesture. They'd told us to practice each word but to seem relaxed, to control the flow while letting the audience feel in control.

I started with the best sentence I had, distilled through years of refinement: "My best friend and I were always together growing up, until the moment in high school when we were sent off on different paths for no good reason."

Folks quieted, wondering what had happened.

"My mom had been a career school counselor who said, 'Right this way, Reid, to get ready for college.'" I opened my arm to one side.

"Jamie's mom had dropped out after eighth grade, and was a single mom raising five kids. So she didn't have time to help Jamie figure out how to navigate a high school system she'd never been a part of.

"In Jamie's words, he's spent the last decade trying to make up for what was lost at that juncture in our lives. And it became my passion and professional obsession to ensure that no student misses out on the learning opportunities they need and deserve—especially when they're just across the hall."

When I opened my other arm, folks nodded, examining me.

As I'd learned in front of unforgiving classes of teenagers, people don't learn, grow, or change by just watching something. So, as tempting as it was to keep control over this high-stakes meeting, I invited conversation.

"That's what brings me here today," I said. "Let's go around the room and hear brief introductions: who you are, and what brings you here today to this conversation about finding students like Jamie who are missing from their schools' college-going classes."

Looking down at the floor as I waited, I saw the ankles of superintendents shod in dress socks or nylons, then above, those thirty-nine executive's faces. They dressed in relatively conservative colors—grays and blues and blacks, some with brighter ties or shirts or scarves beneath in lavender, orange, or aquamarine.

The next hour, and much of the broader effort to find missing students, would be determined by what this crowd decided this conversation would be like now. I'd put all our chips in to get each of these folks here to this amazing campus, this moment of real possibility.

"I'll go first," said an older gentleman who had his legs crossed at the knees, his cuffs bunching a bit. "At first, I honestly thought you were the summer intern for this big Equal Opportunity Schools organization we've been hearing about." He chuckled good-humoredly. "But I think I'm seeing a bit more of what's going on here and why you started all this. Anyways, I look forward to learning more. And the question? Oh yes: introductions."

"And why you're here to talk about equity and excellence in schools."

"Right. I'm Don Stinson, superintendent from up Stockton-ways. And part of why I'm here was this Google invitation." He chuckled again, and my stomach wrenched in. *Maybe they'd all just come to see the famous cafeteria, and the rest of this would come to nothing . . .*

"But seriously," he continued, "I'm nearing the end of my career, and I won't go to things unless I think they have the potential to be really valuable to the kids in my district. I learned that lesson a long time ago. And we, like I think a lot of folks here do," he said, looking around, nodding at a couple folks he knew, "we kind of have two separate systems running. There's the kids and the families who know how to work the system. Like you did, Reid."

OK, he's actually on to the issue, I thought, as he rounded his second minute. I was regretting my decision to open things up. If each of the 37 folks took two minutes, like Don was about to do, we'd run out of time just doing introductions.

"And then there's the part of our schools for kids whose parents didn't grow up working it and knowing how to navigate everything. And they don't necessarily know how to open every door for their kids who are with us now. Like your friend. What was his name?"

"Jamie," I said sternly, then cut Don off. "So you're saying that you want to solve the issue of schools not working for some kids whose families don't know how to navigate them. Great."

Don nodded his assent and said something about taking too long, blushing a bit. I pointed to the gentleman seated next to him.

"How about you?"

"I was wondering if I'd get a turn at all," he said. "I'm just kidding, Don. You hit the nail on the head with that one." He made a hammering gesture on Don's shoulder. "Garrett Taylor here, up from Briarwood Unified. And ditto what Don said. Interested in the Google campus, but most importantly the separate systems for separate kids. How'd I do on time, Teach?" he joked.

"Great," I said. "Thanks, Garrett, and thanks, Don." Then I looked to the next person. We were rolling. *I might actually end up with time to tell them what Equal Opportunity Schools has to offer.*

"Marta Remington here, Los Juntos School District."

"Thanks for being here."

"Well, I almost wasn't," she said. "You see, I know exactly what this work is about, because I've lived it. When I was growing up, I was one of those students like your friend. My counselor took one look at me and told me that my dream of going to college wasn't going to work. And I gave up on it. Figured I was going to follow my family into the fields in the Imperial Valley, until Señora Ventura—the one Spanish-speaking teacher in our entire school—told me otherwise. And if I'm really honest, I'd have to say that I didn't believe her as much as I believed what that white counselor had told me. But Señora Ventura kept at it. And now I'm a superintendent, one who understands exactly what you're trying to do here. So, thank you for your work. And now I'll stop talking."

I felt grounded by Dr. Remington's comments, as well as those of other folks, who told stories of being missing students themselves or of working with missing students.

Some just gave their name and district and said "ditto" to someone else's comment about the importance of the achievement gap. Some said they honestly weren't sure what this was about from the flyer they'd received, or just that their county superintendent had suggested they come.

I asked, "But is there something about access to college-level courses that relates to what you're working on, or that speaks to you? Something you want to learn today?"

"Yeah—I'd like to learn what your program is, and what you actually do."

"Good. We'll get to that. So," I said, trying to integrate all the comments I'd heard, "some people are pretty keen on checking out Google." There were chuckles. "The tour comes after our meeting here. And most folks seem to have a strong understanding that kids are missing out on college-level learning opportunities—including some folks with personal experiences of being overlooked as students. I think the real question is how we can actually do something about it. Because we all know about it, but we're seeing nationally that fewer than 1 percent of schools have actually *solved* this problem and closed these gaps. Our work and our expertise is all about how folks do that."

I advanced the slides to a picture of me and Jim and told them about how he'd reminded me of Jamie, about how Jim's successes had prompted me to try to find every missing student. I told them how we'd doubled the size of our Advanced Studies program in a single year, tripled African American participation, closed some long-standing gaps, and seen passing increase by 20 percent on the advanced exams. They liked that. It was rare to hear of any gaps fully closing, but we'd done just that with our race gap in a single year.

"Each step of the way, when we see that kind of result, part of me is happy for the students who've moved up, and another part of me is sad about the implication for other students. Because this tells us that the idea of 'missing students' is true: there are lots of students each year stuck just across the hall from the education they deserve. They're ready to be successful at the highest levels, if we can pull it together and open those doors to them.

"After we found the missing students at Battery Creek High School in South Carolina, I went off to DC and was adopted by the head of the Education Trust. She asked me to write a paper counting every missing student in the country. We found that there are two-thirds of a million each year. And that became the mission of Equal Opportunity Schools: to find all those kids.

"Why do we focus on this?" I showed them a three-column chart with reasons for:

Schools

- Progress on achievement and opportunity gaps
- Progress on their annual evaluation
- Progress on college readiness
- Build on what's already working
- College coursework as an organizing end goal

Staff

- Like teaching advanced courses
- Most think this issue needs to be addressed
- Further fulfill their purpose of helping kids

Students

- Not getting bored anymore
- Greater engagement and belonging
- Getting ready for their college goals
- Better prepared for jobs of the future

And under it all, in bold, the hypothesis we were testing with the Harvard EdLabs folks: that this might be the most effective way to use existing resources to boost college completion.

Then I brought up a gaps chart from the pilot work I'd done in San Felipe. It was double disaggregated by race and income so that we could see the effects of each. It showed Latino students—both low-income and non-low-income—participating in Advanced Studies at about half the rate of the white students from middle- and upper-income families. "Ninety-nine percent of diverse high schools in the US with significant Advanced Studies programs have these types of gaps, with all other race and income groups participating less than middle- and upper-income white and Asian students," I said. "And after this meeting, we can give each of you your charts."

They were visibly eager, clearly love-hating the prospect of being graded, wanting to score high but knowing that few had on this test, so maybe it'd be OK if they didn't yet . . .

"But I can tell you right now," I said, clenching and unclenching my hands, hoping they'd take this well, "we invited you here because this is very relevant to each of you. You have high-quality Advanced Studies programs, diverse student bodies, and some progress in access. But you have significant gaps remaining."

———

After I was done speaking, I handed it over to a peer of theirs—one of the first school leaders I'd partnered with in California. I'd been learning how to design surveys and how to use Excel in classes, then riding the train down after class.

At first, Dorothy hadn't met with any of the kids on her lists, had told me she was very busy. It took my meeting with her every week for months, talking through her questions and concerns, giving her new lists of students, before she got into a rhythm. Then, she'd say, "I just had the most amazing conversation with three girls who immigrated to the US last year. They told me no one had ever talked with them about college or anything like that— that they were so grateful to meet with me and find out what's really going on and what they need to do to get ready. How many more names do you have for me today?"

Now, as she spoke to the group at Google, I watched the clock, trying to tame time for this make-or-break presentation with the superintendents that would decide whether we'd have work this year or not. I was hoping Dorothy would wrap up her comments quickly so I could take back the reins when, suddenly, her words got to me.

"So I'd spent my career for forty years as a teacher and principal, pulling kids out of class on discipline issues over and over, assigning detentions, filling out paperwork. There was so much to do, and this Equal Opportunity Schools thing got added on as yet *another* thing I had to do."

Folks nodded knowingly.

"And Reid kept bugging me. Honestly, he was really bugging me for a while." Folks laughed, and I laughed nervously back. "But when I finally made the time to talk with kids, this wasn't just another thing. This was *the* thing— the reason I got into education in the first place. You see, somewhere along the way, we can lose that. We lose our purpose because we're just trying to keep on top of everything. But why? We get into education because we want to change lives for kids. We believe in the power of learning. And I wasn't getting to my discipline referrals for a while, sure, but I had kids in front of me who had *never* had an adult put their name in the same sentence with anything like 'Advanced Studies' or 'college.' And I told them we had the data saying that they could do it, and they lit up. And I even caught up with my kids who'd been written up for discipline issues. I started meeting with them to ask *why* they were acting out. Were they bored in class? And sure enough, misbehavior started to go down because I said, 'You're in trouble? Why is that? Are we meeting your learning needs? Let's get you into a class that will meet your needs and send you on the path to college that you came here to be on.' And I was finally doing the work that I came to education to do. And it became the highlight of my career."

Awash in gratitude for what Dorothy had said, lost in thoughts about all the teachers who were so eager for data and support to help open up further opportunities for kids, I suddenly remembered we were in the middle of a presentation. "And thanks in part to Dorothy's work," I said, "we were able to close the gap in San Felipe." I clicked forward to a slide that included an additional eight hundred Latino students in their Advanced Studies programs. "And they joined that 1 percent of diverse schools with significant Advanced Studies programs in the US that fully reflect that diversity at the highest levels."

The administrators in the room pointed and whispered. Some snapped photos with their phones. Some even started to clap.

"For the schools who have closed these gaps," I said, "we've seen that it starts with leadership at your level. Because we've talked a lot about the achievement gap in this country. And that's given some folks a lot of data to think of low-income students and students of color as low achievers. Even well-intentioned folks who are strapped for time—like counselors here in California, who can have caseloads of a thousand kids—might just have a couple minutes with a student. And they know about the achievement gap, they've seen the lower average test scores for Latino students, and they have to decide quickly which class to put a kid in. Maybe they pick a lower-level class, where the kid will end up with lower-level assignments, which lead to the lower levels of achievement.

"And around we go in a cycle, until a leader comes along here"—I pointed at the part of the diagram that said "Expectations"—"and says, 'I know about the achievement-gap data and all that, but I also expect that kids of every background can do high-level work, and so we're going to provide those opportunities now.'"

"OK," someone interrupted. "I think we're with you that this is a problem. But what you're giving us is all theoretical. What do you actually *do* to help us with this?"

She looked as if she were about to walk out, so I reluctantly but quickly clicked ahead. "Yep, OK. You got it."

———

At first, I just wanted superintendents to feel on fire about kids being overlooked. I thought that if I got them to feel on fire, they'd figure out how to put it out right away—that the rest was just details. But Zendaya helped me understand how much they need actions and processes. They need to be able to take the inspiration and the idea and hand it off to someone who was fired up about lots of things, and to get that person to focus on what specifically would need to get done by when.

I told the audience at Google that if we partnered together, EOS would measure their gaps and the causes. Then we'd bring in the best practices from places who'd closed the gap, build a custom plan for their context, and then get the kids signed up together.

"For that first study phase, we'll do a survey of all students and staff"—an idea I'd taken from Allie's project, though I didn't realize it yet—"and examine the academic records, and pull that all together into a report and recommendations. I'm going to show some real examples from the report you'll get in the study phase, but with the national data. But before I show you the first finding from that report, I'd like you to guess: what portion of your students do you think want to go to college?"

They were quiet because they weren't sure. It can be pretty hard to get educators to guess, because they really don't want to be wrong. So I waited. Over the years I'd spent at the front of a classroom, I'd learned to entertain myself in the silences that came after certain questions, to rejoice in the reprieve, to breathe, smile about the thinking that's happening.

"Sixty percent?" asked a young administrator.

"Good guess," I said. "That's right around what staff on our survey of a couple thousand educators so far have been guessing, but it's not right."

"Seventy-five?"

"It's almost ninety percent," I said, pushing on the clicker in my palm. "And it's pretty consistent, as you can see, across race and income groups. And about ninety percent of parents expect their kid to go to college too.

"So the next question is, what proportion of students nationally do you think actually go on to *get* a college degree within six years of graduating high school?"

It always surprises me when folks don't know the answers to these questions. I thought of all the banners and posters I'd seen strung over plaster

walls, under crown molding, in entrance halls and auditoriums, over da-
ises and stages, all attesting to the goal of college for the kids in those
buildings.

Half a minute passed before someone finally decided it'd be better to look
foolish giving a wrong answer than sit through any more awkward silence.

"Fifty percent?"

Other people snuck their answers in quickly.

"Forty."

"Two-thirds."

"It's about *thirty* percent," I said. Most of the 90-percent bar that'd been
on the screen faded to a dashed line representing the 60 percent of kids
whose goal is college but who don't leave high school with enough momentum to achieve it.

"And what is the biggest factor in determining whether kids will actually
achieve this college goal that 90 percent of them have?"

Again, silence. An aggravating silence. Together, the superintendents in
this meeting had responsibility for several *billion* dollars in educational resources each year. *So how are they picking where to focus what they do with all
of it?!*

"Pggrzz?" someone whispered.

"I'm sorry?"

"Oh—I was saying poverty?"

Someone saw my expression and decided to put in a different guess.
"Eighth grade CAT scores?"

"Uh-huh," I said noncommittally. "We're guessing income, and eighth
grade test scores." *So, they don't think high schools can make much of a difference?* "Others?"

". . ."

". . ."

"Parents' education?"

"Third grade test scores?"

I advanced the slide to a citation from the US Department of Education.
"Academic intensity in high school drives college completion more than any
other factor," I said. "And we don't ask kids whether their classes are 'academically intense'; in our survey, we ask them whether they're challenged by
their classes. And our findings across tens of thousands of kids match pretty
well with the college completion rate." I clicked up another bar on the chart,
almost identical to the college completion rate, showing the percent of kids
who said they're challenged or very challenged by their classes.

"The cool thing about this," I said, trying to move on from the fact that they didn't know what most impacts their goal, "is that this is really within our control as educators at the high school level. We often think about poverty or test scores or parenting as the factors that'll determine whether a kid achieves their college goals. But the most important thing is something we can change: whether or not we give them a rigorous high school education. Which makes sense, right? Because if a kid's going to have a good shot at tackling eight college classes when they're nineteen, shouldn't we get them doing one or two when they're eighteen, while they have the support of their high school community all around them?"

Three administrators gathered their things and quietly left, taking some of my confidence out the back door with them.

————

We'd made this special event, at one of the world's most popular companies, invitation only. I told them that their gaps were something most schools faced, so they wouldn't feel too criticized. "So, we know what's most important to accomplishing the college goal, and everyone here has a strong set of academic programs that is working well today to provide that rigor to some students. The strength of your advanced programs is a key reason we invited you to apply for this project.

"And, as we've talked about, we all have this problem of missing students. In total, today there are more than fifteen thousand missing students in the school systems that you all lead."

I saw folks swallow, look down, rub a cheek, and I wondered if I'd created an opening or triggered too many defenses.

"And here's how we can find them together: we'll figure out exactly what's causing these particular gaps in your particular schools." I pulled up a slide showing race and income differences in student knowledge about how Advanced Studies works, the benefits, and how to sign up, all under the header "Information Gaps."

"Whether it's differences in who knows what about your best academic programs, like with Jamie, or whether there are differences in encouragement for different students," I added, clicking to a slide headed "Encouragement Gap." It showed different race and income-group answers to the questions of whether they'd been encouraged to participate in A.S., and whether they felt that "students like me" are welcome in those classes.

"Or whether there are issues around academic preparation for Advanced Studies—real or perceived. We'll provide a holistic view of student readiness."

"This is my favorite part," said Dorothy's old boss from the side, his palms flat on the foldout table as I clicked forward.

On the mostly blank screen was a student named Taualai Tumiavave—a photo, GPA, and test score he said he wanted us to share to help tell his story. I said, "Taualai started out in a school where they judged him by how he looked, and maybe a couple numbers they had in his file. And as he tells it, he used to walk around with his hood up in ninety-six-degree weather, just to create a barrier between himself and a school where folks didn't see his potential."

Next, the slide filled in with lots of other information—bar charts, stars, comments—the contours of the information from our surveys bringing Taualai's story to life in a way that made the folks in the room ooh and aah.

"When his family moved, he transferred into a school that came to know Taualai much more fully and to believe he could do amazing things. They found out that he was really interested in chemistry, politics, and more, that he had a growth mindset, that no one had ever talked to him about A.S. but that he trusted Ms. Smith for advice. So Ms. Smith used that information, sat down with him, and got him into A.S. chemistry. In Taualai's words, he came out of his shell. And he ended up becoming class president, and is now in college, with his younger brother fast behind."

"Wow, OK. This is really something."

"I gotta get a picture of this."

"So, what you're offering here is really a technology platform?"

"Are these 'Student Insights,' as you have it labeled there, available for every student?"

I smiled. I'd been having nervous fun before, but now this was just pure fun.

I talked about how educational change is "technically simple but socially complex," and that in addition to the technology, they would also have an amazing coach to help them figure out how to put strategies in place to fit their data and their context.

Then, finally, I pitched, like with the kids I'd recruited: Do you want to take on this challenge? We think you can do it. We'll help you. To get where you say you want to go, this is what you need to do next.

The room roiled with interest, energy, uncertainty. In my pitch, I told them they'd have to apply to get in, which made them—expert navigators of such applications—want it all the more. I knew that they'd already gotten dozens of emails from their staffs in just the past hour dealing with everything from lockdowns to threatened teacher strikes to executive sessions of the board to principal vacancies to the latest round of state-funding fiascoes threatening their ability to keep things going next month. So I told them they should decide now (before they had a chance to forget), and forward the application materials we'd emailed them to a point person on their team who could take responsibility for submitting the materials on time.

One of the superintendents said, "I'm looking at the info here on my phone, and it says 'match-funded technical assistance.' Is that what we're applying for?"

I swallowed, nodded. We'd prepared a couple scenarios for the ending, depending on how much folks wanted to know about the money.

"So, what does that mean, exactly?" he pushed. "The 'match-funded' part."

"Good question," I said, clicking forward to an optional final slide. It all came down to this.

The slide had four dollar signs on it in different boxes, along with our slew of partners' logos. I started in before they could. "So, *if* you're selected for this project, you would receive match funding from our foundation partners, who would cover half of the cost of EOS's technical assistance—"

"And *we* would be responsible for the other half?" they cut in.

"That's the eighteen thousand dollars there?"

"Eighteen thousand dollars *per school*?"

Heads swiveled away from the projector, eyes meeting knowing eyes. Pout-lipped exhales of *whooooo*. We were doing the first-date dance. They were like, *Wait, is he trying to get* me *to pay?*

"Yes," I said, hoping to show my confidence in the big impact those dollars would have if folks decided to spend them on Equal Opportunity Schools. "Eighteen thousand dollars per school supported by the foundations. We believe it is critical for you to also invest in this work, if it is truly a priority for you. And then we will be providing additional grant funding to support student and teacher success when you close your access gaps."

"So you're gonna pay us back? How much?"

"That depends somewhat on the final set of schools we accept into the program and how many missing students get served. But you may receive something like $200 of support for each found student."

"If we find a hundred missing students, we can get our $18,000 back, then?"

"I wouldn't quite think of it that way, but . . . yes. You see, you'd be investing in half the cost of the technical assistance. And then you would receive resources to support the additional students succeeding in advanced studies—books, beakers, teacher trainings, etc."

"Well, I'd have to think of it as payback, because my board has a freeze on new spending, and that'd be the only way to get this through—for the grant to be at least as big as the cost."

"We're all in," said Garrett from Briarwood. "I think it's so important for us all to find our missing students. This is the type of work we've all been saying we're about, and this is our opportunity to lead and ensure our kids from all backgrounds are being served really well."

"Great!" I replied.

I wanted to hear the objections that might be holding some of the other superintendents back, even if they felt reluctant to claim them as their own. So I asked: "What questions or objections might you hear from *others* in your districts if you brought this initiative back to them?"

"I know I would get questions about whether these kids could actually do Advanced Studies."

"Yes," I said, "that's kind of the heart of things, isn't it?"

"Uh-huh."

"And what ideas," I asked, turning the question back to the group, "do folks have about how you could address that with your teams? What would you say if they claim that these missing students can't cut it in Advanced Studies?"

This technique got a little look of betrayal from the person who'd asked the original question, like, *I asked you, dude, and now you're asking us? What the hell?*

Don spoke up. "I think I might say—and this is just a suggestion; it's of course different in every district—that we've been thinking they can't do it for a long time, but we'll never know unless we give them a chance at it. And that we'll be there to support those students and their teachers. But the way we've been doing it in the past hasn't been working for a lot of kids, and we need to try giving an equal chance at these college-level classes."

"I like that," said the woman who'd asked the question, taking notes.

"And," said another woman, "I think we could shift the question from whether or not the kids could do it to: What do we need in order to be successful as we grow and diversify Advanced Studies? In other words, how can I support you to be successful in this new context of equal opportunity?"

"Yes!" I said. "I love that! Not 'Is the *kid* good enough or not?' but 'How can I support *you* to be successful with a more diverse set of kids in Advanced Studies?' Sitting down as the leader and being clear that you'll support them—I've seen that be very effective."

I saw that we were approaching ten minutes over time and decided to wrap things up. "We'll be around here for a bit, so feel free to talk with us further, but we're going to end the all-group session, knowing that you all have very busy and demanding jobs. Thank you for your leadership—particularly for the historically underserved students who need us to stand up for their opportunities at the highest levels."

There was a light smattering of clapping as everyone got up, deciding where to go next.

—— CHAPTER TWENTY-NINE ——

Though I hadn't paid attention to this while I was in the room with them, odds are that thirty of the thirty-nine superintendents in attendance were men, and thirty-six of them were white. Like other executives, those who lead our school districts tend to be taller than average. And as a group, superintendents have a reputation for ego and big talk.

I shared a common perspective with many of them. And I fell for partnerships with some of the biggest talkers in the group.

They talked about diversity. They talked about leadership and about making changes that are hard to make because it's the right thing to do. They talked about building plans based on research, investing financial and political capital in the most important things, making real progress. They even talked about how people talked too much about this work instead of taking real action.

I'd been told by a mentor that I'd learn the most in some of the wealthier communities. She failed to mention it'd be the hard way.

One such superintendent out of the Northeast won my heart, so I was shocked when the team said that his district wasn't making any progress in actually enrolling missing students. Every time I'd call the superintendent to check in, there'd be a new reason. My team hadn't given them all the Student Insight cards soon enough. The process of enrollment and the various requirements for entering Advanced Studies classes were too opaque and wrapped up in board policy, and the superintendent couldn't figure out how to navigate them.

When, by the end of the year, they'd found about one in ten of their missing students, the superintendent blew up at his team and said, "Who's responsible here?!" It turned out the course enrollment forms were passed around to half a dozen different folks, any of whom could change a student out of a class, without anyone else being the wiser as to what had happened.

So I asked the EOS team to build a software system so we could track who had talked to whom, when, and with what result. Our new software proved useful in other districts, but in the second year, this superintendent abandoned the effort—"just temporarily," he assured me, "until the board election is over."

I was mad at what seemed to me the school's unwillingness to take responsibility for several hundred students missing from Advanced Studies. Most of the missing were Black students who wanted to go to college, weren't being challenged by their classes, said they didn't feel welcome in A.S., and had never been encouraged to participate.

After each of the partnerships, we'd write a reflective case study about what had happened and why. Even though I wasn't the partnership director on this project, I wanted to write the case study—try to understand what had happened.

What had happened was right out of Jim Crow, even though it was the Northeast in the 2010s—the same things I'd seen in South Carolina showing up with a Connecticut twist. The superintendent had previously pushed for a bit of integration in the middle schools, and after a big battle, he changed the middle school from having four separate tracks (which closely followed race and income strata) to three. For this level of change, he'd gotten two new board candidates who ran on campaigns to overturn this type of thing. And now he had two more candidates running against his efforts. If they won, the six-member board would have four people who wanted to—and therefore could—fire him.

More than this, the high school principal, a Black woman, was receiving death threats, and understandably decided she'd rather retire early than put her life on the line to see if she could get Black students into college-level classes. I couldn't believe it when the principal on the EOS staff told me about it. But she assured me it was true.

I talked to a close friend who was a superintendent in Washington State, and he told me about a contentious board meeting held to discuss their plans to include far more students of color in advanced programs. They'd said they loved the A.S. programs in their district, thought they were great—but that in order for those programs to continue, they would have to fully include students of all backgrounds. I wouldn't have believed him if I didn't know him well, but he said that after the meeting, he'd come out to discover (thankfully before leaving the parking lot) that his brake lines had been cut.

When I talked to Zendaya about this, she nodded: "Mm-hmm." When I told Natalie, she said, "No waaay." When I told Jamie—who'd recently moved back to the state and into a low-income apartment complex a couple of neighborhoods away—he said, "Fascinating—tell me more," and we read about how advanced high school programs had arisen around the time of desegregation, and that many families defended exclusive access to them in similar ways to how parents had broken off separate school districts to avoid integration.

I hoped one day I could tell my toddler, Oliver, about this as old history. One morning, I was with Oliver and Natalie at a local coffee shop; a big set of toy train tracks had been set up on a table between love seats and armchairs. Not noticing in the moment that everyone in the coffee shop was white, I watched each of the parents carefully teach their child how to share the tracks when another child wanted to pass. And I wondered, *How could those brake lines have gotten cut in a nice place like this?*

———

Though the fact is that New York is the most segregated state for Black students and California the most segregated state for Latino students, rumors persist that such things are worst in the South and in the middle of the country.

Superintendent Paul Hansen of the Darrentown, Kansas, School District hadn't said any great things at the big group meeting at Google. It took several follow-ups to get another meeting. And then, instead of meeting with me himself, he sent a few team members to have lunch with me at a mainstreet cafe where horse-drawn carriages would have fit right in.

The team was very kind and respectful, even though I was half their age. They discussed technical aspects of some of their recent initiatives and how those might fit with what I was proposing—if we waited another year to start.

I had been hoping for big statements about the importance of doing this work right away, but I tried to follow Zendaya's advice about believing the best of those we worked with. I said it was clear from their comments how much they cared about their students, and that I knew they wouldn't want any missing students to become permanently lost to education in an intervening year. They agreed, but returned to the logistical challenges. They were opening a new high school and said they lacked the capacity to tackle a new initiative like this. After I scrambled to modify our proposal to meet each specific point they raised, they reluctantly agreed to get started now.

Month by month, on the whiteboard in our office where we tracked progress, I saw Darrentown gaining steady ground. Fifty students found. A hundred students. A hundred and fifty students. Two hundred. Stories of the ways they pushed our work excited the team during our check-in meetings.

One of our analysts who'd been developing the student lists for Darrentown visited the schools there, and one of the more skeptical principals had asked him, "So you're telling me these kids on this list are ready for Advanced Studies, and we've been overlooking them?"

"I think possibly yes, ma'am."

At the principal's next pronouncement, our analyst began sweating.

"Well, given all that we've already done on these issues at our school, we'll just see about that," she said, picking up the phone. "Patrice, can you please send Roderick Marshall down to my office?"

The analyst told us later in our team meeting by the whiteboard: "I'd only ever looked at these students' names and survey responses and teacher recommendations and everything in a spreadsheet. I thought we were using the right information to identify missing kids, but I guess you never really know. And so I had no idea who was going to come through that door or what it would say about everything that I'd been doing with the data."

Roderick came in looking very serious, likely wondering what he'd done to get called in. Staring at the principal's desk instead of her face, lips tight in a frown, he said softly, "Ma'am? You wanted to see me?"

"Yes, Roderick, I do. Have a seat."

Our analyst scampered out of his chair to offer it to Roderick, then stood by the wall.

"How are you today, Roderick?"

"Fine, I guess. I hope . . ."

"You're not in any kind of trouble. You should know that off the bat."

He let out his held breath, nodded, and looked at the principal.

"Are you enjoying your classes, Roderick?"

"Yes, ma'am."

"You seem to have all As and Bs here. Are your classes hard for you?"

"No, ma'am. They're fine."

"What would you say to the possibility of an Advanced Studies class this fall?" the principal asked him.

"Honestly, I'd like that. You see, I want to get a degree in math or physics, maybe become a programmer."

The principal examined him.

"Maybe?" he said.

Her reverie broke, and she said, "That would be wonderful! Your science grades are excellent. And several of your teachers are recommending you for Advanced Studies, so—"

"Recommending me?" Roderick interjected, casting any remaining tension from the room with a huge smile. "For Advanced Studies? Who's recommending me?"

His hands were now up by his chin, gripping each other.

"Well, Mr. Carter, for one," the principal said, after looking at the sheet. "So, advanced physics with him for next year, then?"

"I'd appreciate that very much, ma'am—yes, I would."

"I'll see to it. Thank you for coming down, Roderick."

Our analyst returned to the chair without saying anything. His smile was as big as Roderick's had been, and soon the principal decided she could be happy about what'd happened too.

"Well, I'm smart enough to admit when right's right! Let's set up that plan you were talking about to meet with all the kids, assign them out to the staff who've volunteered, and get this thing going full steam ahead."

———

It didn't surprise me that the analysis our team produced was hitting the mark. Eventually, we'd survey millions of kids and tens of thousands of teachers. The data short-circuited abstract, roundabout conversations about what students *might* be able to do and made everything specific to the facts of what was happening with each kid and teacher in a school. We saved a lot of time that would've otherwise been lost to speculation (including the stereotyping and generalizations we all tend to rely on when we don't have enough information) and instead used direct insights that emerged from deep data.

But there would never be a perfect formula to predict whether a kid would succeed at a higher level. It will always be a combination of what the student brings to class, the skills and expectations of the educators, and the context created by the school. So we saw it as our role to help leaders develop an amazing context in which each student's incredible potential was drawn out and made manifest.

When the finding of missing students in Darrentown eventually stopped, with about one-third of the missing students remaining unfound, I asked the team to use our data to figure out why. They dug into the system we'd developed for tracking educator outreach and student course requests and saw that some of the adults who talked to kids had great results, while others could probably use more practice. At the extreme end, there was a counselor who had less than 10 percent of the missing students she met with sign up for advanced classes; and then there was someone who had more than 90 percent of her missing students sign up.

Even with this new information, though, our partnership director, Rachel, put the odds of closing the rest of the gap at one in four. The morning I saw that stat on the board, I focused the team meeting on Darrentown, trying to understand what was going on.

Rachel seemed exasperated. "I think," she sighed softly, then started tapping her heel, retying her bun, "I think they just feel like they're done. They've done a lot and made a lot of progress, and they're wrapping up the year. They're talking a lot about how they can support kids once they're in the classes, and ignoring what I say about continuing to meet with students."

I pushed for her to speak with the superintendent in person. "Come back with those kids accounted for, eh?"

She'd told me before that she thought it was a little weird how much I focused on the numbers—how everyone's numbers and confidence levels for their districts were on the wall, and that I got involved like this and pushed on folks.

She gave me one of those smiles that isn't really a smile and booked another ticket to Kansas.

———

When she got there and met one on one with superintendent Hansen, he said, "Rachel," scratching his goatee, "this is a lot of progress. And all in one year. It's pretty amazing. You just don't see these types of results in education—and you know that, as a longtime educator. I think you should be very happy with what we've accomplished here. What *you've* made possible for us to accomplish."

She gulped. "Sir? With all due respect, the progress is really, really great, but it's not the goal we set. It's not what we agreed to. There are ninety-four more students who—by your own criteria—belong in Advanced Studies. And you're the only one who can ensure that happens now. Can we do that?" A very successful education consultant up to this point, she worried how he'd respond.

Years later, Superintendent Hansen would join the Equal Opportunity Schools team and tell rooms full of other superintendents all over the country about that conversation, when Rachel had confronted him. He'd tell them he'd "felt about *this* big," holding out his thumb and forefinger an inch apart. "But then," he'd say—to a thousand school district leaders, as we asked them to join us in finding their missing students—"I realized she was right. We'd taken on the partnership with Equal Opportunity Schools to *close* our gap. Not to leave a hundred students out, patting ourselves on the back because we'd found a couple hundred others. Not to leave gap closing for another year. We get into education to change lives, and ultimately the responsibility was with me—as it is with each of you—to change those lives, and to act on the information we have. Equal Opportunity Schools gives you the data and the plan to actually, finally turn ideas about justice into reality in our schools. Now's the time to stop talking about it—to actually get it done, if you'll make the decision to join us."

I'd been so suspicious that he hadn't made big proclamations up front, that his team wanted to get into the details of the challenges of making something like this work. It turns out they were just a team of educators who were especially committed to learning—so much so that their leader had responded to feeling small not by puffing himself up but by owning a mistake and growing from it.

I really admired that, and wondered if I could ever be the type of educator who changes minds first by sharing openly how his own has changed.

—— CHAPTER THIRTY ——

That summer, Max graduated from college in South Carolina and came out to Seattle to intern at Equal Opportunity Schools. He didn't have much money, and said he wouldn't crowd my family by staying on our 650-square-foot houseboat, which was quickly filling up with our tabby, our Aussie, and Oliver.

Though I offered to help him find a summer sublet, Max said he was enjoying camping out in the back of his truck. He'd frequently hang out at the boat, and occasionally showered at our place or bathed in the lake.

We went across the street from the office for lunch one day, and while I waited for Max to put in his order, I thought about what I'd recently learned at a student conference in the Midwest.

One of the Black students there had talked about the funny look that the counselor gave him when he tried to sign up for advanced classes, how she'd asked him why he wanted to do that, whether he was sure, whether he was *really* ready. Another talked about his doubts that arose when he entered a class where no one looked like him. And another said that when he talked in class, he got funny looks from classmates, who seemed to doubt most everything he said. "And they want evidence, which is fine," he had told the assembled educators, "but it seems like it takes, like, four times as much evidence for people to agree with anything I say. So it's kinda like we have to work to overcome the doubts of counselors and teachers, our own doubts, and doubts from classmates—and all that's before you even get to the tough academic work."

They'd recounted the doll experiment replication that Allie Duncan had researched, and said that separate was still inherently unequal and that their school was both.

As I watched Max at the counter, I noticed that everybody in my line of sight was white. The folks waiting for their coffee, the folks making the coffee, the folks on the busy city sidewalk out one set of windows, the folks in the busy parking lot out the other side. All white like me, and like Max.

The social environment felt normal to me. I'd seen it every day. But I'd never paid much attention to it at home in Seattle. And then I didn't want to think about it when a friend of color visiting from out of town mentioned it. Defensively—and ironically, given the work that I'd chosen—I said I'd appreciate if he said some nice things about the place where I was born and raised.

Here I was, with one of my few students who was a white guy like me, who fit into the homogenous scene at this cafe. Perhaps I was missing several of my Black and Latino former students from my internship program because they didn't feel like they belonged here.

When Max sat down with his food, I smiled: we'd ordered the same thing.

As I chewed, he said, "That was cool, meeting your sister."

"Oh yeah," I said. It was the first time I'd seen her in more than fifteen years. I was so ashamed that our family hadn't kept her during those intervening years that I was scared to ask about that time in her life. We'd talked about the chili I was making, how it would've made my mom fart if she was there, about the houseboat, anything but those intervening fifteen years. I'd wanted to make her feel comfortable at my house, but she'd left pretty early.

"You said you wanted to ask me about some work stuff?" I asked.

"Just curious, you know. Nothing big, but that conversation we just had with the team got me thinking."

"Uh-huh," I said, unfoiling my burrito and taking a big bite.

"Y'all were talking about the things you could do as a team to get ahead of time on the calendar, to make the data even more clear, to respond better when you hit a bump. Building relationships, pushing but not being too pushy, all that stuff the team said: it's really impressive."

I smiled again, nodded.

"And Zendaya was talking about how you guys are perfecting your approach so that it can be strong enough to work at schools all over the country. But I guess my question is, like, why are there those cases where it doesn't work? I'm sitting here with this as my first, like, professional type of job, and I'm just blown away by all y'all got goin on. And sometimes I'm wondering how I got to be here, but that's beside the point—"

"Because you're awesome," I said instinctively.

He blushed. "But I guess what I'm saying is, even though I'm new to this kind of thing, it seems like what we're doing should work *all* the time. Why doesn't it work sometimes?"

I was obsessed with the places where this change was hardest. The superintendent we'd just been talking about—I'd followed him for several years, tried every avenue to getting a partnership, finally surrounded him with other districts and county leadership who were doing it, the prestige of Google. Even then, though, it seemed as if he just signed up to *appear* to be doing something about his nearly one thousand missing students.

"I don't know," I told Max, hungry, taking another big bite. "Wharrrr rr ooo tink?"

"I mean, is it just racism?" he asked. "Like with all the evidence you guys put together making it clear more kids can do it, but he just doesn't want to let them in."

"Look," I responded after wiping my mouth, "I was so pissed, honestly. We did all the things. And it all came down to that meeting we were talking about, and we showed the superintendent the hundreds of students who were missing. And I told him all about Miguel on the top of the stack of student cards, and would he take responsibility for him and the others. And I'm not a violent guy, but I just about wanted to leap across the table and punch this guy when he waved his hand dismissively over Miguel's face, saying he couldn't possibly be responsible for knowing anything about individual students. But that's not going to get Miguel or any of the other kids served. So I keep trying to understand where this guy's coming from. I think maybe he's in kind of a tough position? Because they have one of the wealthiest zip codes in the country in their district. And he answers to the school board, which is elected by a lot of these really involved wealthy-zip-code folks, right?"

As Max ate, beans fell from his burrito into the crinkly basket paper.

"And school's working for those folks. And they are electing the school board, for the most part. So the superintendent's gotta cater to them to keep his job, to be able to move forward any changes."

"So, then, the parents are racist?"

"I mean," I started, then stopped and held the side of my forehead. "We haven't really talked about people being racist in our work. They never even really talked about it at a big civil rights organization I spent a lot of time with when we were getting started."

"Why not?"

I set my burrito down. The coffee grinder in the shop was incredibly loud. It sounded as though we were sitting inside it. "Do you wanna go out of here? It's *so* loud."

"Yeah, sure."

We crossed back over the parking lot and street, then ascended the wooden stairs to the roof of our building, sat next to the top of an old tugboat, and squinted out at the marina. We'd both forgotten sunglasses.

Max hadn't forgotten what we were talking about, though: "You were saying you don't talk about people being racist in schools?"

"Well I saw some stuff in Beaufort—specific words and things—that would be considered classic racism. But honestly, Johnston and the community were way more open to increasing options for students of color than places like the west coast district we've been talking about. These districts have a lot of well-to-do folks mixed up about what a good education is and misguidedly keeping their own children away from Black and Latino kids. And the folks who represent those parents say things to us like 'The high quality of our A.S. programs is as much due to who's *in* the A.S. classes as to who's *not* in the A.S. classes.'"

"Wait, really?"

I thought of the analyst who'd looked queasy after telling me that story, saying, "I just can't believe the principal said that . . ."

"Yeah," I said. "And they say the most liberal congressional districts have the highest private school attendance rates and . . ." The sun sparkled every which way off the water below the deck—it was overwhelming. "Anyways, these gaps are in almost all schools. I say you change people's behavior, who they're teaching in these classes, and that'll change their minds. Maybe you don't need to lead with a word like 'racist,' which is so charged and doesn't especially open people up to change. It puts people in more of a defensive posture, which is not a great position for learning."

"Can you ever get to the real problem, then?" He knew he'd asked a big question, and took the opportunity to unfoil the next layer of his burrito and enjoy eating for a bit as I looked hungrily at what was left of mine.

"I mean, there's some people we can't get to. But I just found out that the Office of Civil Rights finally caught up with one of my earliest and most stubborn districts, which had hundreds of missing Black students, and finally made them change. And federal leaders we've worked with even released a memo to every district in the country saying that gaps in access to advanced courses aren't OK and that—without some strong, exculpatory explanation—those gaps are a violation of the Civil Rights Act of '64, and of

Brown v. Board of Education. But that's not how Equal Opportunity Schools works with people. We try to get them to actually learn and face this stuff in an open and nondefensive way.

"Like, take a counselor who's responsible for, like, a thousand students. And a student comes in, and the counselor doesn't have much time to dig in deep, but does know that everyone's been talking about the achievement gap lately and the lower average for Black kids. She has to make a quick call, so she assumes this Black kid has low achievement results—or even that he might not feel comfortable in the advanced classes because they're all white kids—and puts him into low-level classes. In those classes, the kid doesn't get challenging stuff that will boost his achievement much, and so you get this self-fulfilling prophecy."

"So the counselor's not a bad person, then?"

"We don't focus on that so much as on showing folks that their leadership can change kids' opportunities for the better."

"So there's lots of heroes and no one's to blame, then."

"People just don't do well with blame. Especially when something matters a lot, like education. How would you feel if someone came up to you and was like, 'Hey!'"—I pointed at him—"'You screwed things up for a bunch of children'?"

He grimaced. "I see what you're saying."

I leaned back in my chair and finished my burrito, looking out over the tugboats and the pleasure boats.

"But then, in that other district, you were saying that some adults came back and said only a few kids on their list of a hundred kids wanted to take A.S. And then, the same type of list, another adult would come back with 90 percent wanting to take A.S.?"

"Yep."

"So, isn't that first counselor who doesn't think hardly any of the kids can do it being racist?"

"We might say more so that they could use some new skills. Like, get the person who had 90 percent of kids excited about A.S. to share some of her techniques with the first one."

"OK, I see what you're doin' here. Everyone can learn and everything. Like you did with us as students. But what about someone like that math teacher we had—Ms. Rooney?"

Cheryl Rooney was an A.S. teacher at Battery Creek. I hated to think of her, and I never talked about what had happened to Jim and a few other students I'd put in her class. It was an advanced statistics course that didn't require as much math background as calculus, so it should have been perfect for kids who could use some challenging mathematical thinking but hadn't been given many previous experiences with it.

"What about her?" I asked, knowing, closing my eyes to the sun coming off the water.

"Like, you could say everyone can learn and be better, but she didn't want to learn or be better. And she kinda screwed kids over along the way."

Ms. Rooney and I had had a total breakdown over Jim's math project. He and some of the other Black students followed the instructions from the Advanced Studies program, which said that you could gather original data for your statistical analysis, *or* use an existing data set. Rooney said that because they had used an existing data set they were cheating and should be disqualified from the entire A.S. diploma.

Even after the principal sided with me, Rooney refused to grade Jim's project, telling me he was a cheater who didn't deserve an advanced diploma.

"So, do you think she's just innocent and can learn to be better?" Max asked. "She basically tried to disqualify a bunch of Black kids from Advanced Studies altogether, even when you were in charge of the program and said what the kids were doing was OK."

"I'm not saying innocent, no," I said, writhing inside, angry at Rooney but of course not thinking about my having failed Buddy. I remembered the desperation in some of the students' voices as they envisaged everything they'd worked for coming apart because their teacher was calling them a cheater. Not wanting to admit what I actually thought of Cheryl Rooney, I asked, "What do you think is going on with Jim these days, anyways? You haven't talked to him?"

I already knew he hadn't. We'd already talked about this a couple weeks ago. I was just hoping for a different answer, I guess. On the road, presenting to educators, I still talked about Jim and about how he'd said my getting him into Advanced Studies changed his life.

"Nope. He's kinda fallen off the grid."

I'd called and messaged and emailed him on and off for years, and received only a couple short responses, years ago now.

We watched a yellow-and-black tugboat pull a massive cargo hull through the channel. The tug's nose was up in the air as its stern bore deep into the cold water. The hull must've been eighty feet long, solid steel, loaded end to end with tons of broken rocks brought in from the Pacific.

For the tugboat to bear such a load, things had to go almost perfectly. The tensile strength of the rope, the reliability of the engines, a long, clear path in front of a load that would take quite a while to change course. All the drawbridges along the way had to receive advance radio calls to stop cars from crossing so that they could split up into the sky just in time to make way for the boat and barge below.

I'd sent Jim's math project to another school, where another Advanced Studies math teacher had agreed to grade it so that we could still submit it for his A.S. grade, and hopefully college credit.

I think the principal might have sent Ms. Rooney away to another school after I left.

But I think something snapped before any of that. The run-in over the math project, Jim's English teacher refusing to grade papers anonymously after several Black students felt they'd been graded unfairly, and the law enforcement involvement in typical teenage shenanigans at the College Fair— these all pulled Jim in a different direction than he wanted to go.

I couldn't stand it. I missed him awfully. Felt like a helpless hypocrite for building this work from the spark he'd created in my life, though we were now so disconnected.

──── **CHAPTER THIRTY-ONE** ────

I was fascinated by the type of person Max was asking about: an educator who was stuck in their viewpoint, an educator who might need special support to have a chance of noticing their mistakes so that they could begin to learn and grow again. I hadn't the slightest inkling that I'd become one.

I was driven by a mission to find all the missing students, but that mission was increasingly tangled up in the lessons I'd internalized from my own segregated education, the elitism taught at places like Harvard and Stanford, and the prejudices in the entrepreneurial, philanthropic, and educational leadership sectors.

In the second half of my decade leading Equal Opportunity Schools, I would work with governors and state school chiefs, do big media stories, launch a $100 million coalition effort to find 100,000 more missing students, and twice go to the White House to represent our work.

I would also descend into the only serious depression I'd ever experienced, break out in a full-body rash, and culminate my run as CEO with an infection that went septic.

At times along the way, exhausted and unable to fully wake up, raising kids with Natalie on our houseboat, I clung to the narrative from my schools and from the fellowships and funders who'd supported me that the work I was doing was heroic, and that I was the best one—the only one—to do it. That if I just pushed hard for a bit longer, I'd get there, like on a run up a mountain.

Thing is, we never paid much attention to our teammates on mountain runs growing up. Sure, we might meet up at the top or ride home together, but it's really between you and the mountain.

My only hope of saving myself (let alone all the missing students we wanted to serve) would be to find a way back to learning. Luckily for me—though not always for them, as I unwittingly made and ignored some significant mistakes—I'd surrounded myself with sixty incredibly talented and diverse educational leaders at Equal Opportunity Schools. And like I believed in missing students' incredible capacity to learn, and like Zendaya believed in educators' capacity to learn, the team generously, graciously, and patiently kept the faith in mine.

———

Our team invited me to a workshop they were putting on for a large group of school and district leaders in Georgetown County Public Schools. On the flight out, Zendaya joked, "You know we're not going to stay at that dirty-ass motel next to the strip club this time, right?"

"Oh come on," I said, blushing. "Those were our earliest days, before I even knew about how hotels work. I didn't know what I was booking, man!"

"Mm-hmm," she said.

I eventually conceded that mistake, because it was silly, but finding missing students in one of the largest school districts in the country is high stakes. So, when Zendaya started sharing just how the district was making progress, how they were experienced and savvy at this type of work, I asked a couple questions, then—in true difficult-learner fashion—eagerly moved on to trying to appear experienced and savvy myself.

I talked about how I'd met with leadership in Georgetown eight years prior, just after I left Battery Creek. "And they were all like, 'Well, yes, everyone wants to learn from us—we're presenting all around the country about all we're doing to get more kids into Advanced Studies.' They didn't want me to come help them, but they offered to help me by letting me visit one of their high schools."

"What'd you learn there?" asked Zendaya.

"Well, they gave me this color brochure about all these programs they had for Black students. And while we were meeting, I used the data on the brochure to figure out they were missing three hundred Black students from Advanced Studies. When I tried to bring it up politely to them, they basically showed me the door! Said they didn't have any more time to meet and teach me about their work."

"It does seem like too often education's become about trying to tell people how much you already know, not about being open to learning," Zendaya mused.

"Exactly!" I said. "It's backwards."

———

When I returned to Georgetown County eight years later with Zendaya—this time to share the results of the first phase of our partnership, to launch the extension of our program to all their schools, and to celebrate the recent commitment of their governor and their state commissioner of education to find all the missing students across the state—I was deeply invested in presenting myself and my company as having it all together.

I'd prove that I knew all about the important stuff, that I was an amazing educator who could teach *them* a thing or two. But not before Zendaya and the team had their turn to try to teach me and the others something.

At the start of the EOS-run early-morning workshop, there were maybe a hundred educators seated at separate tables in groups of six to eight. And in the middle of each was a tray of beads, segmented by color.

Facilitating the session, Zendaya held up a different bead as she read each line from a notecard. "The white bead is for when your answer to the question is: folks who are white."

That's me, I thought.

"The black bead is for Black folks." *Like Zendaya, and most of the EOS team here.* As she went through several race groups, everyone listened.

Then she began asking us questions. For each one, we were supposed to pick the bead that represented our answer from out of the bowl in the middle of the table, and put it into our small, clear plastic bag.

She asked about the race that we identified with, and we took a bead.

The race of most of our classmates in school.

The race of most of our teachers in school.

The race of most of our nuclear family. Our extended family.

The race of most of the characters on the TV shows we watched.

The race of most of our coworkers.

Those we'd dated.

Those we'd roomed with.

Those in our neighborhood.

Our best friend.

And on through our lives.

I tried to stealthily pick my beads so folks wouldn't notice the color.

The white beads were now running much lower than any of the others at our table.

I could hardly wait until this activity was over, when I was going to get up in front of the room to give a talk. Giving a talk, I knew what I was doing and could show why I deserved to be here, leading my diverse organization, leading this district in this type of work. But at the table, my bag filled with white beads, it might appear as though I still had much to learn, more types of people to know, more work to do to understand those from different backgrounds. So I kept my bag under the table.

Until Zendaya asked us to hold it up! "Right in front of your eye," she said. "Hold them up."

I hesitated. But even the grimacing folks at my table who had only white beads in their bags were holding them up. And so I brought mine up, half hidden in my hand, making sure not to cover any of the few colored beads that I had.

"There's nothing definitive about this," Zendaya said. "It's just one thing to keep in mind. A way to think about the lens through which you view the world, where you get your information. You see things through the lens of the experiences you have, the reference points you have in your history. How do you know about, say, Latinx students or Native students, when you're making decisions that affect them? I realized by doing this that I have more to learn from Native students and adults, to be informed about the issues and perspectives they're bringing, and to serve them better in my work. For some of us, these bags are pretty heterogeneous. For others, maybe more homogeneous. We all have our perspectives. And this is part of yours, and the ways that you see the world, based on the experiences you've had with the people you've been around . . . so far."

I kept Salvador Dalí's *Hallucinogenic Toreador* on my wall at Battery Creek and now at EOS to remind people of the different perspectives inherent in a single image, and the importance of seeking out perspective shifts if you want to more fully understand the world. But even though Zendaya was saying the right things to try to make this a moment when we could open up to learning—that this bag of beads didn't define us forever, that this exercise was one thing to consider, that we could change and evolve—as soon as I could, I pulled my bag down from my face, jammed it into my pocket, and readied myself to take the stage.

———

Screw these beads. I was going to show the group that the organization I'd put together was worth the million bucks this district was spending on Equal Opportunity Schools. That for all they'd done, I could still impress this room full of principals and teachers and counselors and district leaders with how much further my ideas could take them.

I told them that I'd talked with their team a decade ago when they were being recognized for doing cutting-edge work on Advanced Studies access, and that they'd done a ton of good work since. And that all of this made it even more incredible that during just one year with EOS, our four pilot schools had increased participation in Advanced Studies a further 32 percent, or a thousand students.

Thinking of all the faculty at Battery Creek who hadn't known how well the found students did on the advanced exams and never much shifted their perspective on what students could achieve, I said to the Georgetown folks, "I want to ask you a question. Given that we added so many kids to Advanced Studies—and this after all the progress the district had made adding kids previously—do you think that this larger, more diverse group of students passed more Advanced Studies exams than in previous years, was it about the same, or was there was a dip?" Passing an A.S. exam generally meant that a student had shown mastery of college-level course material in a given subject area while in high school. After some hesitancy to answer, they hazarded some guesses.

"Maybe about the same?"

"Maybe less, actually. Adding so many new students to the program, I imagine there were more struggles."

"I don't know—maybe I'll guess 10 percent more passing?"

I smiled and said, "Since last year, there's been a 26 percent increase in A.S. exams passed. That includes an increase in exam passing for every race and income group. And when you look at Black, Latino, and low-income students, they had a 30 percent increase in exams passed compared to last year."

After my talk, the audience was quiet. I'd given them an insight: proof that more kids could do advanced coursework than even they had thought—that their hard work and ours could make college attainable for far more kids. Then they clapped. And I clapped back at them. Their missing students could do great things, and I'd shown I knew it when they didn't. I could do great things too.

As I backed off the stage, I felt the beads in my pocket.

—— CHAPTER THIRTY-TWO ——

Although Zendaya said we could keep the beads, I emptied my little baggie back into the tray, telling myself that the team could use them again—that other people needed them way more than I did.

One of our earliest team members had told me that if I kept hiring so many high achievers they'd start to become a real headache, because they'd all want to have their say and they'd really push me. I'd told her I could handle that, and it'd make EOS stronger to have all that energy and capability driving our mission forward. And some days I handled it fine. But over time, some of these team members—dedicated, talented professional educators committed to adult learning and justice—continued bringing the strength of their professional educator skills to bear on *me*, bringing up more and more problems.

As they offered new perspectives—beyond what I could easily see through the angle of my past experience—I started to become confused, annoyed, tired. It seemed to me we were doing great things in schools across the country. We'd doubled the number of advanced high school programs in the country that fully reflected the diversity of their schools. To me, that sounded like a nice hero's story in which I belonged at the helm, making the world a better place, justifying the extra bedroom I'd had growing up, the access I'd been given to senators and governors and the White House. It was a cognitive frame that—as Dolliver taught—can be especially stubborn when what we're framing is a positive image of ourselves. Other things, beyond my beads, didn't seem to fit.

A group formed within Equal Opportunity Schools calling themselves the Racial Equity Team. They said, "If we're going to help schools deal with issues of race, then we should deal with issues of race at EOS too." And I thought, *What issues of race at EOS? We're all good people, here to do the right thing (especially me).*

I nodded big when some of the most experienced educators on our team told me, "These younger folks criticizing EOS have no idea how good they have it here. Wait'll they try working most anywhere else, and then they'll see."

But some of the younger staff kept meeting and talking about issues and organizing book clubs that read books like *Things That Make White People Uncomfortable.* When we had an all-staff training where we read "White Privilege: Unpacking the Invisible Knapsack," I thought, *Pshaw. I think I first read that in fifth grade. And I'm gonna tell everyone that when it's my turn to share. And how the one on the list that always stuck out to me was that "flesh-colored" band-aids match my skin, but not people with darker skin. Then maybe they'll understand that I got this stuff a long time ago and will stop tryna make me learn. Focus on the people who really need it!*

Then there was a book called *How to Slowly Kill Yourself and Others in America,* which made me wince when I started reading it. After I'd missed a few book club meetings, I heard from people there that the meetings now started with a spoken recognition of how we were occupying land stolen from the Duwamish Tribe of Native Americans who'd lived in the Seattle region before the white settlers. Some people complained to me: *I mean, once, maybe twice to say this, I can see. But* every *time? Like, are we just going to dwell on bad stuff?* I shrugged and walked off to my next meeting. The Racial Equity Team wasn't my group.

But then they said they wanted to be someone's group, and Zendaya—who I'd recently promoted to chief operating officer—said she'd do it.

I tried to go to the meetings when I could, but that was happening less and less often. A big part of privilege is the privilege to ignore, to not take the time needed to learn and understand in areas where you don't feel strong. You can simply choose not to focus on things that don't fit well in your frame. But some of the team kept bringing up issues I didn't want to dwell on, in new ways.

Black Lives Matter was picking up steam when we hired a Black person as a senior leader in the organization. He and I pushed back on the proposal to get the word "all" out of our mission. We thought it was good to say that students of all backgrounds should have equal access. And since unequal access is a problem for some groups more than others, we also said, in the mission, "particularly low-income students and students of color."

The new senior leader said that when you lead a district you have to take responsibility for all students and that MLK had talked a lot about the movement for justice as a shared and inclusive movement that affects everyone. And some folks said the leader wasn't woke enough, and I didn't know what to do, and he ended up leaving.

Then some team members said if we were serious about students of color, we should put them before "low-income students" in the order of wording in our mission.

Some said we should de-center whiteness, which I hadn't heard about before. It sounded like an accusation that I was self-centered or something.

Folks put together an activity for our all-staff retreat in which we reviewed our hiring process to try to remove bias and promote diversity, which seemed useful. EOS was about 35 percent Black in a city that was 7 percent Black. We weren't attracting a lot of Latino applicants, and I was hopeful we could fix that; the suggestions put forward in that collaborative session improved our hiring process. I thought that had gone well, maybe because it was a specific problem showing up in the data followed by specific fixes we could act on.

The next activity was much broader. We were to divide into two "caucuses"—one for white folks and the other for people of color—so that there could be more open conversation about what each group was experiencing. I noticed that there were several folks in my group who really stumbled when they were talking about race, especially the guys who did the computer programming and the work on our data.

They'd say things like, "I ... um ... never really thought about race stuff," while the guy sitting next to them had that wide-eyed, blank expression you get when you're praying no one calls on you.

And we weren't sure if the guy was done talking, or who was next, and after a minute, he'd continue: "Yeah ... so ..."

I can't remember what I said, but I do remember that there were a couple of people who seemed to be looking at me the same way I looked at the computer programmers, which I didn't appreciate. And I got the sense we all wanted to know what was going on in the group with the people of color.

Someone said, "This feels off. I think I maybe miss our colleagues?"

I regularly found myself in groups of all-white friends and usually felt at ease. Did it seem strange now because we were paying attention to it?

We heard raucous laughter, while we waited, quiet and stilted. And when the rest of the team came back to join us, they kept talking with one another, laughing and smiling, saying, "Oh, I needed that!" They looked at one another knowingly, wiped their eyes.

The white folks started breathing normally and smiling again, all apparently grateful the activity was over. Then some of the folks of color said we should definitely do more racial caucusing again soon, how nice it was.

I wanted to take team concerns seriously even if I didn't fully understand them. So I tried to lead a conversation with the senior team—most of whom were Black—about defining what we meant by racial justice, and what we wanted to do about it at EOS. I told them my goal was to get it down in a few sentences we could all agree on. None of my sentences worked, and they didn't offer others. I couldn't figure it out. Was it that such things shouldn't be reduced down? Should I not be the one doing the reducing? Or had something totally different made that conversation incredibly awkward? In any case, we all left the endeavor for a simple answer behind when that meeting ended.

I tried to listen and learn, but sometimes found myself feeling impatience, thinking: *We're supposed to be serving kids and solving injustices that're happening in schools, but that work's coming up less and less in the team meetings.* Instead, things were coming up like "Shouldn't everyone be putting their gender pronouns in their email signature line?" Other people would say that a lot of our districts wouldn't appreciate seeing that info in our emails. And: "We need to get districts to hire us in order to find missing students, which is our mission. A lot of the missing students are in conservative districts. We can't take on every issue, but we can help them find their missing students, and shouldn't we focus on that?"

And I thought, *Yessss!*

Then someone would say, "Do we even want to work with districts that don't get it? If they're not into anti-racism, should we work with them?"

I thought, *Of* course *we should! Our job is to help them see new possibilities for the kids they've been missing. That's our whole thing: to help them change their minds about that. Draw on the best of what's in them as educators to help them find specific ways to do better. Not to just work with people who see things like we do to begin with. Otherwise, why would they even need us?* And I decided to say that, but when I did, I got a couple of stink eyes in return.

Increasingly, I'd go home and have a horrible headache, not sleeping well and thinking about this stuff, then getting woken up by a baby crying in the middle of the night.

After the migraine cleared, I'd try to come back to what I thought was the main thing: What would work to find missing kids and get them the education they deserved?

And then more issues would come up. The complexity confused me, and things started to blur.

The building didn't have a gender-neutral bathroom. Would we take out some of our working space to build one?

Should we partner with districts that didn't have strong Advanced Studies results, or should we refer those to another nonprofit that specialized in strengthening A.S. programs first? I thought making sure the programs were strong before folks worked with us was important, so that we weren't just shuffling kids around between classes with lower academic standards. But then someone said that a lot of the schools with weaker A.S. results had more Black and brown kids, and it'd be wrong to exclude those schools.

A couple people got mad that I was including white kids who weren't poor in the reports on the numbers of students we'd added to A.S. They asked, "Doesn't that fly in the face of our mission?" I wondered, *Leading Equal Opportunity Schools as a white guy who wasn't poor, do I?*

I thought, *If a funder supported our mission, which focuses on Black, Latino, and low-income students, and also thought it was good that other kids were added to Advanced Studies too, wasn't that a fine thing for us to talk about?*

Was I a fine person to talk about these things? In one of our feedback surveys, a staff member said my strength was talking to white male superintendents. And I thought: *Come on! Are you saying I can work well only with people who're like me? That I want to be in an all-white caucus? Because I don't!*

Some folks wanted to make sure we didn't help schools recruit any students of my race and class to Advanced Studies, saying, "We should purge our recruitment lists of those students. And if schools are focused on recruiting a lot of them, we should walk away!"

As we grew, I gave up my office so that anyone could use the room for meetings. One of my board members suggested a name for the room to make clear that I had some priority when I needed to host donors or board members. So we called it the Reiding Room, and let anyone sign up to use it when I wasn't meeting in there.

And then someone said, "We really should change the names of the rooms to the names of womxn of color, don't you think?"

I took two ibuprofen.

I met the husband of one of Natalie's friends, who didn't realize where I worked. He was a school counselor and told me about this "crazy" project his school was doing with Equal Opportunity Schools to try to get more students into advanced classes. I listened and encouraged him to share his thoughts. He scoffed at a Black girl who'd complained to him that her A.S.

teacher was picking on her. He said if a student couldn't figure that kind of thing out, they didn't belong in advanced classes. He said he and his colleagues couldn't talk openly about where the kids really belonged, but that "every day we're fighting it."

I thought, *With some external folks every day fighting what we were trying to do, how could we afford to waste time fighting internally?*

I was trying to put together an event with the White House cabinet secretary to recognize the work we and our partner schools were doing toward the president's My Brother's Keeper goals. When I shared with Zendaya that the secretary had confirmed and then asked if she was surprised or impressed, she said, "Not really. Things always seem to work out for you!"

And I thought, *What's that supposed to mean?* What were folks after? Were they thinking I hadn't earned my position through hard work, that maybe they needed someone better—someone who understood something I didn't?

I had a cup of coffee and a hot water—anything to open up those vessels in my brain. I made it through four more meetings at the office. I had an hour of work time before my last two meetings, which were going to be individual check-ins with our head of finance, and then our head of sales.

I stepped out behind the building and stood under the awning, watching a tired little boat splash through waves on its way up the canal. The cold air felt nice. I stepped out into the light rain. That felt nice too. As the minutes passed, I started to get wet and eventually realized I should go back inside. But it was too hot in there. I wanted to let the rain soak through, maybe even jump into the river.

So I started walking slowly along the bank, barely moving the heel of one foot up to the toes of the other. I held on to the railing as I crossed the bridge back toward my houseboat, rain from above, river below. I turned down a wet metal staircase, through whose slats the droplets fell to the dirty gravel below.

When I made it to ground level, I stood in the gravel by the hundred-year-old cement foundation of the bridge, realizing I wouldn't be making it back up the steps that day. I sent an email from my wet phone to my two colleagues, letting them know I was sorry but that I wouldn't be able to meet today because I had a bad headache.

On the floor of the houseboat, I watched the oven glow around a frozen pizza for a while, then gave up, turned the oven off, drank some water, and brought the refilled glass up the ladder to bed. I closed all the curtains—not because I had the energy to, but because I felt I absolutely needed to. But even then, it was too bright on this overcast day.

Lying down didn't feel as much like death as sitting or standing, but I couldn't stay lying down because I was sweating heavily. I sat up to take off most of my clothes, then lay down again, feeling fully like death from the effort. Putting my head under the pillow felt a little less like death. And then I passed out.

———

As things got hazier and my energy lagged a bit, I narrowed my focus. My personal development, or that of anyone else on the team, seemed beside the point. I thought it needed to be all about finding more and more missing students as quickly as possible.

Bob was last on the agenda for the staff retreat one spring day, following a bunch of exercises discussing possible microaggressions within EOS, how people felt about how we should define race groupings, and more.

This was the time of year when we'd either get each kid enrolled in Advanced Studies for next year or we wouldn't. And we took each of those thousands of kids and their enrollment seriously. With that, plus all these internal conversations about charged racial topics, I think we were all a little raw. And most of us, myself included, had no idea what Bob was about to say.

Bob was our database administrator. He loved dogs, and even trained them for show competition. He had a great smile and not much hair left. Like some of the best people in technology, he took great pleasure in providing practical solutions to complex problems, figuring out what didn't make sense and fixing it up.

He stood in front of his bench seat, hands in his jeans pockets, wearing a large blue-striped synthetic polo.

"So, they asked me to talk about my small role in the Grant High School partnership. I think it's great that you let someone like me go out into the schools and see how our work really happens. It's a lot of fun to build the code behind the model, but to get to see what things look like in practice has added so much learning for me, and I appreciate the opportunity to share that with you."

He took his hands out of his pockets and massaged the webs between his thumbs and forefingers. His open attitude was infectious, and the fifty other staff members, of varied ages and backgrounds, all seemed interested.

"So here I am, a middle-aged, balding, white programmer guy with a stack of these Student Insight cards we make, getting ready to meet with actual missing kids. And I was sorting through the cards, figuring out who I wanted to talk with first, and I got to LaShandra's card and I put it in the 'no' pile. But right after I set it down, I stopped, and I picked it back up to reread it. And I thought, 'Who am *I* to look at her and decide she shouldn't have this opportunity to get ready for college?'"

I heard some snapping fingers around the room.

I shifted on the bench seat cushion, hoping he wouldn't say something off key. He was one of the tech guys who generally seemed to stumble when it came to talking about things involving race.

"Now, LaShandra's career interest was listed as 'fashion consultant.' And, well, you can see here"—he pointed to his striped belly—"I clearly have no *clue* what a fashion consultant is."

Everyone laughed, breaking the building tension of this guy about to cross professional, racial, and age lines to talk with this girl.

"So I decided I shouldn't prejudge whether college was a good idea for LaShandra before talking with her about it. She hadn't marked college in her plans, but she let us know on the survey that no one had really ever talked with her about college or college-level classes before, so I decided I would."

"Get 'em, Bob!" someone shouted, and I felt as if I were back in class in Beaufort.

"Ha-ha," he chuckled, his cheeks getting rosier, his sagged shoulders popping up a little bit with the laughs.

The room was popping a bit too now.

"When LaShandra came in, I told her I obviously knew nothing about fashion consulting, and asked if she would talk about her ideas and goals. And she opened right up, saying no one at school had ever asked her about it before. Apparently there's a lot of design aspects, marketing, illustration. And I told her about the design parts of my college program in computer science, and she got really excited and told me the reason she hadn't marked down college was that no one had ever told her it might be an option for her."

Bob gulped, then appeared to choke for a second on his emotions.

"I told her I'd do some research and see if there are programs out there that might make sense for her and that I could follow up with her about it. And she was happy about that."

He went on—beaming—to tell us about finding a great local community college program for her, about how excited she was, about how they found the perfect advanced course to help get her ready for that college program. The moral of the story, for him, was that we shouldn't prejudge people's capabilities and needed instead to focus on giving them a chance to show all

they're capable of. He said he'd take that lesson back to his work programming the database and the tools like the Student Insight cards, which we
used to identify tens of thousands of missing students a year.

I thought about all the technology companies who'd given us grants but
were having a hell of a time trying to do in their own workplaces what Bob
had figured out in a day at one of our schools.

Folks in the room seemed ecstatic, and I thought about why. Here's this
dude who wasn't especially tuned in to racial justice, didn't have the names
of the latest concepts on the tip of his tongue, but he was confronting his own
doubts about LaShandra, changing his mind, and creating opportunities.

Now, I like the idea of people opening their minds and seeing greater
possibilities in others—especially across lines of race and age and privilege—but as I watched the smiles and heard the applause for Bob, I felt tired,
even angry.

This local school district had a huge budget—about $20,000 for every
student. And despite all their employees and programs, they had students
who weren't getting basic guidance on decisions with the biggest possible
implications! No one had talked to LaShandra about her goals, even as she
headed into her senior year. Clearly Bob had had fun solving LaShandra's
problem and matching her up with better opportunities, but there was a
billion-dollar professional system of schooling that was supposed to have already done that. To me, the fact that someone with no background or training in education could make this type of difference in LaShandra's life was
an indictment of the failures afoot in our city.

And if we couldn't get schools in our own backyard to fix these things, I thought,
what could work in thousands of other cities possibly come to? It was unacceptable that LaShandra hadn't been matched up with appropriate coursework
and guidance before Bob came along. And in fact, EOS had been in the district the year prior—we hadn't yet succeeded in building the system that
LaShandra and her peers deserved.

Why was everyone smiling? This was like when the missing students at
Battery Creek had been successful. That was great for them, but in a bigger
way it was horrible: it confirmed that students really are missing out on an
education they're ready for. That hundreds before Jim and before Joaquin
had been lost. Solving the problem so easily meant we were generally allowing easily solvable problems to persist and take our kids down. This was
more evidence of a systemic failure of tragic proportions to get opportunities to kids.

Equal Opportunity Schools had to get going, get growing much faster, because finding LaShandra so easily meant we had much more to do to ensure that students' efforts—all the time they put in at school every day—weren't in vain.

We can't afford to waste any more time trying to make our team culture perfect, or perfect these conversations about race inside EOS. When we do that, we're talking about the experiences of dozens of adults. This is supposed to be about the experiences of the two-thirds of a million kids who go missing each year.

I rushed out of the room to my computer, where I pounded away for a while, writing words that I hoped would get us $12 million to rapidly expand our reach.

———

There was something really holding me back, though. Trying to get out of the house for work in the mornings became so hard.

I'd wake to fuzz behind my forehead. When the new day's light and the sounds of the neighborhood's many vehicles made themselves known to me, I'd feel annoyed—the sun a giant overhead fluorescent fixture, buzzing interminably, and the engine sounds so close I'd feel I was about to get hit.

Dis-ease.

In bed until the last possible second, having an awake-dream of continued sleep.

One at a time—and then too many all at once—I'd start to remember the things that I needed to do with my day.

Lots of growing children and animals, and not a lot of space. I'd have to interact with all of them, helping them to complete the tasks that I'd barely been able to complete for myself—feeding, watering, making and disposing of waste, cleaning, dressing—mouth by mouth, cup by cup, limb by limb, over and over again and again in the mornings.

I'd barely get out of the houseboat in time to make my way over to the many other things I was responsible for doing at Equal Opportunity Schools.

Why the fuzz?

A kiddo woke us up in the night again. And there was a lot of work as our organization kept growing. But something else, accreting daily, was getting big enough to crush me.

Was it the weight of these people at work pushing, pushing, pushing? I can understand the children and the dog and the cat, but what's with these professionals who want to make everything into an issue? So many needs

that they want me to address. They're talented folks who have good jobs doing good work, making things better for kids. Isn't that enough? Must they
always be talking about learning more and digging deeper into our organization and the leadership, and race and all this stressful stuff? Can't I just
do my work and find missing kids—and perhaps a little peace along the way?

— CHAPTER THIRTY-THREE —

Students are often the best teachers. Thankfully, while I was stalled in my own learning journey, my former student Sandee reached out to ask about an internship at EOS. She told me she was still into the activism that'd begun for her and some of her peers with our "significant positive change" projects many years ago. She said she wanted to make a difference in the world, to change things, and that after college she was trying to find her way and thought maybe she could learn from us.

Near the end of her internship, she came over with some more of my former students, who were in town for a visit. We were going to hang out and have a barbecue on the roof of the houseboat. She'd just cut her hair to emulate our office manager with a shoulder-length bob.

It was Sandee, Allie, Traci, and another one of my former students, Georgia, as well as me, Natalie, and Jamie—who was now working with underserved students at a local community college, and was becoming a master educator, adept at guiding people beyond blockers to new insights. The boys were taking their naps downstairs, and the sun lit up the trees around us, which were filled with the past winter's rains. Planters I'd put in on the roof were sprouting things swaying in the light breeze; rosemary, mint, basil, and lavender attracted the bees, while the banana peppers stood stoic and scentless by themselves, building up their heat inside.

Like everyone else, my legs dangled beyond the roof, over the lake twenty feet below, as I reclined on my elbows. "Isn't this amazing?"

"This is SO amazing," said Sandee. "I just love it."

"Are you being sarcastic?" I asked lazily, eyes closed to the sun.

"No, totally. Totally, totally, totally amazing," she said. "Really, completely, totally. Am I right, ladies?" she asked, looking to her left and squinting in the roof's glare.

"I love it here," said Traci. "I've never seen anything like it." The others nodded. Wearing their South Carolina sunglasses, they looked out over the water and the boats and the lake to Mount Rainier's iced peak, which graced the horizon next to the downtown skyscrapers.

"If you love it now, just wait till we get our jump on!" I said.

"Saaris, you crazy. I'm not jumpin' into that cold, wet mess," said Allie.

"Me neither," said Sandee quickly.

"I might be up for trying it later," said Traci. "Is there a way to get in without jumping from all the way up here? There's gotta be, right?" She looked down past all our feet for a ladder.

"Yeah," said Georgia in that lazy voice you get sunbathing.

"We don't have one," I said. "But our neighbor lets us use theirs, over there." I pointed, feeling proud of my hometown and our incredible summers, as well as the 650-square-foot boat Natalie, Oliver, Oscar, and I called home.

It was quiet for a bit, then Sandee said, "So, Saaris!"

"Yes?"

"Mis-ter Sah-ris," she said, stretching things out awkwardly. "What. It. Is?"

"What it is? S'all good over here. What it is with you, Ms. Liu?"

"Just tryna figure out my life is all. My whole. Entire. Life. Now that my internship with Equal Opportunity Schools is ending."

"Yeah? What're you thinkin'?" I asked, realizing I hadn't thought to wonder about her next steps.

"Are you going to stay in Seattle?" asked Natalie. "Are you looking for a job?"

"Yes, I definitely want to stay in Seattle, but the whole job thing: it's, umm, not so easy to get a job around here these days."

"Yeah," said Natalie. "It took me forever to find mine, and I was getting so discouraged being on the job market for, like, six months."

"Six months? Oh shit. I couldn't last here six weeks with my bills. Ain't cheap here," said Sandee. Looking over at me, she said, "We can't all own a nice houseboat like this."

I responded immediately. "Well, technically, the bank owns it. And we got into this during the recession for not very much at all. And since it's only 650 square feet, we were able to afford it—as long as we were up for the small-house thing, that is. We really lucked out."

"Yes," said Sandee. "Lucky, lucky. You, Mr. Saaris, are very *lucky.*"

Traci and Georgia looked at Sandee, wide-eyed.

"Well," I said, looking down the line at the young folks I'd taught, "sometimes, yes."

"I think it's great that you were able to get it," said Traci, tipping her head back. "It's *so* nice here." She looked up at the blue, blue sky.

Sandee seemed to be studying her toes high above the ten thousand shattered crystal glasses of the undulating lake water that refracted light every which way, whipped up gently by boats passing a couple hundred yards off the marina's alcove.

Minutes passed quietly, the only sounds coming up from little waves rhythmically undulating into the houseboat below our dozens of toes. Things were calm enough that I felt pretty good, though tired.

Then Sandee asked, "Do you really think you're that *lucky*, Saaris?"

". . ."

"Like, this *lucky*?" she opened up her arms and gestured at everything in front of us, underneath us, at the immense, majestic architecture of the Aurora Bridge overhead, whose beams seemed to scaffold the heavens.

We all took sips from our beer bottles, which were sweating in the roof's radiant heat.

"I mean," I said, remembering an activity the team had put together recently about different advantages that people in the room might have, during which I was startled to see how many I had, "I know I have advantages."

Though I usually recognized advantages when it came to looking at others, the idea that the inequities I worked on were relevant in my personal life was an entirely different matter— something I seemed chronically quick to forget.

"Like what?" Sandee asked, apparently unaware of—or uninterested in— my discomfort as I shifted on the roof's edge, lifting glowing red sheaths from my sun-tired eyes, trying to dilate back into focus.

"Well," I said, putting an arm around Jamie, "this guy called me out on how we were able to get this house, when he wouldn't have been able to, which is an advantage I didn't earn and that he doesn't get." I swallowed, and Jamie put his arm around me too. I went on: "Which sucks. It really sucks. I mean, Natalie's parents worked their butts off—her grandma cleaning rich people's houses, and her mom watching other people's kids. And

Natalie works her butt off, so why shouldn't she be able to get ahead without having to marry a schmuck like me?"

"Right—that's definitely the reason I married you, Mr. Nonprofit!"

I think we all felt on display in front of my former students, and it was becoming cutesy awkward, so Jamie and I disentangled our arms.

"But," I said, "my parents weren't that well off or anything. They were stingy, didn't really spend money on anything. I mean, my mom kept her car for forty years, and they—"

Sandee cut in. "Yeah, OK, Saaris, so your white, middle-class upbringing in this place, whatever this crazy place is, where the sun shines brighter and the skies are bluer and there's clean-ass water *everywhere*—like, look at all this water! She waved wildly around at all the stuff we were enjoying, and her voice rose. "And you had good schools. It's all because your parents were cheap?"

"No, I'm not saying that. And my school *was* the worst in our town."

"Well, it sounded like you were saying it's because your parents were cheap."

Allie nodded from the seat farthest from me, while Georgia and Traci looked on. Natalie nodded.

Jamie clapped me on the back, then said, "Look, it's true. I couldn't have gotten this house or made this rooftop barbecue happen in all its glory. Because my mom was raising me and four other kids by cleaning mansions. And even though she's doing better now, there's not enough money to go around to help make a down payment on a house for me and my siblings. Of course it's not just because your parents are cheap. You probably didn't mean it like that. It's because the systems we have in this country advantage the status quo and keep a lot of things the way they are for folks who're well off. And while a bunch of my money disappears to rent each month—even though I'm in low-income housing, which is really the only way I could afford to live in Seattle—yours goes to . . . well, the bank, like you say, but you know that you're going to get more out of this than you pay. And that's how things work. Those who're doing well financially usually get to keep doing better and better. And some folks have obstacle after obstacle placed in front of them."

"That's what I'm talkin' about! I love this guy!" said Sandee, reaching around me to high-five Jamie.

"I know that!" I said. "I mean, you guys honestly think I don't know this or something?"

"No," Jamie said, "you know it. We talk about this stuff. And you're trying to dismantle some of these cycles in your work, which is awesome. It really is." He made a point of putting his hand on my shoulder and looking me in the eyes, nodding so I could see that he saw that I knew. "And the work we do to help other people with this sort of stuff is sometimes easier than dealing with it ourselves, right?"

"OK, brotherly love fest over here—come on now," said Sandee, and I looked reluctantly away from Jamie and over to her. "I know that you understand it. But do you *understand* it?"

I tried to hide my sigh. What did she want me to say on this day, when I just wanted to get my barbecue on with friends?

"I mean, I used to teach you guys about this stuff in class! And I built a whole organization working on this stuff. What do you mean, do I *understand* it?" I said mockingly.

Then I caught myself. "Sorry. I'm interested in this. I just I didn't expect to be talking about it now. But I do want to talk about it, because it sounds like you've been thinking about it, and it's tough stuff. And I imagine it's tough to bring up with your old teacher."

"And my boss."

"Well, not technically your boss—"

"Oh, my boss's boss—that's much better, right?" she said, tipping her head and looking at me askance. "You keep dodging things. Like, does the bank own your boat or do you?"

"OK, OK. You're right," I said, breathing in and puffing my cheeks, attempting to fill my mouth with something besides words so that I could listen.

No one was reclining back on their hands or elbows anymore. We were all sitting in a line on the roof's edge, looking straight ahead.

"I guess what I'm trying to ask," said Sandee, looking at her three friends from Battery Creek for a moment and then swiveling back to me, "is how come you didn't acknowledge all your advantages to me, or to us, before?"

"Acknowledge them? They're pretty obvious, aren't they?"

"I think so. Seems obvious to me," she said, trying to make a ponytail but, feeling that there wasn't enough hair left after her cut, letting it all fall, then tucked some of it behind her ears. "But that doesn't mean it was obvious that *you* knew that. You were always going off about we can do anything and, *Oh, just go change the world and get a great education*, even if we were in a *really* shitty school. You may've been able to go off and do all this stuff and get into all these schools—like *Harvard University*, for God's sake—and build your own company, but our situation was different."

I looked at her for a moment. I wanted to say, *Are you kidding me? Are you saying you didn't* want *me to talk about new possibilities and all that you could do?* But instead, I looked at her a few seconds more and gave it some thought.

"You're asking if I should've talked more about *my* advantages?"

"Exactly."

"I suppose that could've been helpful. I won't give up on the idea that you all can do—and are doing—amazing things: folks from Battery Creek learning new languages, seeing the world, doing ecology, business, nonprofit work, graduate degrees, teaching. I heard earlier this year from one of my students doing his PhD in psychology about how hard it is to know your own mind and cut through our defenses against change; and from another, who felt like what we did together enabled them to embrace their identity for the first time, despite some of the prejudice and things that'd been holding them back. I believed—still believe—in you guys. Big time. And we did talk about the obstacles and the barriers and all that too."

"We talked about it in general—like for other people, mostly," said Sandee. "But the disadvantages for us were real. And the flip side was all the advantages you had but didn't talk about. Things came easier for you. And if you knew that—or talked about it, or whatever—you just wouldn't have seemed so . . . naive, I guess," said Sandee, while a couple of the others winced. "Then I think people could've learned even more from you," she added, scratching her forehead under her new bangs.

For a moment, the only word I could hear was "naive," and I felt angry and wanted to leave. My face went neutral, as when you don't want to show what's going on beneath the surface. I held that expression, waiting for the magma and shifting plates below to calm a bit until I could muster something nicer.

I could see that Jamie and Natalie wanted to help me out but didn't quite know how.

Then I remembered one of the other things from an EOS workshop—the contradictory idea of "being comfortable with the discomfort"—and I just sat there for a minute.

"I didn't think you were naive, Mr. Saaris."

"You didn't seem naive to me. Or if you were, it was a good kind of naive, to be able to talk about all we could do and focus us on our talents without so many limits."

"How about you, Allie?" I asked, leaning out over the water to see her, wanting to know.

"You bet," she said.

"You bet I was naive?" I asked.

"To be fair, how could you *not* be naive? You came from far off. Different race from most of us. Different class. Different education." Allie looked right at me for the first time in a while.

"I appreciate your saying that," I said, feeling immense relief. "That's true. I do believe that across cultures and circumstances, we can all do amazing things, and we have far more in common than we do different. But"—I shook my head—"the point I'm hearing is that talking about some of the differences could've helped. Just saying that my road was easier than a lot of folks' and that I knew many of you would face bigger obstacles than I'd had to."

"It would've been more truthful, right?" asked Allie.

"Yeah," said Sandee. "All the advantages you had are just true, Saaris."

"I guess so, yeah. I feel so lucky to have you guys willing to talk to me about this stuff," I said. "The fact that you trust and value me enough to push me to think differently, and to put some of your energy out there to help me learn about this stuff means a lot to me."

"Maybe there's hope for you yet!" said Sandee. "You didn't give up on us, and maybe we'll keep trying to hold out hope for your sorry ass, Saaris." She smiled. "Sorry-ass Saaris: I like that!"

"Oh boy," I said. Then I stood up, took a breath, and jumped. Some folks screamed as I fell into the water. Jamie dove in after me and we swam. Natalie showed Georgia and Traci to the swim ladder on our neighbor's boat, as Sandee and Allie kept dangling their feet above us, chatting.

We grilled, and the sun slipped behind the bridge for a bit. The roof cooled, and Sandee and I eventually found our way to adjacent camping chairs, watching the magenta cast of the early evening on Mount Rainier's glaciers.

She leaned toward me on her armrest. "Look, Saaris, thanks for letting me get that stuff off my chest. I'm blunt, right? Is that a good thing?"

"I think so. I learn a lot from you, honestly, because you're blunt about stuff."

"But really, I wouldn't have said any of this shit if I didn't think you'd get it." She punched me in the shoulder. She was silent for a while, then: "Honestly, you should thank me, cuz I'm doing you a favor. It's probably the nicest you're ever going to hear this from anyone. You're going to have to think things through some more and talk to other people about this stuff too."

"Like who?" I asked, eyes closed, arms resting, feet up, glad to have learned some things but inclined to forget them for at least the rest of today and just enjoy the evening.

"Like, I'm done with my internship. You're not my teacher anymore. You don't have any power over me. Did I tell you all this stuff while I was interning for you? No. So maybe think about other people on your team who might not feel so free to talk to you about all this stuff."

"I don't know if I can figure it all out today, you know?" I said, opening my eyes to see if that was OK with Sandee.

"Fair enough," she said.

I closed my eyes and leaned my head back on the dark green fabric of the camping chair.

"Let's talk more about it soon. You can tell me the other people you're talking about—"

"So let me get this right. It's, like, my homework to bring it back up to you, and explain it to you?"

"Well, not homework, no . . ."

"I'll tell you what. *You* figure out who else might need to hear some things about this from you. *You* do the homework, and then you can reach back out and run it by *me*, OK? How does that sound?" she folded her arms smugly, knowing she had me.

"Yeah, OK."

"Really OK? Like you're *actually* going to do it?" she pushed.

"Really OK!" I said.

"Cuz you can't come to my class unless you come prepared," she said.

"Ha. Fine," I said, then got up to go check on Natalie and the boys. On the way down the ladder, I used my phone to send myself a blank email with the subject line:

SANDEE HW: People I should talk to about advantage.

—— CHAPTER THIRTY-FOUR ——

As the team continued to grow, and the number of schools we partnered with increased, I began to stumble along the fog-ensconced edges of my mind's limits, finding myself in different rooms in different states with a lot of new people.

One day, I was invited to a regal room filled with dozens of representatives of the richest people in the world. Everyone was white, and they—offering me an obscenely crystalline water glass—asked me to tell them how I thought they should spend their money to improve other people's thinking. And I wondered, What were *we* thinking? And because it was an increasingly popular topic, they said, *Oh, and be sure and talk about racial equity too*, which I did. I thought I did a good job, and they told me I did a good job, and then a lot of people there gave me a lot of money to bring back to Equal Opportunity Schools, where I didn't feel like I was doing such a good job lately.

I met with famous researchers to talk about where the important feeling of belonging comes from, and how all our data could help us figure out what schools could do to create belonging. We'd talk about how experimenters had made kids of color think about negative stereotypes they faced, and that made them bomb their next test. And how this sort of stereotype threat was like knowing there's a snake in the room, and being alert, and using up mental bandwidth to stay aware of the danger, to try to keep yourself safe. And how one of the big triggers is having too few people around who look like you or share your experiences, too few people who look like you in the textbooks, or at the front of the classroom.

Meanwhile, I was trying to feel like I belonged at the head of the table at Equal Opportunity Schools, in the CEO's chair. But why was I sitting there when the folks on the leadership team around me were bringing such stellar insights and ideas, were getting such incredible things done for kids? I was flagging in the face of all they were doing.

When I doubted myself, I'd make a couple calls to powerful people who said I was doing great, that I was uniquely qualified to run EOS. And then I'd come back to the team and tell them which things I was going to put all the money into, and which I wouldn't. And when tough questions came up, I tried hard to look like I knew what I was doing and like I deserved to be the one making these decisions, even though I was the youngest, most inexperienced person in the room.

I wondered how long I could keep it up. I really wanted us to do incredible things for kids. But I kept getting twisted around something—I couldn't quite see what—that was making it progressively harder to get enough air.

———

When I finally got the diagnosis, I misused it to explain everything—all the doubts, the uncomfortableness, the uncertainties. The headaches.

One morning, shortly after I'd begun my nightly treatment, the leadership team was mingling in the room that used to be called the Reiding Room but was now called Tubman. I came in and smiled at the Dalí print on the wall that—after some study—reveals the hallucinogenic toreador. It reminded me of the power of learning: how everything can suddenly appear different and make a new kind of sense.

I had my insight now, and could take my seat at the head of the table with confidence.

"How was your vacation?" asked Zendaya, Eddie, and a few others.

"Oh boy!" I say, stretching up to the ceiling and smiling.

"That good, huh?" asked Eddie, smiling back.

"Yeah," I said. "I'm not sure everyone knows, but I was diagnosed with sleep apnea. I think it explains my migraine headaches, and some of my stress. Basically, for years I haven't been sleeping even ten minutes at a stretch without kind of choking and waking myself up!"

"Holy shit."

"I'm sorry to hear that."

"That's rough, man. Wow."

"Oh yeah, thanks," I said. "But now I'm back, baby! They gave me one of those CPAP thingies and I started using it on my vacation, and oh my gosh.

I went into a parallel universe—dove so deep into my sleep that I found my mojo way down there."

I didn't mention how bad things had really gotten—what had almost happened. I liked to wait until I had issues all fixed up before sharing, to try to show I had it all together.

Now here I was again, with an incredible team, doing incredible work, taking my seat at the new conference table, smiling again, capable of having a really good day.

We breezed through most of our agenda. I helped answer questions about nailing down tough contracts, updated folks on the financial and grant work I was leading, deferred to others' judgment in their areas of the organization's work, and talked about what we would share at the upcoming board meeting—an incredible client story, our financial health, our being on track with a new and ambitious strategic plan, the new folks we'd hired with incredible experience.

And then, near the end, race came up again.

I felt a bit less defensive than during the most recent conversations on the topic. I had more energy to engage, to listen, to learn. My colleagues around the table radiated good intentions and insights, and we worked together to carry things forward.

Then Zendaya asked, "I just wanted to make sure that you saw the email from Devon?"

"No, I don't think I did," I said. "What's it about?"

"Well, you know she—I mean *they*—quit, right?"

"Yes."

"*They* wrote an email to the staff about their departure and their concerns. A big one was that Jamie is not Black."

"Jamie what?" I asked.

"Well, they were under the impression that Jamie, from our founding story, was Black."

"OK . . . but what does that have to do with anything?" I asked. *Why does that matter?* I'd brought Jamie by the office a few times over the years, and he'd met a lot of folks on the team. His race wasn't supposed to be a secret or something, but his story did inspire a lot of people and enable them to identify with our work. I'd seen Black, white, well-off, and raised-in-poverty educators who had been encouraged to tell their stories—sometimes in tears—after hearing Jamie's.

"I'm just saying what they were concerned about. I dealt with it while you were on vacation."

"Got it," I thought, feeling slightly more curious than defensive.

"And in general, they wanted EOS to take a more aggressively pro–gender diversity stand on things, like requiring people to put pronouns into their emails."

Eddie said, "I'm one of the people who told her I wasn't going to do that, unless EOS developed a policy. I mean, I get it and I support the effort. But we can't take on everything all at once. We are not an all-encompassing equity company. Do you think administrators in the South want to return my team's emails about hiring us when the conversation turns to discussing our pronouns in our signature line with them? It doesn't correspond to the reality we have. We're about poverty and race here."

Bernadette spoke up. "And I think we need to consistently put race first, because it tends to be the hardest of the inequities. If it doesn't come first, then it just won't get addressed at all. People don't want to tackle hard stuff when they're already tired from everything else, so I figure it's best to tackle it first, while you have some fresh energy for it."

"I agree with that," said Zendaya.

"Me too," said another team member. "I've definitely been noticing that race seems to be the hardest for people, and so if you give them another type of inequity to talk about, they'll probably avoid race and go for the other one."

After another person agreed, I decided to jump on the bandwagon. "Let's do it," I said energetically.

"That's great," said Bernadette, "if we actually mean that and want to talk more about how to do it?"

At first, I thought, *You're saying I don't mean what I say?* and pulled up my best recent evidence of how well we were doing on race at EOS: a Latina team member who'd just told me that EOS was the first job where she felt safe and like she belonged. But this time, my thought didn't end in defensive refuge. I started to wonder what we could do differently as an organization, how I could lead better. Something deep in my mind started to shift—to return to a previously forgotten state, when I'd been a truly curious learner. I was no longer defending myself and my extremely limited energy supplies from further impositions. This was a great group of people I knew well, and they weren't attacking me. They were inviting me to think about this tough issue together, and I felt grateful.

"That's a good question," I said. "I know we're short on time, but this seems important, right? Can people stay to talk about it?"

Everyone agreed, and a few folks picked up their phones to text their next appointments that they'd be late.

I was excited about this decision, and eager to learn more with the staff about what it would mean for Zendaya to launch some of the new professional development ideas we'd brainstormed.

That night, as the CPAP helped me off to sleep, I was still replaying some of the comments from that conversation:

"Are we actually serious about race in this organization now? Because it has seemed at times like maybe we're not."

"My experience has been that white folks need to either lead on race or get out of the way."

"If we *really* want to do this, let's do it."

I'd told them I did really want to do it, that I was open to undergoing some of the types of analysis, scrutiny, and leadership coaching our team provided every day to principals and superintendents around the country.

To date, I'd used every trick I had to fend off the idea that I could fail my sister (I put that on my parents, then on Erin) or fail my students (I blamed Paula Barnes). I'd defended and deflected and dodged the notion that I might be a leader trying to bring fairness across the American high school hallway while failing to bridge the distance across the hallway outside my own office door.

My ability to parry these ideas was mighty, but the forces of a diversely talented team are mightier.

————

They started us off with a session with all of EOS's managers, led by LueRachelle, a facilitator Zendaya brought in. LueRachelle reminded me of my Auntie Suzy: brilliant and brimming with love, but also gravely serious about the things that she knew to be right and important in the world. Eyes flitting on the surface with learning's latest possibilities, over a deep well of past insights.

A lot had built up to this day. We'd said that we helped other management teams work on race issues in their schools, but for seven years we hadn't done so ourselves. And now we would. Though we all seemed a bit wound up, LueRachelle brought us down into things gently and firmly.

"So, Zendaya tells me you'all want to work on race within Equal Opportunity Schools. Is that right?"

Seated, we all nodded and said nothing, filling the border of the room. We had so many managers, I couldn't believe it. I felt deeply proud of EOS.

I was often counting diversity in the rooms I entered these days, because Claude Steele had told me that people of color do this instinctively, seeing if the room they're in is a place where people who look like them belong. I'd done this instinctively too, the times I found myself in the minority in Beaufort. I wanted EOS to feel like a place of belonging for everyone. I counted that staff of color were overrepresented on our senior team, and underrepresented in middle management, when compared with our city.

LueRachelle asked again: "Tell me more. Why are we here today?"

I looked at Zendaya, and she looked at me. Other people started looking at me too.

So I shared something I'd been thinking about recently, hoping I'd get it right. "Privilege gives you the ability to ignore privilege and pretend it doesn't exist, while others have to deal with its repercussions daily. I've been able to pretend that the issues of racism that we battle in our schools aren't present within the organization I lead, and that we're above these pervasive forces. Because I've been able to choose whether or not to engage in conversations about race at EOS. But folks of color don't get to choose whether or not to engage these issues. They are confronted with them ongoingly. And folks like me who ignore that aren't ignoring racism—they're abetting it by supporting the status quo. I'm sorry I didn't acknowledge that and didn't create space for us to address this sooner."

Zendaya said she appreciated what I said, which she hadn't said to me about anything for a while, so I figured I was on the right track.

I always liked to be specific when working with schools because specifics make the *oh-yeah-of-course* nodding stop and the thinking start. So I said, "What is the status quo that we've left unaddressed? We had 100 percent of our staff say that racial inequity was an issue in the schools we serve. We had 75 percent of people say racial inequity was a problem in our organization. Virtually all the folks who said it was *not* an issue at Equal Opportunity Schools are white.

"The data from our colleagues of color about the experiences they have at Equal Opportunity Schools is clear: race is an issue here. And we're gonna talk about our issues. Starting today, as a whole management team, and with LueRachelle's help. Thanks so much for being here, LueRachelle, and thank you, Zendaya, for putting this together."

We heard other people's introductions and opening thoughts about the work, and I was nodding along and everything. And then LueRachelle made us get more specific.

She handed out a rubric to evaluate "anti-racist organizations" and asked us to break out into groups and talk about where we thought EOS fell on the six-point scale.

Our group decided maybe four or five points, and I could settle for that. I had just said we had work to do, after all.

And then some of the other small groups came back and said they were giving us a three. A two, maybe. One group said they could see ways that we were a two, and ways that we were maybe a one.

I sat there, thinking, *What?! Seriously? This project I've been leading all decade getting the lowest score on anti-racism? Which means racist, which is, like, the worst.*

I didn't say anything for a long time as the activities continued.

We had a nice lunch break in a garden. And then, back in our chairs, I was made the student again. And like I'd done to so many kids, I was pushed. The boundaries of my ideas weren't as supple as they had once been; they held pretty hard. In the room, though, we had district leaders, racial equity leaders, doctors of philosophy, folks I'd known for a long time and who knew me.

At some point, Zendaya brought up that she'd heard from Sandee that maybe Jim was working at McDonald's, and she said she wondered why I was at EOS talking about his experience with advanced courses and the opportunities it had opened up for him. This was the first I'd heard in quite some time about how Jim was doing. I felt a deep pang for him to have what he wanted—everything EOS thought it could help him and students like him have.

And I felt ashamed for letting him down while sharing his story with others to advance my work. During my pitches, I always shared quotes from him, quotes he'd said I could use. *I'm using actual experiences to try to help people understand how amazing kids could be, and we're out there making things better in hundreds of schools,* I thought. *Isn't that good enough? Does Jim need to have completed college? I've tried so many times to reach him to talk about what he wanted and whether I could help. What does this team want from me, anyways?*

As good teachers do, LueRachelle went on to address questions I hadn't asked. And—just as I'd done by counting missing students and the gaps that had caused them to go missing—she made the issues concrete, so there was no eluding things. It was the facts and their implications she was after.

"We can't live anyone else's experience but our own. But what we can do—and what you all probably should do, especially if you're going to be teaching other people about race and things like that in your schools—is to learn from others about their experiences. And we do some of that together as a team, with your colleagues. But that can get tiring, especially for people of color. And so we have to build relationships outside of the workplace with people from different backgrounds. How many of you would say that at least one of your close friends is from a different race group than you?"

I *so* wanted to give a good answer. I thought about how the mother of a close friend was Mexican. I thought back to one of my best friends in grade school who was adopted from Korea, but LueRachelle—seeing a lot of us thinking hard and partially raising our hands—cut us off.

"And if it's a maybe, then *that*'s a no. I mean, like, someone you spend time with and talk to—not from work—at least every month. And that they're obviously from a significantly different background than you are."

My wife grew up poor, immigrating from Poland. But I'm pretty sure she said "race" . . .

With her concrete and well-defined questions about what we were actually doing—making us account for how we spent our time and related to others—she wasn't leaving much space to hide.

I kept my hands nonchalantly in my lap and was perversely pleased to see most others doing the same, including Zendaya, who'd smilingly said, "Darn," after LueRachelle said that a maybe was a no.

A smattering continued to hold their hands in the air. They looked as if they were trying not to appear as satisfied as they felt.

"How many of you," LueRachelle went on, "have *several* close friends from different racial backgrounds?"

One woman still held her hand up.

"And how many of you have several close friends from several different racial backgrounds?"

The woman put her hand down. Now no one looked satisfied, except Lue-Rachelle, who said, "You see, the point is we all have some work to do if we want to understand others' experiences and we want to really engage these issues that you are working on in your schools. Tilting her head a bit in my direction, then in the direction of a few other folks, she added, "And *some* of us have a little more work to do than others."

Although it felt as if there wasn't any air left in the room, LueRachelle somehow had enough to continue.

"Let's expand it beyond your best friends and into your broader community. Now, we're not talking about people who serve you food at restaurants or cut your hair or something like that. I'm not even talking about the books you read, but the actual people you relate to. How do you go about learning about folks from different racial backgrounds—to inform yourselves, and to inform your practice and your work on issues of race?"

I was devastated when I saw she was using my old technique of having everybody talk, starting off at one part of the circle, then going around. The beads I'd quickly sorted back into the big, anonymous container were about to return to my lap. The question was only six people away from me. Five. Two. I hadn't really heard what anybody said. Unusually, it was like there was a snake on my side of the room. I couldn't focus past my fear. I strained to hear what the person next to me was saying.

"—try to go . . . would like to do more . . . it's . . ."

They'd stopped. Everyone was looking at me. How did I *what*? Learn about race?

But *not* from books.

And *not* from my colleagues at work?

"I, uh, I'd like to get out more and expand more of my horizons on this stuff, like you're talking about. I really believe in it. In learning from difference. But it's been pretty hard lately, with the two young kids and trying to get enough sleep and doing EOS and everything."

"Oh yeah, it can be hard with young kids," said LueRachelle sympathetically. "How old are they?"

"Two and five." I smiled and looked to the person to my left, who said something I couldn't make out.

As we continued around the circle, I tuned in as another colleague said, "I think it's *most* important to get out there and connect and learn across differences when you have kids. For the sake of your kids."

I felt criticized, indignant. *She has no idea what all I've been doing for my kids!*

Then there was a discussion about centering whiteness, which I still wasn't sure I understood. So I said, "I'm interested in trying to change this kind of thing, because I'm hearing that it's hurtful to some of you. I care so much that you have a good experience, and I want to do something about it. But tangibly, what does that look like?"

I heard someone heave an exasperated sigh.

And then Eddie jumped in and said, "Look, I'm not sure what centering whiteness means either. And maybe that's because I'm a bit mixed up and have had to do a lot of things to try to fit this white culture to get ahead

over the years—I don't know. But I do know that our job here is about getting schools signed up to do our process and find missing students. And to
be honest, most of the folks who run school districts are white. And it's just
part of the reality that we need to cater to who they are if we want to work
with them, to reach the kids in their schools. So I don't know why we're getting all tied up about this stuff. Honestly, it's getting a little exhausting."

I sighed in relief to know that I wasn't the only one feeling tired of the
topic. I let myself off the hook about Jim, about needing to have more relationships across racial lines if I were to credibly claim to have something significant to teach others about all this. As things wrapped up, I said goodbye
to folks, and drove off.

—— CHAPTER THIRTY-FIVE ——

A couple months later, standing alone, I looked behind me, at the distance between me and the rest of my colleagues. I saw how I'd come to be at the front of the room. One step at a time, one "yes" after another.

At the start of the activity, we were all together on the back wall. Then LueRachelle told us, "Please step forward if most of the students in your elementary school were of the race group that you identify with."

I remembered just a couple of Black and Asian faces from my classes, and stepped off the wall. Looking left and right, I could see that most of the folks off the wall were white, with two Black folks.

"Thank you," she said. "Now please step forward if most of the *teachers* in your elementary school were of the race group that you identify with."

I scanned my memory—the only teacher of color I came up with was Ms. Bahat, from middle school—and stepped forward again. Only white folks were two steps away from the wall.

"Next, the statement is 'I'm pretty sure that if I go to a business and ask to speak to the person in charge, I will be speaking with someone of my race.'"

Shit, I thought, stepping forward with a smaller step than before. I didn't want to be way out here like this.

"Most of the bosses or supervisors I've had appeared to be of the same race group that I identify with."

Ha! I thought. *I had one Black principal and one white principal. One Black board chair and one white board chair. So technically* most *of my bosses were not* white. There were a few people out in front of me now. I glanced back and saw most of my Black colleagues still up against the wall, then I quickly looked forward.

Am I this far out because my legs are long? I have to take shorter steps from now on.

"I can attend college without someone thinking I got in because of my race."

"I can take a job with an employer who believes in affirmative action without worrying about people thinking I got the job because of my race."

I had to step forward.

"I have never worried that I was being stopped by the police because of my race or ethnicity."

True for me.

"Most of the people in the stories I've read or watched over the years have been of the same race group that I identify with."

Also true. I wished the activity would stop. But it went on and on.

When it did finally stop, it got worse. LueRachelle asked us to turn around.

Those of my colleagues with the darkest skin were still up against the wall—except Zendaya, who was out sick; she'd told me I was really stressing her out lately. Some of the folks on the wall looked back at me, and I looked away. Others looked down, glassy-eyed. Some stared at the ceiling, hands tucked so far back through their armpits that they were hugging themselves.

I'd failed—despite years of effort on the part of my colleagues to help me—to see this. It'd been like a Magic Eye stereogram whose third dimension was especially hard for me to pop.

But as Tony spoke, it emerged.

"This activity really sucked for me," he said. "I go back and forth. There are issues I regularly face because I'm Black. It's not necessarily every day, but it's more than often enough. And in between those things, sometimes I try to forget about it for a while. And I imagine that next time . . . I imagine or hope that maybe there won't be a next time, I guess. That maybe I won't be followed in a department store by a security guard again. Or I won't be pulled over and have those tapes of those other Black men being killed running through my head and just holding the steering wheel to—" He let out a sudden sob.

People stepped off the wall to get closer to him, put hands on his shoulders.

"Look: if people really want to learn about this pain, let me try to explain, and maybe it'll be worth something to you. But listen closely, because I'm not going through this kinda shit in front of all of my work colleagues ever again, OK?" He laughed a bit, and those with their hands on his shoulders smiled deeply, affectionately back.

He exhaled and looked toward me. "You know how you get tired? Maybe you took on too much. Like, you didn't sleep well and then you had a hard day at work, and then there's bad traffic on the way home, and your day's just full up and you've had enough, but you still have to go get some groceries before you can go home, because there's nothing in the house for dinner. Like, maybe you've been on the road traveling for EOS for a while."

Some folks snickered and said, "You know that's the truth!"

"You can't handle another thing," he said. "But you *need* to handle another thing."

I remembered a feeling I'd had during the darkest part of last winter, before my treatment: migraine raging, needing to make it through pouring rain that the wipers couldn't clear.

"That's just life," said Tony. "We all deal with that kind of thing sometimes, whether you're Black or white. And sometimes we're right on the edge of what we can and can't handle. And then something comes along on top of the normal difficulties of life, often comes along at those moments when you're on the edge of energy and what you can handle, and pushes you right on over."

Folks along the wall nodded solemnly but heartily, as we do when something seriously sucks but you know you're at least in it with others who get it.

"So in this situation," Tony said, building now, "you had a shit day, you slept horribly, work was really hard, and then there's this bad traffic. You just need to get home to rest, but you remember you have to detour to the grocery store, even though you feel like you've got nothing left in you."

I flashed back to last winter, an evening I'd had to pick up a carton of soy milk. I remembered the milk just as I was pulling away from La Escuelita. Both kids were already strapped in, so I had to ride the long block back around, park again, unbuckle everyone, and carry Oscar on my hip through the rain while Oli hopped in the puddles alongside us.

"And *then*, on top of all the difficulties that normal life brings," Tony continued, "you get into the grocery store, and you get this vibe that the people in the grocery store don't want you to be there. You're the only Black guy around. They're staring at you. They take a long path to walk around you. The security guy's following you. So you didn't have the energy to do the damn grocery shopping in the first place, and now people are piling on top of that, clearly wanting you gone. And it's too much, so you give up."

In contrast, I'd grabbed my Silk and gotten a couple smiles at checkout, even though I was grimacing.

Driving back through traffic with the kids in the back seat, fussing and then yelling, my headache closed in on me. Tracers in my vision looked like people lunging out onto the dark wet road in front of the car. I hunched over the steering wheel, trying to see, leaning into oncoming headlights whose beams hit each eyeball like a hammer-driven screwdriver. I wasn't sure I'd make it home.

"So, in some ways, it's just another thing weighing on you, on top of everything else. But when you can't handle another thing, and another thing gets forced upon you, it can break you. Another thing can become everything, if that makes sense."

When I turned our car into the gravel parking area, everything was on the line: the fulcrum of the small cliff ahead. Below it, across the cove, was our little houseboat, its dim lights shining through the dark rain. But there was no joy in nearing home. In recent months, there had been no destination of relief I could imagine reaching.

Then I thought of one.

I imagined the car continuing beyond our parking spot, off the graveled precipice, down the thorny-bushed rockery, the glow of my home on the other side of the water fading forever as the car tumbled fifty feet to the bottom of the canal.

That night, my foot was reluctant to come up off the gas, and it was so slow to the brake that we hit a small log that'd been recently put on the edge to prevent disaster, jolting the log forward, but not quite enough for us to go over.

As I saw Tony's nearby coworkers embracing him, I felt like I knew what he meant, that another thing could become everything. If, that winter day, someone had piled one more thing on me, made me feel a little more like I didn't belong in this world, that one more push could've cost me everything.

As he wrapped up—"That's everything. That's all I've got"—our eyes met. It seemed like Tony could see that I was starting to understand.

I swore to myself that I'd always remember it. That though privilege meant I had the power to walk out of this room at the end of the day and pretty much forget about racism if I wanted to, I would hold on vigilantly to this insight and all its implications. I would keep close watch on myself and our organization and our work with schools, and ensure that I didn't add more racial burdens to the backs of my colleagues of color.

And then, after the retreat wrapped up, I had to go pick up the kids, take them home, cook dinner, and help put them to bed. After all that, I got into bed and started scrolling through Netflix. Joining me, Natalie asked how my day had been.

And I said, "Huh?"

She said, "I was asking about your day."

And I said, "Oh man, it was pretty intense. Really intense, actually."

"Oh yeah?"

"Yeah, but I don't really want to talk about it. It's a lot. I'm tired."

"OK."

"Just want to take it easy for a little bit here."

"Sounds good."

"And you're good?"

"Yeah, I'm good," she said.

"Good."

Then I watched *Cheers* and forgot about it all for the last long time.

––––––

I'd like to think I almost made it. That I was right on the verge of figuring out what I'd been missing and acting on it in a big way. But that's probably wishful thinking.

The last clue I got, before it was too late, came from the powerful formula we used with schools: simple counting applied to complex relationships.

For me, the counting came on a slide I saw at a conference of wealthy donors. A few Black women leaders took the stage in front of the white audience and projected a slide titled "Black Women and Funding," which said that the average amount raised by startups owned by Black women was $36,000. By comparison, they told us, the average raised by failed startups overall in the US was $1,300,000.

So, ideas that don't work are typically given more than thirty-five times as much money as Black women's ideas.

But that's just ideas that are funded. If Black women's ideas were funded proportionately to US demographics, we'd have about thirty times more Black women funded than the twenty-four venture deals with Black women.

So, the thirty-five-fold inequity in dollars, compounded by missing Black women founders who never receive funding to begin with, is really a one-thousand-fold resource inequity.

I was stunned. But it was only through real relationships that I was able to start connecting that abstraction to my personal actions.

I had a discussion with a friend who could see I was exhausted and wanted to be supportive. She told me I shouldn't put up with all those trainings or pay much attention to ten concerned people on the team when we were trying to serve ten thousand students. She wanted to help me feel better, and so she talked about things I'd accomplished, like raising almost $50 million so far, and said that folks leading racial equity efforts, like Zendaya, could raise money and start their own organizations if they didn't like how I was leading EOS.

When I said I didn't know if they could, she said, *Exactly! That's why you're in charge, because you have the entrepreneurship and vision and capabilities and . . .*

And it clicked.

All the conversations I'd had with educators in which they suggested that maybe missing students were meant to be missing because they didn't have what it took. And I'd always ask them if they were assuming that or if they'd actually provided an equal opportunity for kids to show if they could cut it.

I'd always assumed that Zendaya didn't have what I had, because she hadn't done the CEO work I was doing. But the funding sector offered people of her background literally a thousandth of the opportunity they afforded folks like me.

That weekend, I even came across the old homework assignment Sandee had given me to talk with others on the team about advantage, and thought, *I should probably talk to Zendaya about all this sometime.*

—— CHAPTER THIRTY-SIX ——

I was seated at the meeting desk in Tubman when Zendaya dropped by for our check-in. She sat down across from me, smiling.

The energy that'd disappeared from behind her eyes during her time on the executive team with me was back, brimming.

"Well," she started, "I have some news."

We found more students than expected? Our cashflow is looking great? We made an amazing new hire? These were the types of things we'd celebrated over the years. Perhaps she too had found a cure for what'd been ailing her? I widened my eyes to say, *Go on.*

"I've decided to leave Equal Opportunity Schools at the end of October." Her smile widened—she put her hands up to her mouth for a moment, then let them drop.

"Really?" I asked, shocked, not knowing what else to say.

"Yep. I think it's an important change for me at this point."

"You . . . got another job?"

"No, not yet."

Oh, I nodded, meeting her eyes, searching for what I'd just lost.

"I . . . Is there anything I can do to get you to stay?"

"No," she answered quickly. "This is the right decision." Her expression made that obvious.

"Or maybe to stay a bit longer than the end of October? Of course, the work that you're doing and what you're contributing is so important on so many fronts right now." Running half the organization as COO, she oversaw about a dozen major initiatives.

"I don't think so, Reid."

I started to say, "But," then realized I needed to get out of there, get some air.

"OK. I . . . I think I need to process this a little. And then can we talk?"

"OK, sure. I'll be just across the hall at my desk." She picked up her purple folio, hugged it close, and seemed to skip out.

But—I gagged—*she won't be there for long.*

———

My favorite color was purple too. But it hadn't been enough. It seemed like we had the same goals for students, but that hadn't been enough. We had the same graduate degrees from the same university. She'd run the Black student union and I ran triathlon. Our moms were educators. We were educators—leaders in the upcoming generation, committed to fixing whatever needed fixing to fully serve underserved students. What was broken here, and why couldn't we fix it?

After I walked along the canal for a bit in a mist, I came back and asked Zendaya to answer a few questions. She didn't tell me anything new. And I couldn't quite see the answers in what she said.

When she talked about her stress and wanting to go home to Fenton, I said *What if we* . . . and she said, *No.*

When I asked if her stress came from me, she said, *Maybe it did.* I asked what I could have done differently, and she replied, *You are who you are.*

But that wasn't good enough.

And my questions were no longer hers to answer. She wasn't working for me anymore.

So I gave my own answers when the team and the board asked about her departure: We'd worked together for almost eight years, and it was time for her to go home; she and I had built things from the get-go, and the organization was in amazing shape; I'd learned a lot from her.

Inexcusably, my migraine was so bad the day of her farewell that I couldn't bring myself to go to the event—to face up to all I'd missed and say goodbye.

———

Discombobulated, I sat with Jamie in his apartment, a block away from the Seattle police station that—a couple years hence—would be taken over by protesters for weeks following the murder of George Floyd.

We talked about Jamie's pop's cancer, and how his family was learning to live with it as best they could, as hard as it was. How the doctors had gone in with knives and carved out the worst parts, a couple of times, a couple of different organs so far. How they'd given him blasts—and a steady drip—of the chemicals most likely to tame his rogue cells.

We talked about Jamie's work as a part-time English instructor at a community college, reaching students like himself who'd been disillusioned by school—students who engaged when invited into the deeper questions and quandaries.

After he talked about bringing his class to the library to do research, I said, "That reminds me—I met this local elementary school librarian the other day."

"Uh-huh?"

"She said that she saw in the data that she'd been disciplining Black girls much more than any other group. And she had this whole thing about her family of origin and learning about cultural differences, and figuring out how to do better. And people seemed to think that was great, but I was pissed! This woman had been over-disciplining Black girls in her school for, like, thirty years." I raised my hands in frustration. "Since she was the librarian, she probably interacted with all the students in the school. So, hundreds of kids whose library should've been a source of knowledge and insight were instead driven out by the overseer! Isn't that disgusting?!"

Jamie nodded along to my outrage at the librarian, then said, "Yeah. And at least it sounds like she's learning."

"But the kids she's hurting shouldn't have to wait for her to learn. There should be more teachers of color in our schools now who already understand the Black girls that this librarian was harassing. More leaders of color. Learning's fine, but those who are being screwed over in the meantime shouldn't have to wait for some slow-ass, reluctant learning."

"Yeah—we should have a lot more educators of color and urgency around stopping that kind of harm, like you're saying. But I think you should also appreciate the learning that's going on."

He told me about a young Black woman in a class he taught who'd been coming in late—how he'd called her out in front of the other students, and how she raised her voice in response. He hadn't known what to do about these disruptive interactions, which were escalating.

So he talked to her about it.

And he listened to her.

He learned that she and her Black classmates often felt put upon by white teachers, and that they felt they needed to defend themselves against attacks. He started talking privately with students when they were late, and he heard about bus routes that were more often canceled in communities of color; parents who were more likely to be deprived of health care; families on the economic brink, like his had been, where his students were called on to step in at the last minute to take care of younger siblings.

He said he realized he'd been giving the benefit of the doubt to white students who came in late, while assuming bad intentions on the part of students of color—treating them more harshly, exactly as the student had accused him of doing.

"You were being racist?" I asked him, feeling disgusted now with my best friend too.

"Well, yeah," he said casually.

Even though we were alone in the apartment, I instinctively looked around to make sure no one else was hearing this.

"We all are sometimes. White folks, that is," he said. "Right?"

Not me, I thought, my nightmares, test results of implicit bias, and other such things long forgotten. "I've spent my career fighting that sort of thing, actually."

"I've been thinking of it this way lately." He leaned forward in his rocker. "I got mad at this girl for coming late to my class when her public bus didn't show up. And the routes that run to her neighborhood and the neighborhoods of folks who look like her get canceled more often than other routes. I was mad at her when her dad was sick. That got through to me because of all I've been going through with Pop's cancer. And when that happened to her, she had to drop out of school for a while to help the family pay their bills. And the evidence shows Black patients are less likely to be treated effectively—that Black workers get paid less for the same job, and not hired in the first place based on race. So there're lots of things going on in our society dragging on her momentum and her prospects unfairly, right?"

"Yeah: the kinds of things Equal Opportunity Schools tries to address—to really make an equal opportunity for folks."

"Yep. And when she showed up to my class and I called her out more vocally and more embarrassingly than I call out white students who are late, when I assumed she was blowing off my class and not taking it seriously, I was an added drag to her prospects. I made my classroom less welcoming to her, and made it harder for her to get a fair shake with her education."

"But why? You're not a racist."

"I didn't mean to do it. I don't want to do things like that. But this society that does all of these things we're talking about, including keeping tons of kids out of advanced classes—you and me, we're a part of that society. And those things that are happening, we're a part of it, and it's a part of us."

"So you're saying, 'I'm a racist, you're a racist'?" I asked.

"That's one way to put it. Maybe people can hear it better if you say that racism is a part of us?"

"Just like that?" I made a straw-slurping sound through gritted teeth. "But I don't want it to be part of me."

"Me neither. It's gross. But can you really think you're unaffected by it if you're raised in and around it? And look: the point of my relationship with this student is that by acknowledging it, I was able to begin to address it, and to change. And now I share the story with each of my new classes of students."

"You tell them about your being harsher on Black students?" I said, appalled.

"Yeah. And that I'm working on it."

Part of me wanted to get out of Jamie's apartment. Not only was he doing racist things, but he was talking about them, like the librarian. But then he let me see my hypocrisy.

As my best friend, he'd shown me over and over how much he loved me, had generously interpreted my behavior in a positive light—had done what every true friend and good teacher does: help you see your best self, and then become it. More than you ever could've seen or done without them.

"Reid," he said, looking me in the eyes and lifting his dark brows, "we all have racism in us. Even you. And the sooner we recognize that, the sooner we can do something about it, don't you think?"

And then I saw myself from a new angle. It'd taken lots of study and evidence over the years, as well as the relationships I'd had with my students and with the EOS team of talented mind-changers. And it took this space of psychological security too, in which it was pointed out to me again, by someone who saw the world much as I did, who knew me as I wanted to be known.

Suddenly, the eight years I'd spent working with Zendaya took a different shape.

I'd been so intent on seeing myself as simply good—on viewing my actions from my vantage point at the head of the table—that I'd missed her.

What had it looked like from the interviewee's side when we first met at that coffee shop, when I got to control the job offer, then decide which ideas we pursued on the job?

What had it felt like when, as her boss, I botched my school district partnership in Morgan, while saying that it was unacceptable for her to botch hers? Or when I told her she needed to be responsible not only for her actions in Fenton but for mine too?

Then I'd threatened to fire her.

Was I like Zendaya's counselor who told her she wasn't good enough for Advanced Studies, like so many of these other adults who had represented wrongness to me? Vice Principal Barnes at Battery Creek, who wouldn't stand up for missing students. My department chair, Walter Thompson, who told me I was doing a bad job because I wasn't doing it his way, who said and did horrible things to students.

Zendaya got the results: finding more missing kids in San Felipe than I had, closing some gaps in her county faster than I'd ever closed a gap, then recruiting the superintendent to work for Equal Opportunity Schools and sign up more superintendents to partner with us.

After all that, what was it like to be left with a seat at the back of the EOS conference room when the staff got together, while I took the seat in front? While I held forth, month after month, year after year, and she had to listen quietly, as though she weren't more experienced with the issue of missing students, more experienced working in schools and districts. Maybe getting the vibe that even though her results were better than mine, I thought I was better than her.

Never mind our teachers with their ten-thousand class bells that rang us apart throughout our time in school, talking about the best and the brightest, or our funders turning Zendaya down, then telling me to hold her more accountable. Wherever it came from, it came through me. It was in me. *I* told her that she had to do—had to be—better than me with fewer resources. Or else.

My sister's father might have claimed his abusive behavior had resulted from being abused himself, but that didn't make his violence hurt Erin any less.

What is it like to be Black at an organization that receives an invitation from the first Black president to work on issues affecting Black Americans at the White House, and to see the young, white founder go instead of you? Or to go with him the next time and—finding one seat for the organization at the table—be consigned to the back wall as he takes the seat and proffers what he believes to be his uniquely valuable insights about the issues facing Black Americans? To have seat after seat blithely taken from you, despite your qualifications, your effort, your abilities?

Her incredible successes shone through, *even though she controlled but a thousandth of the financial resources that I had been given.* But I hadn't recognized those successes—at least not when they might have cast a shadow on what I was doing.

I'd been a part of the taking from others for my own advantage. Of course I had.

I'd seen this type of thing happen to student after student in school after school, city after city, state after state, and had somehow imagined that I was above it all. That I had completely escaped these patterns. That I was one of the only folks who saw the cruelty clearly, and simply transcended it.

These patterns exist in nearly every schoolhouse in every city. It's all around us. It's in us. We're pickled in it. And no cucumber—even one on the top of the pot, poking a bit out of the brine—escapes pickling.

And so I'd missed out on the capabilities of some of my earliest students and driven some, like Tatyana Crum, away. I'd lost Allie, who'd said, after our visit on the roof that day, that we wouldn't ever be friends, because she'd trusted me but that the Incomplete I'd initially given her change project had put her college dreams in peril.

I'd missed out on Zendaya's capabilities, and seemingly driven her away. From missing students to missing teammates. She was the first employee at EOS. Why didn't I call her a cofounder? Why had it taken me six years to put her on the senior team? And why had I failed for all those years to comprehend why she might feel stressed around me?

"But would people ever really want to talk about racism being a part of them?" I asked Jamie, wincing at the realizations about Zendaya flooding painfully in. "Racist is one of the worst things. You'd be likely to lose your career and be completely torn down."

I'd done it to others myself: identified racism in them and written them off. From my roommate I met in the trailer park who'd kicked me out after he thought I might have my Black students over, to Paula Barnes, to Jim's math teacher, to Walter Thompson, and a wide variety of school and district leaders who I saw as obfuscating, avoidant, and injustice-perpetuating. These people's rot seemed to me irredeemable.

So if it's in me, then am I irredeemable?

It felt then as though I were Jamie's high school counselor, who hadn't seen college potential through his hand-me-down clothing. My mistaken failure to believe in Zendaya felt like my mistaken failure to believe in Erin. The world made sense when its horrors could be ascribed away from me and the other innocents onto the monsters, like Erin's father, who'd shoved her face into the toilet and flushed, over and over.

But I could no longer ascribe all the horrors away. Sure, I *wanted* to clean up all the nastiness, but some of it was on me, and I was spreading it around onto others.

The many founder colleagues and I, who shared a skin tone and a bathroom, weren't the best or the brightest. And the sooner I recognized that, the sooner the talents and capabilities on the Equal Opportunity Schools team could take the project of finding missing students to the next level.

— CHAPTER THIRTY-SEVEN —

Everyone who's known deep learning is at least a bit scared of it.
Shallow learning—like finding the pop of a Magic Eye book's third dimension—is fun and inconsequential.

But if you're talking about the way you see the broader world and what your perspective misses—big mistakes of consequence that you have yet to learn from—you're not talking about the rearrangement of a picture in a picture book. You're talking tectonic shifts in the ground you depend on. A betrayal by a loved one breaks not only that relationship but your ability to trust your own understanding of any relationship.

And when learning breaks through like a flash flood after a drought, it's all chaos. Topsoil ripped and thrown. New channels opening unpredictably as tributaries roil together across what had, until that instant, seemed firm ground.

Through the tumult in my mind over Zendaya, I can't account for which pieces of my intellectual terrain gave way when, or exactly why. But just as finding a group of missing students was a gateway into a superintendent thinking differently about how to fully serve all students, realizing I'd missed Zendaya opened my path to thinking very differently about all my colleagues.

That path was too long. I wrestled for months with the board's question of how we should structure EOS's leadership following Zendaya's departure. I was losing confidence in my own judgment as the world seemed to be shifting around me. Some others were probably losing confidence in me as well, but they gave me space to think things through and submit my recommendation, which the board accepted.

After ten full-time years building Equal Opportunity Schools, I would resign as CEO. I'd continue to serve on the board and as an adviser to help them transition to a long-term successor.

Many of us were wrong in thinking that the strongest candidate for CEO would come from outside Equal Opportunity Schools, and I think we caused the team a fair amount of heartache and difficulty by pushing for someone with "more experience" than anyone on our current team had. Everyone on the senior leadership team had more years of experience than I did. All but one were Black.

And yet the organization lost precious time, energy, and experienced staff searching for, recruiting, hiring, training, and soon off-boarding a couple of external CEOs.

Why didn't we clearly see who was right in front of us?

Eddie Lincoln had been the most successful of partnership directors, fully closing gaps in almost all the schools he had been responsible for in his first year. At that point, I estimated that his work had created 10 percent of all the equitable Advanced Studies programs in the entire country. He built strong relationships with principals and superintendents so that when partnership got difficult, they had the trust needed to communicate openly and he could help push them toward their best work.

He, like I, had cried alone in his car after long, fraught meetings in which we couldn't convince superintendents to give missing students the chance to take the highest-level courses.

Several years prior, the board and I had recruited Eddie to become the senior director responsible for developing new partnerships. I remember the first big meeting in his new role, when he and I presented together to a room full of leaders in the West—none of whom shared Eddie's skin color. The leaders were attentive to what I had to say, making eye contact and nodding. But when I turned things over to Eddie, they began to pick up their phones, looked out the window, and responded to his questions with silence.

In an organization aspiring to close gaps nationwide, new partnership development is perhaps the most important work, and it was an area I'd excelled in. But Eddie—facing far greater and unmerited skepticism from many of the superintendents we worked with—quickly built more partnerships than I had. Additionally, working with the notoriously biased fundraising sector, Eddie brought in millions in grant money *before that was even part of his job responsibilities.*

Eddie wasn't missing something he needed to do the job I'd done for the past decade. By not understanding that, the search committee, advisers, and

I were the ones who were missing something during an extended two years of transition.

But since Eddie has stepped up to lead the company, he's raised tens of millions of additional dollars, and collaboratively developed a plan to double EOS's impact. In just a couple of years, we anticipate the team will find as many missing students as the organization did during its whole first decade, while I was at the helm.

I've learned a great deal from Eddie about leadership. About putting other people first by focusing on their dreams and aspirations above all. About openness and clarity. About how to gather input, make tough decisions, and clearly explain and invest others in them. About empowerment and accountability.

And about grace, compassion, and forgiveness—at the time when I needed it most. Somehow, even though I hadn't fully appreciated Eddie's incredible leadership potential—or, for that matter, the CEO potential of the other senior leaders of color on our team, all of whom have since gone on to become CEOs and executive directors in their own right—he's said he still believes in mine, and wants to help me achieve it.

He says that, despite the difficulties along the way, we've already achieved a lot together. It's ironic, but two things pointing in opposite directions are both true, different vantage points on a larger whole:

- At times, I literally increased the distance between many of my colleagues of color and where they wanted to go. Our analysis showed that when I put the Equal Opportunity Schools office next to my houseboat, I substantially and disproportionately increased their commute. Because of my decision, staff of color, like Eddie, had less time in their day than white folks to do their jobs.

- And also, in founding EOS and working with those colleagues on our core effort to find missing students, I'd helped to significantly shorten the distance between over a hundred thousand students and where they aspired to go.

── CHAPTER THIRTY-EIGHT ──

My son Oliver is now about the age Jamie and I were when we'd brag to each other about about "scoring" with girls. (We'd run around the playground and find a girl who was up for singing the *Fresh Prince of Bel-Air* theme song with us.)

A couple years ago, Oliver's best friend from elementary school and his single dad had to move out of the increasingly expensive Fremont neighborhood of Seattle, where we lived. That summer, Oliver and I were passing by his elementary school and noticed some parents who'd gathered there for a march in support of Black lives, and we decided to join them. We lapped the school once, twice, three times—and yet saw no Black people. None in the march, none on the playground, none on the walk back to the houseboat. Where were they?

What did this march mean? That folks were willing to spend half an hour walking around in a circle to appear in support of something? Of what? I started thinking, *These people live in a segregated neighborhood*, then remembered I lived there too. I knew, from sessions at EOS, that neighborhood covenants had been written into rapidly appreciating property deeds during my grandmother's time going to school in this neighborhood—covenants specifying that "no person of any race other than the White or Caucasian race shall use or occupy any building or lot."

All of us adults in the march sent our kids to a school where there were still almost no Black children.

What did we think we were doing walking in circles?

More importantly, what did I think I was doing, sending my kids to this school? Oscar was slated to start here with Oliver next year. And then Millie.

And as long as we kept walking around these blocks, we were unlikely to get far.

When I first learned that my decision about EOS's office location added about an hour to Eddie's and other Black colleagues' commutes, I'd thought, *Hey, come on—it's just where I happen to live! I didn't know about the neighborhood or its history. I just found an affordable little houseboat, and now here we all are!*

I didn't have to intend to make the jobs at my company tougher on Black people to have done it, to have the historical forces work their way into and through me, on to my colleagues. But now I knew to pay better attention.

I'd told so many people what they should do with the kids they were responsible for. And here I was, holding the child-soft hand of my son, walking summer circles around the public school I'd chosen to live by, without having paid enough attention to what Oliver would learn there.

I thought back to Dolliver's dwelling on "the medium is the message"—that how things are conveyed, and the context around them, is more important than what's actually said. What does a lecture class convey, as compared with a lab, or a discussion class? Who gets to talk? Who gets to teach? Who is included in the discussion? The class? The school?

At this school, Oliver would learn from the medium of instruction that those who teach and lead classrooms are white. With almost 90 percent white teachers, the odds were quite high that he would never have a Black teacher—just as I never had.

He would learn that he belongs mostly with people whose families are financially well off. Though he'd connected with a friend from a lower-income family before they'd had to leave, odds were that such a relationship wouldn't happen in that school building again.

Given that the school didn't much include people from diverse race, class, and linguistic backgrounds, why would some folks call it great? At this school, Oliver wouldn't ever have much chance to get to know kids like his uncle Jamie, or his mother.

Maybe that'd be less of a problem if we were preparing kids for a less diverse world. But the reality is that most American K-12 students come from low-income families, and most are not white. In this context, wouldn't it be good to prepare kids to know, understand, and collaborate with the peer groups comprising the significant majority of their generation?

When I got back to the boat and talked with Natalie, we started to wonder about the strong ratings that Oliver's school showed on popular websites. With a little research, we soon realized that not only did those websites not put any positive value on the inclusion of people like Natalie, the presence of students like her tended to lower their assessment of a school. Since income is one of the strongest correlates of achievement test performance, many schools with larger populations of low-income students have lower average standardized test scores. And this can have little to do with how much learning actually happens at the school.

We did our best to compare Oliver's current school with one I'd visited in Skyway.

Years ago, when Zendaya and another colleague first told me they were moving to Skyway, I'd asked where that was, and Zendaya asked, "Didn't you grow up around here?"

"Yeah, I've just never heard of it," I said. Turns out, Skyway—an unincorporated neighborhood in south Seattle—was just across the city. As it happened, the one neighborhood I didn't know about was the one with the largest proportion of Black residents in any zip code in the state.

The school in Skyway was rated lower, as are most schools with large populations of low-income students and students of color.

But we decided we wanted to go there anyway. This move was the first time that my family and I took what's often considered an educational risk, in contradiction of the conventional wisdom about race, income, and academic success. I'd advocated that teachers, principals, superintendents, school boards, funders, partners, and state leaders take such so-called risks. That students and their parents take them. Hiring Zendaya, Eddie and others at Equal Opportunity Schools wasn't a risk for me. They had stellar records by any standard.

Natalie's and my online research did not turn up such a record for the school where we enrolled Oliver. Black, Latino, and Asian students each make up around a quarter of the school. Two-thirds are low-income, like Oliver's best friend, his uncle Jamie, and his mother have been. We followed Natalie's experience in a highly diverse school, and our hunch that a diverse school doing good work was probably better than the traditional measures suggested. We followed the advice of my former students, who told me they wouldn't give up the diversity of their education for anything.

Oliver was sad to leave some of his friends when we made the move, but now he says he'd be sad to leave the ones he's made in Skyway. Oscar has now started his school years in Skyway, as will Millie. And I imagine they'll get an education that's better than the fool's-gold-plated one I got, in which folks kept telling me I was the best, and that people I was surrounded by who shared my background were the best, while denying me the critical opportunity to benefit from a broad variety of human experiences, which are accessible to us if we can just figure out how to traverse the distances that divide us from difference.

———

When our youngest, Millie, first looked at the broken pegboard over cement and two-by-fours in the unfinished part of the basement where I set up my desk after our recent move, she told me, "Daddy, your office is broken!" Sitting there now, I can hear Oliver and Oscar playing out on the grass with Darren and Davide.

Still figuring out where to focus my time in the bumpy years since leaving EOS, I've been spending a lot more time with Erin—she'll be over soon for dinner with her husband and daughter. Looking forward to her visit, I laugh at the ridiculousness of the idea that she was ever incapable of love. She has been the most generous, considerate, supportive, insightful, and consistent person through this time of change. We're in touch several times a day and have rewoven our braided history.

Even though I didn't prevent the physical and sexual assaults she suffered in high school, or in the hotel room she desperately needed but couldn't pay for, I've vowed to be there with her every way I know how, for the rest of our days. She expands my sense of the possibilities of compassion and love, generosity, and unmatched determination.

With her encouragement, I've been spending my time writing, volunteering, coaching executives from underrepresented backgrounds, and also engaging with some of the most advantaged folks in the state about what we can do to make as much progress as possible in education, on youth mental health, equity, homelessness, and the divisions we face when trying to come together to solve our most pressing challenges.

That cheap print of the Dalí painting that's traveled with me, from Battery Creek High School to my office at Equal Opportunity Schools, now hangs on the broken pegboard. I keep the painting around to remind me that the elements we readily observe in the world are often a part of something bigger that we can't yet make out. But once you really see that the flies and the broken statues and swaths of fabric—together—comprise Dalí's hallucinogenic toreador, you'll never mistake it for anything less.

Applying the concept of "missing" to our lives—biasing toward a belief in profound talent and possibilities, especially in people and places we may be most likely to overlook—has already proven a boon to our kids, who won't have to grow up in as segregated an environment as I did. And Natalie's and my hunch that the students in their new school, and the school itself, were probably being underestimated has been borne out. Even if you just use the traditional lens of achievement test scores, recent data shows that students at our new elementary school actually learn *more* each year than students in the higher-rated and heavily segregated school we left. That's true for low-income students as well as for middle- and upper-income students.

Beyond test scores, I find myself thinking back to what learning is at its most fundamental level: the incorporation of difference into our existing mental map of the world. For learning to happen, our minds need to change their patterns to better reflect what we're observing. And if what we observe is fairly narrow, our minds will be too. If what we observe from others is mostly like what we've observed at home in our own family, then our mind doesn't have much fodder for change or growth. If all our teachers share similar backgrounds, ways of talking, and ways of thinking, our learning will be stunted—as mine was. Not only are we not preparing students in segregated environments for the world as it actually exists—full of complexity and diversity—we're artificially narrowing the scope of their minds. I've always aspired to the type of broader mind my wife has developed.

Schools may be broadening the curricular content of our classes more than in previous generations as a way to try to expand our children's mental horizons, but without changing the composition of our classrooms and of our teaching force, we're missing a far bigger opportunity: the chance to substantially expand the bounding frames of our thinking, to incorporate angles heretofore unobserved by separated and demographically isolated students. New lessons covering new content are important. But we are shaped socially, above all else. So the breadth and truth of our ideas—our morality, who we think we are, what we think matters, where we focus, what we dream, and where we aim our lives and those of the rising generation—will be considerably determined by the breadth and representation of people with whom we engage.

Our parents these days generally look back on the perpetuators of de jure (by law) segregation as deeply, morally wrong in having made that choice. When it was outlawed, that form of segregation is generally understood to have been replaced with de facto segregation. And some people take "de facto" to mean just "in fact"—some sort of an immutable result of forces beyond the law and therefore beyond us as a society to change. But "de facto" means in fact, or in practice. We can practice separation—which, in me, has caused a sense of small-mindedness, loneliness, and incompletion.

I'm eternally grateful to my students, my team, my board, my wife, my friends, and my sister for helping me into broader practices. It took fifteen years to undo some of the most harmful things I'd been asked to practice in school, and to begin to build personal relationships across some of the starkest divides our society prompts us to practice daily. After we moved, it took Oliver less than fifteen days to do the same.

And as relationships in the rising generation change, so do our mores. Our children may look back at contemporary de facto practices of segregation as being deeply, morally wrong. What excuses would folks with any significant choice in the matter offer for having sent a child to a school with mostly white students (as Natalie and I did) and mostly white teachers (as we still do), though their generation is mostly nonwhite?

My excuse for having done that was that it was just the way I came up. That maybe the alternatives seemed worse. That I didn't know any better. But now we do.

Writing about this gets me worked up, and I think about a call I had earlier today with some of the folks working atop one of the highest skyscrapers in the city. They'd asked where I live and where my kids went to school, and I said Skyway. And they said they'd never heard of it. I couldn't help but shake my head and wonder, *How can people not know one of the most diverse neighborhoods in their own city? What's wrong with them?*

I laugh at my own arrogance and hypocrisy, remembering I didn't know, just a couple years ago! So, I wonder, instead, *Why do I still get drawn into this trap of looking down on others and pretending I'm morally superior?* What a waste of time, when there's so much I still don't know, and so many opportunities to learn and grow and change, when we surround ourselves with diversity and grace, understanding that mistakes are inevitable—sometimes awful—and the basis for progress.

—— CHAPTER THIRTY-NINE ——

Near the end of my third year at Battery Creek High School, I walked into my advanced psychology class, indignant.

Indirect light came into the classroom out of the fog that was hugging the big brick building. Through it, the world was unseeable—we might as well have been drifting at sea or floating in space. Perhaps it would burn off later.

Jim was truing up his desk to the circle, and Max his. Allie was already seated across from Juan, and Sandee searched her compact mirror for something she had yet to find.

I hoped we'd been making progress in the school these past few years, but progress didn't seem to be reaching the class across the hall, where I'd spent the past hour.

"So, I was just subbing in on someone's class, and maybe you guys can help me out here, because I'm at a loss."

"Thompson's class, right?"

I slid into my desk in the circle.

"Heard he was chasin' that boy down the hall, kept puttin' hands on him and—"

"Police involved."

"Jordan just had his headphones on's all, and Thompson kept—"

"All right. Whose class it was doesn't matter. Point is that it was US history. And after observing for a while, after they'd finished up their dittos and stuff, I just asked them a question."

"Did the teacher tell you to do that, Saaris?" Allie tipped her head sideways at me.

"No, but—"

"Tscht! Always stirrin' somethin'."

"But he didn't tell me anything about what to do because he had to go—"

"So it *was* Thompson, after he took off on Jordan."

"I knew it."

"*Anyways*, I asked the class why they thought all the Black kids were sitting in the back and white kids in the front. In their classroom, that is." I laced my fingers together on the desk and sat back, balancing my feet on the toes of my shoes.

"Oh boy," said Allie.

"Watcha think they goin' say to that, Saaris?" asked D'Shaun. "Like, we talkin' 'bout *Brown v. Board,* and desegregation of schools and classrooms, and psychology of prejudice and all that in here, but . . ."

"They could say anything, really, after they've supposedly been taught the history of the country all year long. But they said my question had nothing to do with history. That they didn't learn anything about civil rights or anything that had to do with the present, and that basically there was no reason. They just felt like sitting where they were."

"And that surprises you?" asked Juan, adjusting his glasses.

"Yeah. I mean, those kids are so close to each other—in the same classroom. And in our class here, we've talked about the only thing really shown to reduce prejudice and discrimination."

"Wasn't that that 'super' thing?" Allie asked. "Super . . ." She leafed through her notebook quickly.

"Superordinate goals," said Jim.

"I had that," she said after a moment. "And I thought of it first!"

He held up his hands, and she smiled back.

"Yeah," I said. "It's all about cross-group interaction. Actually having contact and taking things out of *ideas* about other people and into *relationships*, working together across difference. It's, like, the only thing that really works against prejudice."

"Wasn't that that sheriff guy?"

"Sherif," I said. "Folks, remember that one?"

"That camp," said Jim. "With, like, the two teams."

"Got it! I got it!" said Allie raising her hand, then pulling it down to trace her detailed notes as she talked. "The campers were assigned to the Eagle and the Rattler groups, which became out-groups to each other."

"Great," I said, "and we talked a few times about how easy it is to create out-groups, how quick we are to categorize and denigrate others."

"Yup," said Juan. "I ended up using some of those examples in my experimental write-up."

"Me too," said Jim. "The 'brown eyes, blue eyes' one in the classroom, where the teacher told everyone that blue eyes were better, and then all the blue eyes ganged up on the brown-eyes folks."

"Yep, and the next day," I said, "she switched it and said she'd been mistaken and it was brown eyes who were better, and then the blue-eyes kids got picked on and felt horrible."

"We knew that, Saaris. Why you talkin' so much?" asked D'Shaun.

"OK, you're right! What else?"

"I think the one that summarizes how crazy it all is is that Tajfel guy," said Juan. "You can assign people to groups based on nothing—even a random coin toss—and they'll *still* show tons of in-group favoritism and out-group prejudice and discrimination. Just like that!" He snapped his fingers, then everyone was quiet.

Looking around the circle, I imagined we were all thinking how tragic this was: how quick we are to tear others down.

"But *we're* together, at least," said Jim.

I swallowed.

"Only for six more days," said Allie, maybe sad about it, maybe with New York on her mind.

"..."

When D'Shaun sat up and began to talk, everyone looked at him, but he stared at the rug in the center. "Us bein' together, like at that College Fair, was, like, one'a the proudest moments for me. They was all these homogeneous folks there, and we was the only group that was actually diverse. Like our own little United Nations or somethin'."

I held my nose and my mouth in my hand and looked off, by the teacher's desk. "It makes me so happy to hear you say that," I said, frowning, pausing. "But is it enough?"

D'Shaun and I looked at each other, and he said, "How you mean?"

"How I mean is, with how our brains work, we're *so* quick to separate ourselves from others. And all the work of desegregation and everything else to try to bring people together . . . but it's not even happening just across the hall!"

"I knew it was Thompson's class!"

I made a *whoops* face.

Max giggled.

"I'm serious, y'all," I said. "And even in this class. Like Allie said, we've got six more days, including today. And then what? We're getting pruned down every day, like we've talked about. The brain's got so much information coming in, and to start making sense of it as a baby, we have to start ignoring tons of it, paying attention only to the stuff that shows up the most, the patterns that repeat. And most of those other connections—some of the possibilities we're talkin' about here—don't get fired enough and just die off, forever."

"Watcha talkin 'bout, 'die off forever'? You sposta be our optimist here, man," said D'Shaun.

"Das morbid, mane."

"Isn't it all kinda morbid?" asked Max. "The selfishness of humans, and evolution kinda puttin' us on the edge of our wits just to try to get us to do all this stuff and reproduce—"

Interrupting, Jim asked me, "I thought you were all about that plasticity? That don't mean die off forever."

"I am, and that's true," I said, thinking about the good discussions we'd had about how much the brain can change at any age. How lobes that spend their whole existence on eyesight can start processing touch sensations, making you "see" Braille through your fingers after just a week of your eyes being covered up. "It's just what's shaping the plastic that's maybe a problem . . ." I stopped, realizing I needed help.

Max took his hand down from his forehead. "You're basically talking about there's all these things pulling us apart and dividing us up, and kind of this one thing that can bring us together, and is it enough?"

I nodded hard. "My understanding is schools are starting to re-segregate," I said flatly. "So instead of being separated across town, we're twenty feet away from each other across the hall. And if we don't close the rest of that distance like now, the tide of re-segregation may sweep away our last opportunity to come together."

"I mean, we already changed a lot of classes, Saaris," said Jim. "Maybe not Thompson's, but we brought a lotta kids together this year."

"Together's important. Proximity, like we studied about. But then you gotta actually work together towards goals, right?" asked Sandee. "And alotta the changed classes are still divided inside, to be honest."

Allie was studying me so forcefully from across the circle that I was starting to feel embarrassed, but she just kept staring across the notebook open on her desk. Her hands were hidden below, and she was leaning into the laminated panel, her eyes slit in scrutiny.

"Saaris," she said after others had said more, "you ain't never gonna change peeps like Thompson, long as you be lookin' down on him."

I knew exactly what she meant, and it hurt, so I responded with "But I can't help it. I'm just taller than he is."

She busted out laughing.

"But no," I said, "I get what you're saying."

"That's it," said Sandee. "Allie's, like, 100 percent on this. Like when we came into your class and you wanted us to change."

I didn't like the idea of me changing them. "Well, to learn. I wanted us *all* to learn, which is change, I guess, yes."

"*Anyways*," she continued, widening her eyes to chastise me for interrupting, "the only reason I stuck around for that was cuz you seemed to think I could do it. Like, you know, you really believed in me . . . or something cheesy like that."

I nodded.

"But you don't believe in Thompson, do you?" pressed Allie.

". . ."

"Like, you came in here all huffy. I was watching you. You're, like, *disgusted* with this guy because he don't teach the kind of history you think he should. You got yo' in-group too, Saaris," she added, gradually smiling as she unwrapped her idea for us.

Sandee said, "It's, like, you and Fry and Señora Perez and, like—who else's in your crew, anyways?"

I've got others, I thought. *I like Johnston most of the time. And Cutter's OK sometimes, and that new guy. I am sorting my group. And sometimes I do think of those outside of it as jerks. And I'm not friends with any of the Black women— more often than not, we seem to be in conflict . . .*

"If you want Thompson to change, you have to believe in him," said Juan. "Like that Pygmalion effect, or any of those self-fulfilling-prophecy thingies. When they make up IQ scores for kids and show the teacher, and then the way the teacher treats the kids leads to them actually scoring like that."

But I was so mad at Walter Thompson. Desperately mad.

"At the end of this year-long class," I tried, "those kids are sayin' history has nothing to do with their lives and their choices. That different outcomes for race groups come from laziness! No understanding whatsoever of the sweeping historical forces that brought us to this point, that put people in these positions to begin with. And that's on the teacher, isn't it?"

"I'm not about to say it isn't," said Allie.

Juan said, "Class I took with Thompson wasn't so bad."

Barreling on, I said, "It takes a lot of messed up and active effort to stop the learning that comes naturally to us."

"But we came in here having done some f . . . messed up things too. Well, some of us," said D'Shaun. "Maybe things we regret, or need to get over. And I remember you was, like, sayin' how e'ry one of us could still be totally down to learn and stuff."

"And I spose you think you ain't made no big mistakes?" asked Allie over crossed arms.

Back then, I still didn't think I had. "I don't know," I said.

"Spose you don't think you'll never need no grace or forgiveness, then."

I said, "What if—and I'm not talkin' about anyone in particular here— what if the mistake is someone looks down on someone because of their race. Holds them back. Gets in their way. Drags them down. You're sayin' don't get mad at *them*? And that you should be 'totally down to learn and stuff' with them?!"

"Ain't sayin I'm down with all that," said Allie.

Me neither! I thought.

"I guess only if you want them to learn," said D'Shaun as others said, *Mmm.*

"Y'all mighta heard what happened to Thompson in Iraq." I hadn't, but there were a couple of solemn nods.

"Honestly" Max said, "no one's gonna wanna listen to you if you dislike 'em."

"And we're all, like, livin' in this world that's messed up and also good too," said Jim. "So, the messed-up stuff and the good stuff gets on all'a us. So you should relate to other people's mistakes, not just what they done that's good."

"And didn't you even say once that we need to love our mistakes?" asked Sandee. "Like, when you grade everything in that stupid green pen and say mistakes are the source of learning?"

"But it's different when you're talking about making mistakes that hurt people—the things that really need fixing," I said. "Not academic mistakes."

"Is it different in the mind, though?" asked D'Shaun. "Like, in how the brain learns? Whether it's school or life, mistakes are still how we learn, innit? And those makin' the biggest mistakes got the most to learn, innit?"

"So folks who want them to learn gotsta believe in them. Even love em."

"You can do that, can't chu, Saaris?"

Can you?

EVIDENCE ON SCHOOLING IN AMERICA TODAY

In this book, I've tried to tell the story of my experiences in public education:

- from my time as a student when I was bored and disengaged, as most high schoolers are these days;[1]

- to the opportunities I received to learn some amazing things and tackle interesting challenges in advanced classes[2]—classes that cost me most of my opportunities to learn from and with kids of different backgrounds, who were often just across the hall;[3]

- to my time as a teacher, an administrator, and a nonprofit leader looking for chances to make great learning opportunities available to students and adults, while trying to catch up on major learning I'd missed along the way.

I chose to tell this as a first-person story because the facts aren't enough. When it comes to changing our lives by changing our minds, it will always be personal and relational. We need both deep relationships and a rigorous understanding of facts and evidence. This epilogue goes beyond the deep data about missing students[4] included in the main part of the book to analyze a broader set of facts and evidence about the state and future of American education.

WHAT WE PUT INTO SCHOOLS

Seventy-four million students currently attend school in the United States.[5] And with an additional eight million people working in our schools,[6] nearly a quarter of the US population is directly involved in formal education on a daily basis. Almost another quarter of the population is involved as parents of those who are in school.[7] So that's nearing half the country—before you start adding in the many nonprofits and companies that work with schools and students.

To run American schools, we spend about one out of every twenty dollars we make in the US.[8] More than 90 percent of this spending is roughly split between local government and the state government, which typically put more into education than any other spending category.[9] When federal, state, and local spending is combined, education spending by the government is second only to public spending on health care.[10]

WHAT WE HOPE COMES OUT

We put so much of ourselves and our resources into schools each year because we know education is useful to individuals—generally enhancing civic engagement and influence in democratic society,[11] boosting earnings,[12] improving health outcomes, and perhaps even extending life itself.[13] There are also, of course, intangible benefits. As my wife says, education made her brain a much more interesting place to be.

At the societal level, our past investments in education seem to have worked out well. America's position of global leadership in the twentieth century—through hard power, soft power, income, and wealth—coincided with an era in which the American people were the most educated in the world.[14]

A great deal has been written about the purpose of K-12 education, but let's keep it simple: in a democracy, schools should be for what we want them to be for. And if you ask millions of high schoolers, about nine in ten will say they're there to get ready for college—and that that's their parents' goal for them too.[15] They pursue college in part because such degrees can mean a million dollars more in lifetime earnings,[16] resulting from higher wages and higher rates of employment.[17] This is in significant part due to the fact that annually there are 50 percent more job openings for positions requiring a bachelor's degree[18] than there are students graduating with one.[19]

College education in America has many problems too, which have been much discussed in recent years: cost and debt, elitism, political divisiveness, and more. One of the most poignant descriptions of toxic education-related divisions comes in a book that doesn't make for light reading: *Deaths of Despair*,[20] in which economists detail how Americans without college degrees are too often denied opportunities and societal respect, resulting in increased risk of alcoholism, drug overdose, and suicide.

New efforts like Opportunity@Work and Merit America are opening innovative pathways for folks who haven't attended college, which is great, because everyone should be supported to find and pursue the career of their choosing. Some of the most effective approaches in education and professional development focus on supportive navigation at key educational and life junctures. And we should have more evidence on the effect of these programs and how to grow their reach and impact in the years ahead.

Since the vast majority of high school students and families are choosing college as their goal, let's go deeper.[21]

MISSING COLLEGE GRADUATES

This past half century, we have expanded education after high school, more than doubling participation in college,[22] while also more than doubling per-person earnings in the US.[23] In recent years, the expansion of college-going has slowed significantly—especially compared with other countries, and for certain groups within the US. While those nearing retirement age in the US earned college degrees at a rate higher than all but four other countries in the world, their children rank twelfth in the world for college degrees earned.[24] About half of those in their mid-twenties to mid-thirties have completed education after high school, which means that around 40 percent of those in that age group who wanted further education have not yet gotten it.

Educational dreams are especially unfulfilled for lower-income students. While college goals don't vary much by family income level, outcomes do. Fifty-eight percent of the wealthiest quarter of 24-year-olds have earned college degrees, but only 11 percent of the poorest quarter have.[25] And the gap between these two groups has nearly doubled over the past forty years. If the current situation persists for the upcoming generation, three million of our youth from lower-income families will achieve their college dreams, and twenty million will not.[26]

College dreams are also unfulfilled for many students of color. Black students are about two-thirds as likely as white students to earn another degree after high school, and Latino students are about half as likely.[27] Our persistent failure to enable similar levels of attainment of college goals across groups is imposing a permanent economic recession on the US.[28] If past attainment levels persist for today's Black and Latino youth, about fifteen million will achieve their college goals, and twenty-three million will not.[29]

This constitutes a loss of earnings and economic activity in the rising generation on the order of tens of trillions of dollars. Since students of color became the new majority in the nation's public schools in 2014,[30] there is simply no way to significantly and sustainably improve our nation's educational, economic, and civic results without figuring out how to better serve those who our schools have too often neglected as "minority."

MISSING ADVANCED STUDIES HIGH SCHOOL STUDENTS

Educational change in the US is notoriously difficult to come by. The public school system has rebuffed a new major reform effort about every couple of decades since the country's founding—with one exception. The common school movement was successful in its stated aim to make schools more inclusive. Driven in part by this effort, American public schools were among the first in the world to open their doors universally to girls, students whose families aren't wealthy, and students of color—eventually expanding access from primary through secondary schools.[31] Although universal access has not yet reached the highest levels of our secondary schools (advanced studies programs like Advanced Placement, International Baccalaureate, Cambridge/AICE, and dual enrollment), we know that expanding access to the next level of learning opportunities has a unique track record of working well in a school system that has otherwise proven fairly impervious to strategic and intentional change efforts.

And yet, low-income students and Black and Latino students are consistently and systematically under-enrolled in the most academically intense high school courses. With the Education Trust, the US Department of Education, College Board/Advanced Placement, and International Baccalaureate, I built an original data set to quantify and diagnose these persistent inequities. We found that while Black, Latino, and low-income students are about as likely as their peers to attend schools that offer AP or IB programs, the vast majority of AP and IB programs (99 percent of well-established programs in diverse high schools) did not yet provide equal access.[32] And so, each year, about 800,000 students remain stuck just across the hall from the education they need, deserve, and have generally proven themselves highly capable of succeeding at. Though the gaps are large—directly affecting about one in ten juniors and seniors—we found that almost all of them could be closed by focusing on how individual schools enroll kids in existing advanced classes and closing those gaps at the school level.[33]

MISSING LEARNING

Many have asked how we could determine who is and is not ready for college-level coursework near the end of high school. There is no perfect formula for doing so (though there have been many failed attempts to quantify "potential" or intelligence, including a popular tool used to identify advanced studies students, which we found to have missed the majority of students of color who went on to pass advanced exams in one of EOS's cohorts of schools). Some school districts have designed systems that effectively prepare almost all their students for the rigors of advanced studies in high shool.[34] Success in such classes comes from more than just a student's "potential"—it's a combination of what students bring to the table, what educators bring to the table, and the context set by the school.

We've talked in this book about educator mindsets, school district reforms, and efforts to reach the 800,000 students who are ready for more rigorous and more diverse advanced classes now. Let's broaden the aperture to all high schoolers—their level of academic preparation, and how we might go about getting even more college aspirants ready for the rigor of advanced classes and college.

Currently, only 37 percent of American twelfth graders are academically prepared for college in reading and math, according to the Nation's Report Card.[35] While some progress has been made in closing racial achievement gaps (with Black-white and Latino-white gaps 30 to 40 percent smaller than during the 1970s), the gaps are still huge, with twelfth grade Black students averaging an eighth grade level in mathematics.[36]

Literacy and numeracy are certainly not the only skills worth pursuing. As you know by this point, I have a strong passion for social studies, and the ways we learn about how individuals, groups, civil society, and government work, as part of our endeavor to be responsible, productive, and caring members of our society. And I believe deeply in rigorous learning assessments, like advanced exams that use portfolios of work, oral and essay exams, and so on. And yet it is worth focusing here more deeply on literacy and numeracy, because building those core skills in more students would help additional high schoolers become prepared for more advanced learning.

It is said that if you learn to read before fourth grade, then you can read to learn about everything else for the rest of your time in school.[37] A lot of what students do—or don't—learn in school comes through reading. The ability to understand math textbooks, science articles, assignment and testing instructions, and more will be impaired if a student has not yet learned grade-level reading skills. Third grade reading is a critical point, with effects extending far beyond elementary school—third grade students who do not read proficiently are four times more likely not to graduate from high school on time.[38] Unfortunately, two-thirds of our fourth graders are not yet proficient in reading—including 83 percent of Black fourth graders.[39] This means we're missing about 2.7 million nine-year-old readers. And if our schools don't help more students catch up to proficiency in reading, of the 52 million students in our public schools today, 35 million will not be successful, according to the standards of our own Nation's Report Card.

If you attain proficiency in mathematics by the eighth grade, you can use your numeracy beyond math classes to enable understanding of the natural sciences, social sciences, finance, music, and even art; you also have dramatically improved odds of graduating high school and college. And yet, 64 percent of our eighth graders are not proficient in grade-level math—including 91 percent of Black students.[40] This means we're missing about 2.4 million grade-level mathematics students. And if these math results aren't improved for the full 52 million-student cohort in our public schools today, that means over 33 million students not successfully learning math.

FINDING MISSING LEARNING, SCIENTIFICALLY

At times, I have been shocked at the extent to which a focus on the social and relational side of educational leadership crowds out more rigorous scientific analysis of key decisions. As this book makes clear, I myself have often fallen into these traps. I think it's a result of the pressure of taking responsibility for the rising generation that sometimes leads us to sloppy and unscientific accounting for what has caused what, and the implications for how best to use scarce resources in our shared endeavor for learning. After all, every hundred years, it's all new people on this planet, and education is our most resource-intensive undertaking to try to ensure that new people have what they need to survive and prosper. The responsibility of being an educator can be almost too much to bear. This can lead educators like me to downplay or ignore our own mistakes—which we need to confront in order to learn—and double down on what we are doing, despite emerging evidence that it isn't the right approach.

For the sake of our children, and especially given the challenges and learning setbacks following the coronavirus pandemic, I think everyone is eager for real solutions that will work to ensure students can read, write, think critically, and become compassionate and engaged citizens and leaders of the next iteration of our species.

Curious what we could learn from the "science" side of things, I set out with two Stanford teams to try to distill what the extensive body of research on learning can teach us. We focused on how school leaders might make the best use of limited financial resources, including the largest ever federal investment in education: about $300 billion during the pandemic. Consulting thousands of studies and dozens of experts, we built a field-wide comparative analysis of what has been shown to most advance student learning in our schools.

Each step of the way, we had to remind ourselves that what we were building would be far from perfect—but that even so, the work of trying to directly compare the effectiveness of all the major approaches to improving student learning could still be valuable. We want to emphasize this point, because what we have built is *not* a perfectly honed academic research paper on the topic. We don't academically address things like the fact that standard deviations in learning gains are not perfectly comparable across different populations taking different tests (though we do adjust for age-based standard deviation differences). Though imperfect, our model may quite favorably compare with the current ways of operating, in which I have yet to see any school system's leaders conduct a rigorous and explicit comparison of the likely learning impacts of each of their major investment choices.

We first worked with a variety of educational leaders and scholars to create a relatively comprehensive list of twenty major topics of focus for improving learning, including topics from student-level interventions up to federal policy changes. To greenlight an approach—meaning we found strong research indicating that implementing such a strategy well would be very likely to significantly increase student learning—we required several robust quasi-experimental design studies pointing in the same positive direction, or a strong and uncontradicted randomized controlled-trial result. Then we verified our interpretation of the literature with leading experts in each topic.

We found that most of the popular areas of educational investments either lacked enough research evidence to determine effectiveness, or had strong research evidence showing them to be generally ineffective. Though researchers have undertaken major efforts to rigorously understand the impact of educational strategies on student learning (e.g., the What Works Clearinghouse, run by the US Department of Education, research published by most graduate schools of education, including the work of the Center for

Research and Reform in Education at Johns Hopkins[41]), researchers and educators seldom have the relationships with one another needed to translate that evidence into local decision-making and ongoing practice. And so ineffective strategies continue to be broadly used, absent both better comparative impact analysis and the collaboration and communication required to bridge existing analyses to the intensive context of day-to-day decision making in our schools.

For the areas with robust evidence of effectiveness, we converted effect sizes to additional months of learning that students would be likely to gain if such a strategy were implemented well.[42] And we matched those demonstrated learning gains to detailed cost estimates from expert practitioners. This allows us to hone in on the most evidenced and effective uses of incoming money—in terms of progress on students' core literacy and numeracy skills. It has become all the more urgent to measure and understand the extent to which investments can support teachers and students, since the Nation's Report Card has recently shown that the pandemic caused many students to lose as much as a year's progress in academic learning.[43] Now more than ever, teachers and students need the best resources their schools can provide them.

High Impact Strategies

We identified a couple areas for investment with a high and proven positive impact per dollar on students' acquisition of reading and math skills. Effectively implementing proven practices in these areas is likely to be among the most effective uses of incoming education funding. We estimate that these strategies cost around $100 per resulting month of learning gains by a student in a school year.[44]

1. Student well-being and mindset—The highest-impact use of funding we found was the application of targeted interventions to promote students' understanding of brain science and belonging.[45] At EOS, we partnered with a number of Stanford researchers for randomized controlled trials on this topic and saw the power of both growth-mindset and sense-of-belonging interventions. For example, in teaching students about the malleable nature of intelligence (that students aren't "smart" or "dumb")—and that learning results from engagement with ideas and evidence—you can readily improve student engagement. Relatedly—and made especially acute by the pandemic—mental health resources are an increasingly important area for schools and states to consider targeting investments. Though the direct impact of mental health services on academics is less studied, Great Britain has shown that cognitive behavioral therapy can reliably relieve symptoms of anxiety and depression in two out of three youth for nine or more years.[46] Currently, such symptoms are afflicting more than half of youth, making engagement with academic content more challenging.

2. Assignment to more challenging classes—In addition to the literature previously discussed connecting rigorous high school coursework to college-going and completion, there is strong research on the impact of advanced course-taking on secondary school achievement levels.[47] The impact of this strategy is relatively higher per dollar than medium impact strategies because transitioning significant numbers of students up to advanced classes does not require the hiring of additional coaches, tutors, or significant new spending on poverty reduction or ongoing recruitment incentives. Rather, it involves a rather straightforward administrative change in students' schedules. Making this change will often require thoughtful leadership, identification of specific students for a first cohort using data analysis, and potentially some transitional support, the purchasing of new books and beakers for the advanced classes, and the like. However, these costs are relatively small and can be amortized, in comparison to other major ongoing investments required for most of the medium-impact categories that follow.

Medium Impact Strategies

Medium-impact areas of investment are very important to a sustained strategy for further improving learning. Though not as impactful per dollar as the strategies above, these strategies have an important feature that the high-impact strategies don't: by increasing dosage, you may be able to increase benefits to students and teachers. They are not all "one-and-done" like the high-impact strategies above. These strategies cost in the ballpark of $500 per added month of learning per student.

3. Collaborative teacher coaching—Though most sit-and-get forms of teacher learning and professional development have not shown an impact on student learning, collaborative coaching models do.[48] In these models, experienced teachers observe and support other teachers, providing informed thinking and jointly identifying opportunities to further develop their practice. Some of my best experiences in teacher training involved detailed notetaking by others who then helped me to reflect on what was working, what I'd like to improve, and how I might go about it. Researchers have a decent understanding of what elements of teacher coaching programs make them most successful;[49] following that evidence, local teachers are well positioned to design the particulars of the approaches that work best in their contexts.

4. Diverse teacher recruitment—The research on the impact of teacher diversity is fairly strong, especially for the impact of Black teachers on Black student learning.[50] Black students may gain about an additional month's worth of learning in a year if they have the opportunity to learn from a Black teacher, especially at some point in elementary school. Following *Brown v. Board of Education*, white school district leaders who controlled the best-funded and most powerful school systems, which were forced to integrate with other schools, often fired all the teachers of color in favor of all-white teaching staffs. Teacher diversity still has not recovered. Today about 80 percent of teachers are white, while most students are not.[51] Like advanced classes in which students of color often say they don't feel like they belong,[52] teachers of color may not feel they belong either, given the culture and makeup of teacher education schools and teachers' lounges to this day.[53] At the same time, the research is increasingly clear that it makes a significant difference (in both math/reading test scores, and long-run college degree attainment) if students get to see their background and experiences represented at the front of the classroom—particularly at some point in the earlier grades.[54]

Even though the current gap nationally is more than a million "missing" teachers of color,[55] even the more costly approaches to recruiting and retaining teachers of color in the US could readily close the gap in the next decade with a few percent of the federal schools' pandemic recovery funding—if this work were prioritized by state and school district leaders. The strategies could be very similar to the work we did to close the "missing" students gap—focusing on understanding the gap through extensive surveys and research, targeting outreach and recruitment to those who feel least included, and building plans for success based in the data. As discussed earlier, it can be important to "go all the way" by *fully* closing gaps in order to tip the sense of inclusion and who belongs, unlocking fantastic levels of achievement by students and educators who were previously underrepresented. And with teacher shortages and significant upcoming waves of retirement, closing these gaps through new and more diverse recruiting needn't displace existing educators.

5. Poverty alleviation—Poverty is often connected to the amount of student learning that shows up on reading, writing, math, and science tests. Poorer kids on average score lower. But this doesn't necessarily mean that poverty directly causes those results. It could be, for example, that schools that serve poorer kids have less money (despite the federal government's efforts to get more money to poor schools through Title I, some of the property-tax-based inequities outdo the federal funds, and often districts assign lower-paid and less-experienced teachers to schools that have more poor students, lowering those schools' total funding and effectiveness.

And we know that schools can also make a positive difference that outweighs the impacts poverty may have on student learning. When they provide more challenging classes, those classes become more important than poverty in determining the student's chances in college.[56] But even if some things can make a bigger difference to student learning than poverty, does poverty itself affect learning beyond the way that schools respond to it?

The best studies of this look at the impacts of direct payments to poor families, especially through tax credits.[57] In our analysis of these studies, we find a reliable positive impact on student test scores for $1,000 tax credits.

When we look at school strategies through the lens of evidence like this, it can hopefully get us out of the politics of blaming only poverty or only schools. Many school and district leaders can make better choices about how to use their resources for better outcomes with students who are in poverty. And getting students out of poverty would, on average, improve their learning further in schools. And the long-term benefits of improved student learning—especially for students from lower-income families, whose greatest chances of boosting income are with higher education—are greater (in terms of dollars, not to mention the many other benefits we've discussed elsewhere) than the costs of poverty-addressing tax credits for families with children.

6. Tutoring—There has been a lot written in recent years about the effectiveness of tutoring, especially by the late Bob Slavin,[58] who spent his career combing through the strongest education research evidence to understand what helps kids learn. Tutoring came in near the middle of our list of proven strategies because it has a high level of effectiveness, but also a relatively high cost. When programs are conducted well and use paraeducators and some computer assistance, costs can be lower.[59] Tutoring can be effective even when provided by folks who haven't undergone expensive trainings and certifications. Tutors need to know the subject that they're tutoring a student on (like reading or multiplication), but beyond that, what seems to matter most is that kids have someone there who is listening and paying attention, and focusing on the learning with them.[60] Because this analysis looks at average effects, the precise effectiveness of particular local implementations can certainly vary. As with many of these strategies, to get the most gains for students from the effort, it is probably a good idea to track the progress being made locally so that educators can adjust their approach based on what's working well in their context.

Lower Impact Strategies

The following strategies have been shown to have an impact on student learning, on the order of $1,000 per increased month of learning per student (about ten times as expensive as the high-impact strategies).

7. Extended learning time—Beyond tutoring, strategies for additional learning time (like summer school) are sometimes shown to work well for kids, just not quite as well as the other strategies we've discussed so far. Also, the results can vary significantly, depending on how the time is used.[61] Such programs are a lower-impact way to use a limited set of additional funding to boost students' reading and writing skills. That said, they may still be a worthwhile investment under certain circumstances. For example, working parents may already need to spend money on summer and after-school programming for day care. In this case, if that existing spending can be better used to help students make academic progress through well-designed summer and after-school care options, then this could be a good investment, and schools could play a role in helping such programs better contribute to students' ongoing learning.

8. Teacher retention—Teachers tend to become more effective after their first few years on the job.[62] When schools lose teachers with that experience, they can lose a significant opportunity for student learning gains. For that reason—and many others—it can be worthwhile to invest in strategies to support and retain teachers who have successfully completed their first few years. There is no set way to do this, but providing opportunities for mentorship, strong induction programs, learning resources, and influence as teacher leaders can be effective. Such strategies can be locally designed with teachers to address the most significant opportunities, and in ways that could reduce the costs of these strategies and increase their effectiveness by tailoring the approach to local needs, based on teacher guidance and data.

9. Decreasing class size—Class size has been in contention for some time. It is popular among teachers and families who understandably may want a more intimate learning environment. Some researchers have argued that there are significant student achievement boosts to be had from class-size reductions, while others have asserted that such benefits are minimal.[63] Then an effect-size number somewhere in the middle emerged—if class sizes are reduced by almost a third.[64] However, implementing class-size reductions at this scale poses great challenges, given the following:

- the size of reductions needed to make much difference would require hiring half again as many teachers as currently practice in the US

- new teachers are generally less effective than experienced ones

- the difficulty many districts and states already have in staffing classes at existing class sizes.[65]

If schools had abundant resources beyond those needed to fully implement each of the other strategies described in this epilogue, class-size reduction could be an approach to consider, assuming we could also afford construction costs for the many new classrooms that would be needed.

Strategies Not Well Evidenced

A number of commonly discussed education interventions—such as educational technology, teacher professional development, family engagement, continuous improvement, curriculum change, and charter schools—are not included in the list above. There are a few reasons for this. Many common approaches have not been studied rigorously. Some have shown average gains that are small but unreliable (most implementations will have no impact or a negative impact, even though the overall average is slightly greater than zero). And some have rigorous evidence showing that they average zero impact. This does not mean that such strategies cannot achieve success, it just means that the current evidence does not suggest they are among the most likely areas to achieve success if invested in by leaders in the current environment. This may be cause for further study, and we have enough robust insights from the existing research to pick areas to focus new investments now, and get right to the more challenging work of implementation.

PRACTICE

The most challenging work comes in building an implementation approach suited to staff skills, school context, and student needs—where the research meets the relationships. Though in this book we have covered some of the key work of implementing greater access to rigorous courses, we don't have space to detail implementation approaches for the other strategies. Hopefully some of the endnotes provide strong leads for the categories that you may be interested in pursuing further.

I find it tremendously unfortunate when I talk with people who appear to be losing hope in our schools. They seem to have the sense—whether they're a teacher, or an administrator, a parent, a policymaker, or a researcher—that what happens in those 130,000 buildings in all corners of our country will never change.

Like many institutions and places now, there are factions and interest groups, distrust, waning confidence—fights even. Things are getting messy.

There is concern that we are divided and may never come together again.

But the rising generation can—and does—come together daily in the American classroom.

If those of us with the honor and responsibility of supporting those daily endeavors can prioritize and practice relationships across difference, and dialogue in rigorous pursuit of truth, then what our kids find during their precious time in those rooms will unleash our highest human potential, enabling us collectively to grow up to be whatever we choose.

ACKNOWLEDGMENTS

My wife and life partner, Natalie, has given me—and this project—more than an acknowledgment could ever adequately recount or repay. Her ideas commingling with my own these past seventeen years have produced such joy in my life, and insight far beyond what I could ever have come up with on my own. Her ideas about teaching and learning; her ideas about strategy, about leadership, about missing and finding others across difference; her ideas about the nature of human connection—so many of her brilliant ideas permeate this book.

There were times when Natalie had just finished a tough week at the office and was solo parenting our three kids while I was away for work. Exhausted after organizing a full-on weekend of adventures for the kids—the library, the playground, a hike, and a homemade dinner, along with dishes, laundry, diapers, teeth-brushing, bedtime stories—she picked up my manuscript at nine o'clock on a Sunday night, making improvements line by line to help me meet a pending deadline.

Though people who so generously offer their time and energy to others often do so at the risk of being taken advantage of, their courageous kindness offers our greatest hope for a more interconnected, shared future. Natalie's model of love inspires me every day to do my best to be as worthy a partner to her, and a more generous friend, parent, colleague, and community member.

Though this book begins by focusing on a difficult period when my parents decided not to adopt Erin, there is much more to the story of their parenting. I don't have the space to tell that whole story here. But I will say that my desire for Erin to permanently join our family was inextricably tied to the fact that the childhood my parents gave me was an incredible gift for which I am eternally grateful. Beyond their jobs, it seems to me they devoted all of their time and energy to our household. The Eden-like gardens my mom cultivated inside and outside the house, whose verdant vines frame every memory, the delicious and healthy food my dad prepared, their tutoring, mentoring, and loving me. I am grateful for my father's playful curiosity and my mom's savvy and compassion. They developed in me a sense of ethical responsibility that has shaped everything I do.

I'm grateful to my "third parent"—my Auntie Suzy, who inspired my love of good writing by writing every morning in journals now stacked to her ceiling, alongside more paintings than can fit on the wall, and Native American art. She does it all on her public school counselor's retirement income by prioritizing beauty and delicious conversation and prose and the hope that she sees in every child—and even in adults—for a better tomorrow. She put a lot of time and a lot of heart into conversations about this book, as well as deep editorial review.

My sister, Erin, has been endlessly gracious and giving. She told me there were times when she would have been embarrassed to have her story shared with others. Now, as an amazing mother reflecting back, she hopes that what she's been through can be of use to others on their learning journeys: to help people understand that the worst things that happen to us should never be used against us; that healing and love and strength are possible, even when we're told they're not.

After Erin left, if I hadn't had Jamie, I think I would've picked up the worst traits associated with the only child: trying to keep everything for myself; taking as truth the false ideas from school that I was better than others; stopping at the edges of my own thinking and refusing to venture beyond into the complexity of real relationships that require us to give up some control, allowing others to rummage through not only our kitchen cabinets for a snack but also through the recesses of our minds, where we hoard and protect our most selfish notions. Thank you for all the uncomfortable conversations that each brought us closer to who we want to grow up to be.

I am so grateful for the sacred time I've spent learning with students over the past twenty years. Your questions, your ideas, your pushes and vivacity continue to change me. I hope that I've been of some use to you, despite the inadequacies of my own education in preparing me to be a good teacher. If you think I can ever be of help in the future, please don't hesitate to call on me.

Founders get too much credit. The work of Equal Opportunity Schools had a kernel that passed through my hands at some point, but that kernel came from Erin, Jamie, EOS's first team members and board members, and generations before us. I got to hold it for a moment, but it was Niambi and Ross and Sandy and Judy and Laudan and Dina and Barbara and Jack and Chris and Luke that made something of the challenge of this much-needed work. It was Bernadette and Sasha and Maile and Kia and Jessica and Aurora and Allison and Adam and Janae and Graham and Alexa and so many others who actually made finding missing students a systematic undertaking involving nearly a hundred full-time staff today, all over the country. Thank you for sharing your incredible work with me and the numerous other educators and students who have benefited from it. I don't know if I'll ever work with as incredible a team as EOS's. I feel especially grateful for the ongoing opportunity to learn from Eddie Lincoln—his drive, hard work, insights, and humility while steadfastly leading to a higher plane.

Educators daily do the hard work of opening doors to our shared future. They make something that seems like a rectangle into a circle, and everything shifts within us. I'm grateful for Del Dolliver, Nancy Jones, the late Annette Dooley, Sergio Martinez, Ed Ramey, Jonathan Bryan, Guy Thomas, Penny Bullock, and many more. The elementary crew of Ms. Hanner, Mary Lou Constans, Sue Bradley, and Paula Fraser. The team of PRISM middle school teachers. Principals like David Engle, who tried to figure out pathways to greater diversity that were debated up to the US Supreme Court. Gloria Mitchell, who taught us to love ourselves even if we found ourselves in places that tried to teach us not to.

Despite drawing attention in this book to some of the flaws and elitism of college and graduate school, I did benefit tremendously from some of these institutions' incredible professors, who fed and watered my mind and sometimes my soul. I'm ongoingly indebted to the inimitable Gay Hoagland. I hope this book blends the personal and the professional, the tactical and the spiritual, in the ways she taught. You would not be reading this book if it weren't for the late Bill Meehan. He put me on the spot in class one day, saying, "Reid, you think you want to start a nonprofit, right? Do you like to ask people for money?" "Not really, no . . ." "Well, that's most of the job. Come down here in front of the class, and I'll bring in my special guest: the chairman of the Gap. Ask him for money." He could spot inconsistent logic and ineffective relational chemistry alike, and never hesitated to accelerate my aspirations for this work. Noah Dauber taught me to turn statistics into the things we're actually talking about—the people—which unlocked for me the concept of "missing students." The late Sidney Verba advised my college thesis and—through his scholarship on the inequality of voice in American democracy—inspired me to focus on equality of educational opportunity.

I want to thank all those who showed true educator colors in being willing to share and discuss their mistakes with me. They showed me that strength doesn't come from pretending that you're strong and have it all together. It comes from opening up to the power of ongoing and lifelong learning. Kate Goerig, Iris Young, Edmond Burnes, Chris Belcher, Lee Vargas, and many more.

Jennifer Carolan believed in EOS at the outset, startling me by being willing to join my founding board. Then she startling me again by calling me up after I left EOS and saying that I should write a book about the work, and supporting me to make it happen. She's an incredible champion for children in our public schools, and I'm always grateful for the motivation that comes from her passion and her drive to ensure that the change we need actually happens.

I'm grateful to other folks who ran the risk of wasting their time on an early-stage organization's board. And they took it seriously, thereby helping the organization become a serious force for good. Anne Marie Burgoyne, Fraser Black, Deborah Wilds, Ron Fortune, and David Fischer, and more.

I appreciate the guidance over the years from Jay Mathews, Kati Haycock, and Jim Shelton. It's been an honor to learn from you and your leadership in this space.

I'm grateful to Truman Liu, Eric Kotin, Vivek Ramakrishnan, and Alice Cheun for making the epilogue to this book possible through our research collaboration. And to the initial team of Stanford students who assembled the ideas for EOS into a business plan that set an ambitious and achievable course for the first phase of Equal Opportunity Schools: Sean Mendy, Hagar Berlin, John Hsu, Thomas Sexton, and Zach Levine. And for my other classmates in graduate school who shared a passion for social impact that kept my flame lit brightly, even on windy days in the foothills.

I'm so grateful to Marcela Christina Maxfield and the team at Stanford University Press for taking a chance on this book, thinking maybe we could upend the tropes and get real about how hard—yet doable—this work is, and make something enjoyable to read in the process.

And my many readers over the years, including a number of the people mentioned earlier, as well as John King, whose insights have taught me so much, John Fisher, Shawon Jackson, Checker Finn, Bernadette Merikle, and more—folks of a wide variety of political and ideological persuasions who nonetheless seem to share a belief that we can figure out how to expand what's working in our schools to include more kids than ever before. Thank you to Margaret Wardlaw, Sean Murray, Sandy Zook, Becky Taylor, Karin Chenoweth, and Jonathan Zwickel for focused review.

I especially want to thank my many student readers, some of whom went far beyond my initial request and collaborated deeply to help tell the truth of what things were like, providing detailed line edits, spelling changes, revisions, advice, disagreements, and discussions, and long phone calls about the purpose and audience for the book, the nature of creativity, what we're here to do, what my limits as an author might be, and whether or not my metaphor for the Cabbage Patch dance was apt. I want to thank Douglas Goethie, Erin Horton, Troy Kelly, Mark Adams, Makai Yallum, Hyesun Lee, Takeia Skanes Redfearn, Latoya Lynn, and especially Shea Roberson Davenport, who dove into the depths of this project with me as an incomparable thought partner. Thank you so much for all you've taught me, y'all!

NOTES

1. In a nationwide survey of US high school students, researchers from the Yale Center for Emotional Intelligence and the Yale Child Study Center found that nearly 75 percent of the students' self-reported feelings related to school were negative. The three most frequently mentioned feelings were tired, stressed, and bored. Julia Moeller, Marc A. Brackett, Zorana Ivcevic, and Arielle E. White, "High School Students' Feelings: Discoveries from a Large National Survey and an Experience Sampling Study," *Learning and Instruction* 66 (April 2020), https://www.sciencedirect.com /science/article/abs/pii/S0959475218304444.

2. Students enrolled in advanced courses tend to be more engaged in their studies, have fewer absences and suspensions, and have higher graduation rates. Kayla Patrick, Socol Allison, and Ivy Morgan, *Inequities in Advanced Coursework: What's Driving Them and What Leaders Can Do* (Washington, DC: The Education Trust, 2020), https://edtrust.org/wp-content/uploads/2014/09/Inequities-in-Advanced-Coursework -Whats-Driving-Them-and-What-Leaders-Can-Do-January-2019.pdf. Additional original analysis of early EOS survey data confirms a relationship between boredom, being challenged, and advanced course taking in high school.

3. In 2013, we reported that nearly two-thirds of a million more low-income students and Black and Latino students would be in advanced courses if they were equitably included. Christina Theokas and Reid Saaris, *Finding America's Missing AP and IB Students* (Washington, DC: The Education Trust, 2013), https://edtrust.org/resource /finding-americas-missing-ap-and-ib-students/. Since then, EOS's original analysis shows that—with the expansion of advanced courses and the further diversification of the American high school student population—those numbers have increased to more than four-fifths of a million students a year.

4. Which came from millions of original survey responses, data on every school in the US, original randomized controlled trials, and a wide variety of other sources I consulted during my twenty years in the field.

5. As of 2020, there were 49.4 million students in K-12 public schools, 4.7 million students in K-12 private schools, and 19.4 million students in college and universities.

"Fast Facts: Back-to-School Statistics," National Center for Education Statistics, accessed September 6, 2022, https://nces.ed.gov/fastfacts/display.asp?id=372.

6. There are over eight million people working in elementary and secondary schools, including teachers, janitors, administrators, bus drivers, cooks, and maintenance workers. "National Industry-Specific Occupational Employment and Wage Estimates: Elementary and Secondary Schools," US Bureau of Labor Statistics, last modified March 31, 2022, https://www.bls.gov/oes/current/naics4_611100.htm.

7. In 2020, there were 75.5 million parents with children under the age of twenty-five. "America's Families and Living Arrangements: Table A3. Parents with Coresident Children Under 18, by Living Arrangement, Sex, and Selected Characteristics," US Census Bureau, last modified November 22, 2021, https://www.census.gov/data/tables/2020/demo/families/cps-2020.html.

8. The US spends 5 percent of its GDP on education. "Education Spending (Indicator)," OECD, accessed September 6, 2022, https://doi.org/10.1787/ca274bac-en.

9. Federal, state, and local government provides $764.7 billion to fund K-12 public education. The federal government provides 7.9 percent of this funding. Melanie Hanson, "U.S. Public Education Spending Statistics," Education Data Initiative, last modified June 15, 2022, https://educationdata.org/public-education-spending-statistics. Of all expenditures by state and local government, 30.8 percent goes to education (21.5 percent in elementary and secondary; 9.3 percent to higher education), more than any other spending category. "Elementary and Secondary Education Expenditures," the Urban Institute, accessed September 6, 2022, https://www.urban.org/policy-centers/cross-center-initiatives/state-and-local-finance-initiative/state-and-local-backgrounders/elementary-and-secondary-education-expenditures.

10. A total of $4.1 trillion is spent on health care, with $1.5 trillion (36.6 percent) from the federal government and $586 billion (14.3 percent) from state and local government. "NHE Fact Sheet," US Department of Health and Human Services, Centers for Medicare & Medicaid Services, last modified December 14, 2022, https://www.cms.gov/Research-Statistics-Data-and-Systems/Statistics-Trends-and-Reports/NationalHealthExpendData/NHE-Fact-Sheet.

11. Reid Saaris, "Our Latest Generation: The Civic Greatness of Young Americans" (thesis, Harvard University, 2004).

12. Tiffany A. Julian and Robert Kominski, "Education and Synthetic Work-Life Earnings Estimates," *American Community Survey Reports* (Washington, DC: US Census Bureau, 2011).

13. People who are well educated experience better health, as reflected in the high levels of self-reported health and low levels of morbidity, mortality, and disability. By extension, low educational attainment is associated with self-reported poor health, shorter life expectancy, and shorter survival when sick. Viju Raghupathi and Wullianallur Raghupathi, "The Influence of Education on Health: An Empirical Assessment of OECD Countries for the Period 1995–2015," *Archives of Public Health* 78, 20 (2020), https://doi.org/10.1186/s13690-020-00402-5.

14. As compared to those in other countries, Americans aged twenty-five and over had the most years of formal education in the entirety of the twentieth century. Max

Roser and Esteban Ortiz-Ospina, "Global Education," OurWorldInData.org, accessed September 6, 2022, https://ourworldindata.org/global-education.

15. Original analysis of EOS survey data, some of which has been published here: Equal Opportunity Schools, *2018–19 Equity Pathways Report* (Seattle: EOS, 2018), https://eoschools.org/wp-content/uploads/2018/12/2018-19-Sample-Equity-Pathways -Report.pdf.

16. High school diploma holders earn a median of $1.6 million over a lifetime. Bachelor's degree holders earn a median of $2.8 million over a lifetime. Anthony P. Carnevale, Ban Cheah, and Emma Wenzinger, *The College Payoff: More Education Doesn't Always Mean More Earnings* (Washington, DC: Georgetown University Center on Education and the Workforce, 2021), https://eric.ed.gov/?q=Gender&ff1=locMaryland&id =ED615605.

17. The Bureau of Labor Statistics, as of 2021, shows unemployment rates for college graduates as close to half of those who have not graduated college; weekly wages of bachelor's degree holders average 167 percent of those who hold just a high school diploma. "Unemployment Rate 3.7 Percent for College Grads, 6.7 Percent for High School Grads in March 2021," US Bureau of Labor Statistics, last modified April 7, 2021, https://www.bls.gov/opub/ted/2021/unemployment-rate-3-7-percent-for-college -grads-6-7-percent-for-high-school-grads-in-march-2021.htm; Elka Torpey, "Education Pays, 2020," US Bureau of Labor Statistics, last modified June 2021, https://www .bls.gov/careeroutlook/2021/data-on-display/education-pays.htm.

18. About three million openings a year require a bachelor's degree, based on analysis of Table 5 (representing 40 percent of positions). Elka Torpey, "Education Level and Projected Openings, 2019–29," US Bureau of Labor Statistics, last modified October 2020, https://www.bls.gov/careeroutlook/2020/article/education-level-and-open ings.htm.

19. Two million students earn a bachelor's degree annually. "Number of Bachelor's Degrees Earned in the United States from 1949/50 to 2030/31, by Gender," Statista, last modified October 2021, https://www.statista.com/statistics/185157/number-of-bache lor-degrees-by-gender-since-1950/.

20. Anne Case and Angus Deaton, *Deaths of Despair and the Future of Capitalism* (Princeton, NJ: Princeton University Press, 2020).

21. This epilogue will focus on academic preparation for college. For more information on college enrollment and persistence strategies, etc., consider the following: Chungseo Kang and Darlene García Torres, "College Undermatching, Bachelor's Degree Attainment, and Minority Students," *Journal of Diversity in Higher Education* 14, no. 2 (2021): 264–77, https://doi.org/10.1037/dhe0000145; George D. Kuh, Jillian Kinzie, John H. Schuh, and Elizabeth J. Whitt, *Student Success in College: Creating Conditions That Matter* (San Francisco: John Wiley & Sons, 2010); Joshua S. Wyner, *What Excellent Community Colleges Do: Preparing All Students for Success* (Cambridge, MA: Harvard Education Press, 2019).

22. 19.4 million students attended college in 2020. "Fast Facts: Back-to-School Statistics," National Center for Education Statistics, accessed September 6, 2022, https:// nces.ed.gov/fastfacts/display.asp?id=372. There were 7.4 million college students in

1970. "Current Population Reports: Population Characteristics" (Washington, DC: US Department of Commerce/Bureau of the Census, 1971), https://www.census.gov/content/dam/Census/library/publications/1970/demo/p20-215.pdf.

23. Per capita income was $39,052 in 2020; in 1970, it was $3,177 ($18,953 adjusted for current dollars). "Table P-1. Total CPS Population and Per Capita Income, All People: 1967 to 2020," US Census Bureau, last modified September 15, 2022, https://www.census.gov/data/tables/time-series/demo/income-poverty/historical-income-people.html.

24. In 2021, 55- to 64-year-olds in the US were ranked third for college degrees earned and 25- to 34-year-olds in the US were ranked twelfth for college degrees earned. "Population with Tertiary Education (Indicator)," OECD, accessed September 6, 2022, https://doi.org/10.1787/0b8f90e9-en.

25. In 2016, an estimated 11 percent of dependent family members in the lowest family income quartile had attained a bachelor's degree by age 24, compared with 20 percent of those in the second quartile, 41 percent of those in the third quartile, and 58 percent of those in the highest quartile. M. Cahalan, L. W. Perna, M. Yamashita, J. Wright, and S. Santillan, *Indicators of Higher Education Equity in the United States* (Washington, DC: The Pell Institute for the Study of Opportunity in Higher Education, Council for Opportunity in Education (COE), and Alliance for Higher Education and Democracy of the University of Pennsylvania (PennAHEAD), 2018), http://pellinstitute.org/downloads/publications-Indicators_of_Higher_Education_Equity_in_the_US_2018_Historical_Trend_Report.pdf.

26. As of 2019, the total US population of those up to age 24 is 102.9 million. "Table 1. Population by Age and Sex: 2019," US Census Bureau, last modified October 8, 2021, https://www.census.gov/data/tables/2019/demo/age-and-sex/2019-age-sex-composition.html. One quarter of that is 25.7 million. Eleven percent of that is 2.83 million. College-aspiring rates from original Equal Opportunity Schools analysis of millions of survey responses.

27. 33.5 percent of white adults ages 25 and older have a bachelor's degree, compared with 16.4 percent of Latino adults and 21.6 percent of Black adults. Kevin McElrath and Michael Martin, *Bachelor's Degree Attainment in the United States: 2005 to 2019* (Washington, DC: US Census Bureau, 2021), https://www.census.gov/content/dam/Census/library/publications/2021/acs/acsbr-009.pdf.

28. Gaps in US educational achievement have affected GDP more severely than have all recessions since the 1970s. Byron Auguste, Bryan Hancock, and Martha Laboissiere, "The Economic Cost of the US Education Gap," McKinsey & Company, June 1, 2009, https://www.mckinsey.com/industries/education/our-insights/the-economic-cost-of-the-us-education-gap.

29. Derived from the US Census Bureau's Current Population Study, Annual Social and Economic Supplements, 2018–21, using current degree attainment for 25- to 29-year-olds by race, applying those rates to the populations of Black or Hispanic origin ages 0 to 24 for college aspirants as per EOS survey data.

30. As of 2014, white students became a minority of K-12 students, accounting for 49.5 percent of public K-12 school enrollment that year (a percentage that has declined annually since). "Table 203.50. Enrollment and Percentage Distribution of Enrollment

in Public Elementary and Secondary Schools, by Race/Ethnicity and Region: Selected Years, Fall 1995 Through Fall 2030," National Center for Education Statistics, last modified September 2021, https://nces.ed.gov/programs/digest/d21/tables/dt21_203.50.asp.

31. For those interested in the history of failed school reforms in the US and the one exception to this pattern, this course syllabus, by David Labaree, provides a solid foundation for understanding, in concert with the books referenced therein: David Labaree, "Course on History of School Reform in the U.S.," *David Labaree on Schooling, History, and Writing,* June 24, 2019, https://davidlabaree.com/2019/06/24/history -of-school-reform-in-the-u-s/.

32. With "equal access" defined by a test of statistically significant differences between school and AP/IB student populations applied at p < 0.05.

33. Theokas and Saaris, *Finding America's Missing AP and IB Students.* Additional findings of missing students numbers from later years come from original analysis of subsequent years of data sets comparable to those cited in the 2013 paper.

34. See, e.g., Bellevue Public Schools, Federal Way Public Schools, and Summit Public Schools.

35. "NAEP Report Card: 2019 NAEP Reading Assessment," National Assessment of Educational Progress, National Center for Education Statistics, accessed September 6, 2022, https://www.nationsreportcard.gov/highlights/reading/2019/g12/; "NAEP Report Card: 2019 NAEP Mathematics Assessment," National Assessment of Educational Progress, National Center for Education Statistics, accessed September 6, 2022, https://www.nationsreportcard.gov/highlights/mathematics/2019/g12/.

36. "Racial and Ethnic Achievement Gaps," Stanford Center for Education Policy Analysis, the Educational Opportunity Monitoring Project, accessed September 6, 2022, https://cepa.stanford.edu/educational-opportunity-monitoring-project/achieve ment-gaps/race/.

37. Kids Count, *Early Warning! Why Reading by the End of Third Grade Matters* (Baltimore: Annie E. Casey Foundation, 2010), https://www.ccf.ny.gov/files/9013/8262/2751 /AECFReporReadingGrade3.pdf.

38. Donald J. Hernandez, *Double Jeopardy: How Third-Grade Reading Skills and Poverty Influence High School Graduation* (New York: The Annie E. Casey Foundation, 2011), https://files.eric.ed.gov/fulltext/ED518818.pdf.

39. "NAEP Report Card: Reading, Grade 4," National Assessment of Educational Progress, National Center for Education Statistics, accessed February 23, 2022, https:// www.nationsreportcard.gov/reading/states/achievement/?grade=4.

40. "NAEP Report Card: Mathematics, Grade 8," National Assessment of Educational Progress, National Center for Education Statistics, accessed February 23, 2022, https://www.nationsreportcard.gov/mathematics/nation/achievement/?grade=8.

41. "Evidence-Based Education," Johns Hopkins School of Education, Center for Research and Reform in Education, accessed January 20, 2023, https://education.jhu .edu/crre/evidence-based-education/.

42. Based on standard deviations of effect sizes and the age-specific conversions in Table 5 of Lipsey et al. 2012, "Translating the Statistical Representation of the Effects of Education Interventions into More Readily Interpretable Forms," Institute of Education Sciences, last modified November 2012, ies.ed.gov/ncser/pubs/20133000/.

43. Sarah Mervosh, "The Pandemic Erased Two Decades of Progress in Math and Reading," *New York Times*, September 1, 2022, https://www.nytimes.com/2022/09/01/us/national-test-scores-math-reading-pandemic.html. There is some controversy about converting results like NAEP into weeks or months of learning gains (like Dr. Ho's comment that some students fell about nine months further behind). Though I don't understand the statistics enough to speak to the academic nuances, I do think it's important that data be converted to actionable, publicly understandable measures whenever possible—even if those conversions are academically imperfect. Sean F. Reardon, Demetra Kalogrides, and Andrew D. Ho, "Linking U.S. School District Test Score Distributions to a Common Scale" (working paper, Stanford Center for Education Policy Analysis, Stanford, CA, 2017); Ho, "A Nonparametric Framework for Comparing Trends and Gaps Across Tests," *Journal of Educational and Behavioral Statistics* 34, no. 2 (2009): 201–28, https://doi.org/10.3102/1076998609332755.

44. Note that not all strategies gain an additional month for students. Strategies range from a onetime gain of three-quarters of a month for a race-congruent teacher for Black students, to six or more months of learning gains for effectively implemented high-dosage tutoring. Some strategies gain more, and some gain less. The point of presenting all strategies in terms of the cost of hypothetical month of learning gain is to start with the strategies that accomplish the most per dollar, and then work up—to the extent that resources are available.

45. Lisa S. Blackwell, Kali H. Trzesniewski, and Carol Sorich Dweck, "Implicit Theories of Intelligence Predict Achievement Across an Adolescent Transition: A Longitudinal Study and an Intervention," *Child Development* 78, no. 1 (2007): 246–63; Melody Manchi Chao, Sujata Visaria, Anirban Mukhopadhyay, and Rajeev Dehejia, "Do Rewards Reinforce the Growth Mindset?: Joint Effects of the Growth Mindset and Incentive Schemes in a Field Intervention," *Journal of Experimental Psychology: General* 146, no. 10 (2017): 1402–19; C. Good, J. Aronson, and M. Inzlicht, "Improving Adolescents' Standardized Test Performance: An Intervention to Reduce the Effects of Stereotype Threat," *Journal of Applied Developmental Psychology* 24, no. 6 (2003): 645–62; David Paunesku, Gregory M. Walton, Carissa Romero, Eric N. Smith, David S. Yeager, and Carol S. Dweck, "Mind-Set Interventions Are a Scalable Treatment for Academic Underachievement," *Psychological Science* 26, no. 6 (2015): 784–93; Cinzia Rienzo, Heater Rolfe, and David Wilkinson, *Changing Mindsets: Evaluation Report and Executive Summary* (London: Education Endowment Foundation, 2015); David S. Yeager et al., "Using Design Thinking to Improve Psychological Interventions: The Case of the Growth Mindset During the Transition to High School," *Journal of Educational Psychology* 108, no. 3 (2016): 374–91.

46. Richard Layard and David M. Clark, *Thrive: The Power of Evidence-Based Psychological Therapy* (London: Penguin UK, 2015). I also conducted an interview with Layard and Clark about updated impact data on the Improving Access to Psychological Therapies Programme in 2022.

47. T. Domina, "The Link Between Middle School Mathematics Course Placement and Achievement," *Child Development* 85, no. 5 (2014): 1948–64; Soo-yong Byun, Matthew J. Irvin, and Bethany A. Bell, "Advanced Math Course Taking: Effects on Math

Achievement and College Enrollment," *Journal of Experimental Education* 83, no. 4 (2015): 439–68, https://doi.org/10.1080/00220973.2014.919570.

48. Matthew A. Kraft, David Blazar, and Dylan Hogan, "The Effect of Teacher Coaching on Instruction and Achievement: A Meta-Analysis of the Causal Evidence," *Review of Educational Research* 88, no. 4 (2018): 547–88, https://doi.org/10.3102/003465 4318759268.

49. Kraft and Blazar, "Taking Teacher Coaching to Scale: Can Personalized Training Become Standard Practice?" *Education Next* 18, no. 4 (2018): 68–75.

50. For a review of key elements, see Goldhaber et al., "The Theoretical and Empirical Arguments for Diversifying the Teacher Workforce: A Review of the Evidence" (working paper, Center for Education Data and Research, Seattle, 2015). Additionally, recent research by Gershenson et al. discusses the impact on long-run attainment: high school graduation and college enrollment. Seth Gershenson, Cassandra M. D. Hart, Joshua Hyman, Constance A. Lindsay, and Nicholas W. Papageorge, "The Long-Run Impacts of Same-Race Teachers," *American Economic Journal: Economic Policy* 14, no. 4 (2022): 300–42, https://doi.org/ 10.1257/pol.20190573. Impact per month of learning per student per dollar is lower in schools with lower populations of Black students. To qualify for the medium-impact category in our analysis, a school would need to have around 20 percent Black students. This research aligns well with a variety of local survey results I've seen in which students and families of color identify their top priorities for school improvement. Sometimes people pit research against "what people really want." In this case—as in many others—what people want and prioritize seems to align closely with what research is telling us. And, as we saw through our million-plus surveys at EOS, what the research says is most impactful can align very well with—and advance the cause of—issues that are popular among students, families, and educators.

51. Katherine Schaeffer, "America's Public School Teachers Are Far Less Racially and Ethnically Diverse Than Their Students" (Washington, DC: Pew Research Center, 2021), https://www.pewresearch.org/fact-tank/2021/12/10/americas-public-school -teachers-are-far-less-racially-and-ethnically-diverse-than-their-students/. About eight in ten (79 percent) US public school teachers identified as non-Hispanic white during the 2017–18 school year, the most recent year in which NCES has published demographic data about them. Fewer than one in ten teachers were either Black (7 percent), Hispanic (9 percent), or Asian American (2 percent). And less than 2 percent of teachers were either American Indian or Alaska Native, Pacific Islander, or of two or more races. By comparison, 47 percent of all public elementary and secondary school students in the US in 2018–19 were White, according to the most recent data available. In that period, 27 percent of public school students were Hispanic, 15 percent were Black, and 5 percent were Asian. Those shares have increased over time as newer generations of young people have entered the classroom. About 1 percent or less were Pacific Islander or identified as American Indian or Alaska Native, while 4 percent were of two or more races.

52. About half the students of color in our surveys reported worrying about "belonging" in advanced courses. This seems especially true for advanced programs that

do not reflect school diversity (which has historically been the case in 99 percent of schools with between 10 and 90 percent students of color with established advanced studies programs, based on original EOS research).

53. Travis J. Bristol, "To Be Alone or in a Group: An Exploration into How the School-Based Experiences Differ for Black Male Teachers Across One Urban School District," *Urban Education* 53, no. 3 (2018): 334–54, https://doi.org/10.1177/00420859 17697200.

54. Gershenson, Hart, Hyman, Lindsay, and Papageorge, "The Long-Run Impacts of Same-Race Teachers," 300–42; Jeffrey Penney, "Racial interaction effects and student achievement," *Education Finance and Policy* 12.4 (2017): 447–67; Dan Goldhaber, Roddy Theobald, and Christopher Tien, "Educator and Student Diversity in Washington State: Gaps and Historical Trends" (working paper, Center for Education Data and Research, Seattle, 2015), https://www.cedr.us/_files/ugd/1394b9_339286 bfafc24fef9f1076128fcfdf50.pdf; Gershenson, Hart, Hyman, Lindsay, and Papageorge, "Same-Race Teachers" (working paper, National Bureau of Economic Research, Cambridge, MA, 2021).

55. 53 percent students of color − 21 percent of teachers of color = 32 percent gap in representation (percentages derived from Pew research cited above). 32 percent of 3.5 million (NCES "Fast Facts" 2017–18) = 1.12 million "missing" teachers of color.

56. Clifford Adelman, *The Toolbox Revisited: Paths to Degree Completion from High School Through College* (Washington, DC: US Department of Education, 2006), www.ed.gov/rschstat/research/pubs/toolboxrevisit/index.html.

57. Greg J. Duncan, Katherine Magnuson, and Elizabeth Votruba-Drzal, "Boosting Family Income to Promote Child Development," *Future of Children* 24, no. 1 (2014): 99–120, http://dx.doi.org/10.1353/foc.2014.0008; Raj Chetty, John N. Friedman, and Jonah Rockoff, "New Evidence on the Long-Term Impacts of Tax Credits," *Proceedings. Annual Conference on Taxation and Minutes of the Annual Meeting of the National Tax Association* 104 (2011): 116–24, http://www.jstor.org/stable/prancotamamnta.104 .116; G. J. Duncan, P. A. Morris, and C. Rodrigues, "Does Money Really Matter? Estimating Impacts of Family Income on Young Children's Achievement with Data from Random-Assignment Experiments," *Developmental Psychology* 47, no. 5 (2011): 1263–79, https://doi.org/10.1037/a0023875; Jacob Bastian and Katherine Michelmore, "The Long-Term Impact of the Earned Income Tax Credit on Children's Education and Employment Outcomes," *Journal of Labor Economics* 36, no. 4 (2018): 1127–63, http://dx .doi.org/10.2139/ssrn.2674603.

58. Robert Slavin, "Launching Proven Tutoring," *Robert Slavin's Blog*, April 26, 2021, https://robertslavinsblog.wordpress.com/category/tutoring/.

59. Nancy A. Madden and Robert E. Slavin, "Evaluations of Technology-Assisted Small-Group Tutoring for Struggling Readers," *Reading & Writing Quarterly* (2017): 1–8, https://doi.org/10.1080/10573569.2016.1255577; Slavin, "Building Back Better," *Robert Slavin's Blog*, January 21, 2021, https://robertslavinsblog.wordpress.com/cate gory/tutoring/page/2/.

60. https://robertslavinsblog.wordpress.com/2018/04/05/new-findings-on-tutor ing-four-shockers/—reviewing three syntheses of key field evidence: Ariane Baye, Cynthia Lake, Amanda Inns, and Slavin, *Effective Reading Programs for Secondary*

Students (manuscript submitted for publication, 2017). Also see Baye, Lake, Inns, and Slavin, *Effective Reading Programs for Secondary Students* (Baltimore: Johns Hopkins University Center for Research and Reform in Education, 2017); Inns, Lake, Pellegrini, and Slavin, "Effective Programs for Struggling Readers: A Best-Evidence Synthesis" (paper presented at the annual meeting of the Society for Research on Educational Effectiveness, Washington, DC, 2018); Pellegrini, Inns, and Slavin, "Effective Programs in Elementary Mathematics: A Best-Evidence Synthesis" (paper presented at the annual meeting of the Society for Research on Educational Effectiveness, Washington, DC, 2018).

61. Chen Xie, Amanda Neitzel, Alan Cheung, and Slavin, *The Effects of Summer Programs on K-12 Students' Reading and Mathematics Achievement: A Meta-Analysis* (Baltimore: Johns Hopkins University Center for Research and Reform in Education, 2021), https://beib228303049.files.wordpress.com/2021/02/xie-cheung-2020-effs-of-summer-for-bee.pdf.

62. Steven G. Rivkin, Eric A. Hanushek, and John F. Kain, "Teachers, Schools, and Academic Achievement," *Econometrica* 73, no. 2 (2005): 417–58, https://doi.org/10.3982/ECTA12211; Goldhaber, Roddy, and Tien, "Educator and Student Diversity."

63. Lawrence Mishel and Richard Rothstein, eds., "Introduction," in *The Class Size Debate* (Washington, DC: Economic Policy Institute, 2002), 3.

64. Steven G. Rivkin, Eric A. Hanushek, and John F. Kain, "Teachers, Schools, and Academic Achievement," *Econometrica* 73, no. 2 (2005): 417–58.

65. Christopher Jepsen and Steven Rivkin, "Class Size Reduction and Student Achievement: The Potential Tradeoff Between Teacher Quality and Class Size," *Journal of Human Resources* 44, no. 1 (2009): 223–50, https://doi.org/10.3368/jhr.44.1.223.